Created and Directed by Hans Höfer

INSIGHT
GUIDES

California

Edited by Daniel T. Max
Contributing Editors:
Jon Carroll, Tracey Johnston, Ben Kalb, and
Bret Reed Lundberg
Updated by John Wilcock

APA PUBLICATIONS

California

Fourth Edition (Reprint)

About This Book

With its mountains, rich agricultural valleys, unique redwood forests, adventurous surf beaches and cosmopolitan cities, California is one of the world's most inviting travel destinations. The Golden State, if separated from the rest of the United States, would rank among the 10 richest nations in the world with an economy roughly the size of Canada's.

All of these facts made California an essential addition to the world-wide collection of travel literature published by Apa Publications of Singapore. Like its predecessors in the Apa series, *Insight Guide: California* combines outstanding photographs, great writing and clear, frank journalism. This concept of publishing travel books that give readers a comprehensive view of a country or region was devised by **Hans Höfer**, the West German-born founder of Apa who wrote its first prize-winning book, *Insight Guide: Bali*, in 1970. A graduate of Bauhaus training in book design, printing and photography, Höfer seeks the best available local editors, writers and photographers to produce each Insight Guide.

For this book, the production responsibility fell to four Californians, **Jon Carroll** and **Tracey Johnston**, a husband-and-wife team from Oakland; **Ben Kalb**, who grew up in Sherman Oaks north of Los Angeles; and **Bret Reed Lundberg**, who coordinated photography and graphics from his studio in Orange County, south of Los Angeles.

Carroll is a daily columnist for the *San Francisco Chronicle*. Johnston works as a free-lance writer and editor. Kalb is the former editor of *Incentive Travel* and *Racquetball Illustrated* magazines and a former writer for *The Honolulu Advertiser*. Lundberg operates a thriving photography business based in Newport Beach. His credits include *National Geographic*, *Time* and *The New York Times*.

The extensive history section is the combined effort of **Tom Cole**, author of *A Short History of San Francisco*, and **Joan Talmage Weiss**, a veteran travel writer and instructor of English at California State University, Fullerton.

The lengthy coverage of "San Francisco" was written by **Jerry Carroll**, who has covered the city for the *San Francisco Chronicle* since the late Sixties.

Reporting on the communities surrounding San Francisco are **Karen Liberatore, Julie Smith** and **Philip Garlington**. Liberatore ("Peninsula") is the author of four books including *Complete Guide to the Golden Gate National Recreation Area* and *Under the Sun: A Guide to the Sonoran Desert*. Smith ("Oakland and the East Bay") is a newspaper reporter-turned-mystery writer. Garlington ("Marin County") has published several articles in *Esquire* and is the author of the novel *Aces and Eights*.

The "Wine Country" chapter was scribed by **Don Edwards**, an expert on Sonoma County and the author of *Making the Most of Sonoma*, a detailed guide to the area.

Walt Wiley ("Sacramento") spent his boyhood in California and currently writes a weekly column on Northern California geography and people for *The Sacramento Bee*.

Tom De Vries ("Gold Country") lived for 10 years in Mariposa and is a news producer for San Francisco TV station KRON.

Covering California's high country are **Steve Rubenstein** and **Kief Hillsbery**. Rubenstein ("Lake Tahoe") is a reporter and columnist for the *San Francisco Chronicle*. Hillsbery ("Yosemite and the High Sierra") lived in Yosemite Valley for five years and was until recently a columnist for *Outside* magazine.

The southern part of Northern California was covered by **Paul Cohen** and **Paul Ciotti**. Cohen ("San Joaquin Valley") was an associate editor of *California* magazine and is currently the editor of *Atar Connection* magazine. Ciotti ("Monterey Peninsula") has published articles in *Time, People, Us, California* and *True* magazines.

Frank Robertson ("North Coast") has had articles in *California, Rolling Stone, Oui* and *Women's Sports* magazines. Currently he is a

Carroll

Johnston

Kalb

Lundberg

Cole

regular columnist for the *Sebastapol Times*.

The author of the introductory piece and essay on "Downtown LA" was **William Franklin**, a frequent free-lance contributor to *Los Angeles Magazine* and *The Los Angeles Reader*.

Margy Rochlin ("Hollywood") is a regular contributor to *Los Angeles Magazine*, *Women's Sports* and *The Los Angeles Reader*. The sidebar ("An Unusual Side of Hollywood") is an excerpt from **Ken Schessler's** *This is Hollywood: An Unusual Movieland Guide* (copyright 1984, Ken Schessler Productions, P.O. Box 99, La Verne, CA).

Charles Warn ("Beverly Hills and the West Side") is a media consultant who specializes in entertainment accounts and political campaigns.

Jeff Spurrier, author of the chapter on "South Bay", is a free-lance writer who contributes to *Los Angeles Magazine*, *The Los Angeles Reader* and various music journals.

Merrill Shindler ("San Fernando") is the *Los Angeles Herald-Examiner* restaurant critic, the *Los Angeles Magazine* film critic, and head writer for the American Top 40 radio program.

The book's "Orange County" expert is **Orman Day**, a staff writer for *The Register*, Orange County's leading daily newspaper.

Glen Grant, who covered San Diego and the excursion to "Baja California", is a free-lance writer and publicist who has written for *The Los Angeles Times*.

Thomas J. Morrow, who wrote on "San Diego County", published his own monthly travel newsletter, *Travel of Tomorrow*.

"Santa Catalina and the Islands" were covered by **Lewis Lustman**, a bank vice-president whose work has been published in *Los Angeles Magazine*, *The Los Angeles Times* and several other periodicals.

Michele Kort wrote about the "Central Coast". He is a free-lance writer whose work has appeared in diverse publications.

Two journalists wrote on the California desert. **Mark Jones** ("Death Valley and the Mojave") is a former staff writer for United Press International and *The Los Angeles Times*. **Bob Vivian** ("Palm Springs to the Colorado"), recently appointed to the faculty of the California State University, is the author of more than 300 magazine articles and also of a satiric book entitled *The Good Humor Man*.

Ruth Reichl, who discussed "The Gourmet's San Francisco", is the food critic for *California* magazine and the former co-owner of a Berkeley restaurant.

Ray Loynd ("The Industry") is a staff writer for *Daily Variety*, a prominent entertainment industry trade paper.

The task of compiling the Travel Tips section fell to **Bob Wolff** and **Michael Caleb Lester**. Wolff is currently writing a novel. Lester, who edited the "What's New" section of *New West* magazine, has written for many magazines.

Several photographic contributors deserve special mention. **Jan Whiting** is a native Californian who moved back to the Bay Area in 1983 after spending most of the previous decade living and working abroad.

Mireille Vautier operates the Photothéque Vautier-de Nanxe in Paris.

Other contributors include **Lee Foster**, who has authored more than 10 books; **John Sanford**, instructor of astronomy and photography at Orange Coast Community College; **Bud Lee**, whose unusual work has appeared in major publications; and **Gene Russell**, a free-lance photo-journalist based in Carlsbad, north of San Diego. Additional photos were taken by **Bart Bartholomew**, **Paul Von Stroheim**, **Joe Viesti**, **Dennis Lane**, **Tom Lippert**, **Kal Müller** (Flame), **Bud Bachman** (Scoopix of Australia), **Allen Grazer**, **R. Ian Lloyd** and **Ronni Pinsler**.

Most historical reproductions come from the archives of the Bancroft Library, University of California, Berkeley. **Bill Roberts** gave special assistance in obtaining these materials. **Austin Wilkie**, student of University of Virginia Law School, offered indefatigable help in beating the book into shape.

—APA Publications

Weiss

Liberatore

Vivian

Wolff

Lester

History

Northern California

Southern California

Features

Maps

TRAVEL TIPS

WELCOME TO CALIFORNIA

For the last 250 years America has been moving westward. One out of every eight Americans is now a Californian and the fraction increases constantly. The result has been that a once – in fact only recently – wild, mountainous and sandy coastline, nearly deserted but for the daring pioneer, has become America's sociological kitchen, where new experiments are cooked up all the time. The working mother, commuter generation, even *sushi* got, if not its start, at least its grandest test here.

So to see America, there's obviously no better place to start than California. Add to this its unsurpassed natural beauty – a thousand miles of coast, three mountain ranges and a great desert – and you have reason enough to come whether your interest is in people or nature.

This book is split between Northern California and Southern, with the place selection organized around the dual foci of Los Angeles and San Francisco. Most trips start from one of these two great cities. If yours doesn't, just open the guide in the middle and pick out your first site.

But a word of advice. You can't rush through California… even if you want to. So sit back and take it slow. You'll never exhaust what there is to see or do. Some people say there's more in California than in the rest of the United States – more beauty, more interesting people, more of the ingredients that will go into the American melting pot of tomorrow.

Preceding pages: LA reflections; Yosemite National Park; Death Valley crossing; the Pigeon Point Lighthouse; architectural contrast in San Francisco; Los Angeles freeways. **Right**, a Laguna Beach stroll.

par Franquelin d'après Choris.

Danse des habitans de Califo

18

Pl. III

Lith. de Langlumé r de l'Abbaye N. 4

à la mission de S.ᵗ Francisco.

California is the product of a myth – a single, improbable myth of a land of gold.

For ages this region was the tranquil home of a race doomed by the myth. For less than a century it was dominated by a luckless people inspired by the myth. It was built and populated by a ragtag society of men and women who saw the myth spring to life.

In January 1848 a "half crazy or harebrained" man named James Marshall picked up a few bits of shiny material out of a millrace on the American River and started an explosion of greed, energy and longing called the Gold Rush. Marshall had at last found the country of gold in the languid foothills of California's Sierra Nevada.

The world was changed by Marshall's discovery. California was created as a result of it. San Francisco was suddenly transformed from a sleepy backwater into a bustling world-famous dream city. California today is streaked with memories of the Gold Rush. Marshall's discovery is the fulcrum of the California experience. But there is a history before it, however flooded it may be by what came later.

The first tenants of this rich land were the tribes that through the centuries crossed the land bridge of the Bering Strait and slowly filtered down into the North American continent. Estimates vary as to the number of Indians in California before European settlement. So many died soon after white people arrived that anthropologists have had to rely on patchy mission records and informed guesses. A reasonable calculation is that 230,000 Indians inhabited Northern California alone.

California Indians were a simple people. Their houses matched the climate – igloo-shaped abodes made of reed provided breezy shelter in summer; deerskins placed over the roofs protected the occupants during the rainy season; and when it got cool, an open fire was built in the homes, each of which had a hole in the roof through which the smoke was allowed to rise.

On sunny days, the men usually went about naked except for ornaments such as necklaces, earrings, bracelets and anklets. So did the children. In cold weather, however, they wore robes of yellow cedar bark or of crudely tanned pelts, and rain capes in downpours. Some groups practiced tattooing. The women wore two-piece aprons of deerskins or reeds.

The Northern Tribes: Customs, talents and preoccupations varied from tribe to tribe – or more accurately from tribelet to tribelet. The Indians had divided themselves into thousands of small groups, many with distinct languages, all jealous guardians of separate identities. In the north, near Mount Shasta,

the Konomihus, the Atsugewis and the Modocs utilized the environment in a singular way. Further south, around San Francisco Bay, the Miwoks and Ohlones were as varied as the terrain.

The Bay's Indians moved in short nomadic spurts. From the ancestral shell mound they sometimes trekked up to the oak groves on what are now called the Berkeley Hills. There they ground acorns into "deliciously rich and oily" meal and socialized warily with other tribelets. Then they would pack up for the meadowland and its rich harvest of deer and elk. At each stop, along each trail, the tribelet would greet and be heartened by ancient landmarks: a venerable oak, a mossy boulder, a lively stream, a soft meadow.

The land around the Bay probably supported more humans than any other California locale. One area not much frequented was what is now the city of San Francisco. A sandy, windy, desolate place, it was an odd contrast to the lushness of the Berkeley Hills, the mild slopes of Mount Tamalpais, or the woods of the southern peninsula. In fact, San Francisco today has more trees and wildlife than at any time in its history.

The Southern Tribes: The Chumash tribe, living in what is now Santa Barbara, were adept fishermen who used seashell hooks, basket traps, nets and even vegetable poi-

symmetry, neatness of finish, and frequent decoration of the surfaces with relief carving and painting. All of this was achieved with limited tools, the principal ones being chisels, curved knives, abrasive stones, wedges and sharkskin.

The Chumash in particular were expert boat builders. One of their vessels, preserved today at the Santa Barbara County Courthouse, has been rated one of the finest in the New World.

The California Indians' lifestyle continued and prospered for 10,000 years. There were few major changes and by our standards their lives were hard and their possessions few. Then white people came and bewildered

sons. The agile ocean tribe even caught fish with their bare hands. So many tons of shellfish were eaten over the centuries that mounds of discarded shells accumulated to a depth of 20 feet.

Canoe-making was facilitated by the natural endowment of easily worked timbers, especially the red cedar and the redwood. A distinguishing feature of canoes made by Indians in this region was the emphasis on

Preceding pages: Louis Storey rendition of 18th-century Californian Indians dancing for Mission Dolores priests and, above, paddling a hand-crafted canoe.

these simple tribes. The Indians began to acquire manufactured articles such as guns, metal utensils, axes, knives, blankets and cloth. This inevitably led to a decline of the native arts and crafts. With the coming of the immigrant wagons and the encroachment of white settlements, warfare became a unifying force. Tribes that had formerly been hostile to one another often united against the intruders. But even this did not save them and in the end they were overwhelmed. The culture of the Indians was radically changed. They had survived regular earthquakes and droughts, but the whites proved too strong for them.

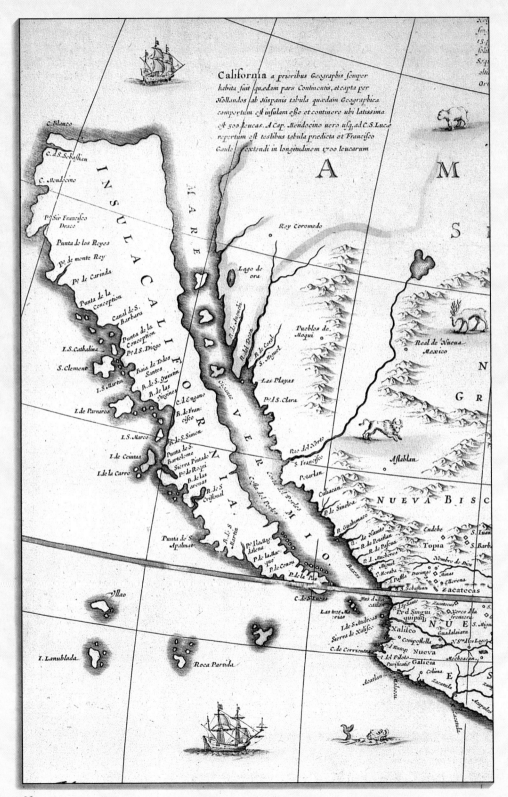

California a prioribus Geographis semper
habita fuit quædam pars Continentis, at capta per
Hollandos ab Hispanis tabula quædam Geographica
comportum est insulam esse et continere ubi latissima
est 300 leucas. A Cap. Mendocino vero usq, ad C.S.Luce
repertum est testibus tabula prædicta et Francisco
Gaule extendi in longitudinem 1700 leucarum

A   M

C. Blanco

C. d S. Sebastian

C. Mendocino

I N S U L A

M A R E

Rey Coromedo

Po Sir Francisco
Draco

Punta de los Reyes

Po de monte Rey

Po de Carinda

Punta de la
Conception

Lago de
ora

Canal de S.
Barbara

Punta de la
Conception

I. S. Cathalina

R. del Peñon

Po d S. Diego

Baia de Todas
Santos

Pueblos de
Moqui

Real de Nueva
Mexico

S. Clement

B. de S. Quintin

R. de Coral

S. Miguel

N

I. S. Martin

B. de las
Vneginas

C. d Engaño

Las Playas

G R

I. de Paxaros

B. de Fran-
cisco

Po d S. Clara

I. S. Marco

R. de S. Simon

C A L I F O R N I A

I. de Cenizas

Punta de S.
Bartolome

Rio del Norte

S. Francisco

Aztablan

I. de la Carro

Sierra Pintada

Po de Roqua
Po de las
arenas

Potarlan

R. de S.
Crisstoal

Culiacan

R. de S.
Martin

P. de Sinaloa

N U E V A   B I S C

M A R   V E R M I O

Punta de S.
Apsilmat

Po Madlig
dalena

R. de Nauito

Po de Lastur,
que

R. de Pastlan

Endche

S. Iuan

Po de Conou

R. del Purles

R. I. Muchoro

Topia

S. Barb

P. de la Paz

R. de Morala

Nombre de Dios

Biguel

I. Passla

Durango

Minas

Ellerena

Yllao

C. de S. Lucas

Mas d
cadas

R. Sebastian

Zacatecas

Zacatecas

Las tres Ma
reias

I S p Santo

Po d Singui
quipac

Xores Fla
frontera

N U E

I. de S. Andreas

Xalilco

Guadalaiara

N Sora los Lagos

I. Lanublada

Roca Partida

Sierra de Xalisco

Compostella

Po d Pilota

Nueva

S Mi

C. de Corrientes

Purificacio

I del Pilota

Galicia

Mechoacan

Colima

E

Acatlan

Zacatla

22

Know then, that on the right hand of the Indies, there is an island called California, very close to the side of the Terrestrial Paradise, and it was peopled by black women, without any men among them, for they lived in the fashion of Amazons. They were of strong and hardy bodies of ardent courage and great force. Their island was the strongest in all the world, with its steep cliffs and rocky shores. Their arms were all of gold, and so was the harness of the wild beasts which they tamed and rode. For, on the whole island, there was no metal but gold. They lived in caves, wrought out of the rock with much labor. They had many ships with which they sailed out to other countries to obtain booty.

In this island, called California, there were many griffins, on account of the great ruggedness of the country and its infinite host of wild beasts, such as much were seen in any other part of the world... and their Queen was called Calafia.

—*from a translation of* Las Sergas de Esplandian *by Garcia Rodriguez Ordonex de Montaivo, c. 1510.*

Incredibly, this fictional account was believed by explorers who were swept into a realm of fantasy beyond their home seas. Calafia, of course, was never found; but some claim they can hear her singing in the La Brea Tar Pits late at night.

Twenty-five years after this legend was written, Hernando Cortés, the Spaniard who conquered Mexico, sailed up the west coast of North America. Stumbling upon a "peninsula" which stretched down between the sea and a gulf, he believed he'd found the fabled island, and he named it "California".

But the discovery of the state of California is officially credited to Juan Rodriguez Cabrillo, Portuguese commander of two Spanish caravels. Virtually nothing is known of his early life. According to what can be pieced together from the various accounts of his California explorations, he is thought to

Early European explorers believed California to be an island. This map was drawn by Dutchman Joannes Jansson in 1638.

have embarked from the Mexican port of Navidad on or about June 27, 1542. He explored most of the coast of what is now the state of California, entering San Diego Harbor on September 28 and labeling it "enclosed and very good".

In 1602, Sebastian Vizcaíno arrived, searching for suitable ports of call for his Manila galleon on its annual return to the Philippines. Vizcaíno gave lasting names to several California sites, such as San Clemente Island, San Diego and Santa Catalina Island. Of more importance was his glowing report on the virtues of the California coast that urged Spain to colonize California.

Another name which lingered was "Nova (New) Albion" coined by Sir Francis Drake, the greatest of the English seamen of the Elizabethan age. As his *Golden Hind* nosed its way up north, after an exploration of the South American waters, it anchored at the site of modern San Francisco. He went ashore and claimed the land in the name of Queen Elizabeth I, the financial supporter of his expedition. However, just where Drake landed is an issue of much controversy. Giving credence to the notion that Drake didn't land at San Francisco, but at Santa Barbara, is the recent discovery of 13 cannons and 5 cast-iron guns near the latter city. These weapons are believed to have come from Drake's ship. If true, this could cause much of California history to be rewritten.

Primitive: Despite these early explorations, California was left very much to the primitive Indians. The actual occupation of the land by Spain began only in 1769 with the Portolá expedition. The final springboard was provided by the Russians who were fast expanding their territory. Rather than let the Russians gain a foothold, King Charles III of Spain was pressured to colonize the country rapidly.

Over the centuries, Spain had developed standard methods for settling a new territory. Where there was hostility from the natives, the sword swiftly cleared the way. Once they had been conquered, their missionary victors brought the benefits of Christianity to the "heathens". This strategy had been successfully used in Mexico. In areas where the natives were peace-loving, the missionaries led the way, accompanied by a small group of soldiers for protection. The second approach was selected for settling California.

Gaspar de Portolá and his party traveled north through what are now the coastal communities. With them was Franciscan friar Junípero Serra whose later missionary work here was to earn him the title "Apostle of California".

Long before the arrival of the Franciscan Order, the Jesuits – in cooperation with Spanish authorities – had begun in 1697 to organize a chain of missions in Baja California, modern Mexico. These missions thrived and expanded for the first two-thirds of the 18th century. But the Jesuits were expelled from all of Spain's American colonies in 1767 on the grounds that their emphasis on papal supremacy ran counter to that of the King, who maintained that absolute authority belonged to the Crown. With the removal of the Jesuit Order, the stage was set for the entry of the Franciscans (also known as "grey friars" because of the color of their religious habits).

March of the missions: Chosen to lead the California movement, Father Serra set up the Mission San Diego de Alcala, the first within the state. A native of Majorca, Spain, Father Serra's statue stands today in the rotunda in Washington, DC. He suffered a leg injury during his first month in Mexico which was to plague him for the rest of his life. But his missionary zeal was not to be quelled. Standing a mere 5 feet 2 inches (1 meter 57 cm), Serra eventually covered thousands of miles on foot and helped establish a series of missions which were to bind Upper (*Alta*) California into one province.

From San Diego, Portolá and Serra continued northward toward Monterey Bay. They had to, first, locate the great harbors of California that were glowingly described by Vizcaíno in this report 167 years earlier; and secondly, they were to establish a series of mission settlements. Between 1769 and 1823, 21 missions were strung along the coast of California like a string of pearls around a beautiful woman's neck.

At first Portolá and Serra worked well together. Later, however, it became a power struggle. While Portolá answered only to the Crown of Spain, God-driven Father Serra had the advice of a "higher, more spiritual

authority". Despite this conflict, Serra founded the first six missions – San Diego (1769), San Carlos (1770), San Antonio and San Gabriel (1771), San Luis Obispo (1772) and San Francisco (1776) – and set in motion plans to build the seventh at San Juan Capistrano.

On arrival there in 1775, Serra was just about to break ground when an Indian uprising at the San Diego mission stopped his plans. Hastily, the traveling priests buried the bells, left the cross and headed back with their accompanying soldiers to assist at San Diego. To their horror, they discovered that a Franciscan, the only martyr of the Order, had been killed.

A year later, the undaunted father returned to San Juan Capistrano with two priests and 11 soldiers to officially break ground. He conducted services within the walls of "Serra's church", since enlarged. While the mission at San Juan Capistrano is not the oldest, "Serra's Church" is considered the oldest mission structure still standing, having survived the 1812 earthquake which shook and destroyed most of the mission settlements. It's also remembered as the only church building in which its founder celebrated Mass.

As these missions became established, each of them gradually grew into a community where all activities and commerce were centered. Each became self-sufficient, as it was meant to be, with its own blacksmith shop, cannery, wine press and warehouses. Priests served as teachers in religious matters and in manual arts. Indians, who had never seen horses or cattle before, were trained to be cowboys. Sewing and cooking were taught to the women.

The decline of the Indians: At first, the Indians resisted conversion. Yet it wasn't long before the last of their tribal customs were swept aside, replaced by a new and bizarre lifestyle which left the natives bewildered. Some *padres* learned the tribal tongues and used them in celebrating Mass. Later genera-

chicken pox, killed thousands. Hundreds more fell ill with venereal diseases and the Indians developed a mortal fear of mission life. But the *padres* persuaded thousands of Indians to accept the benevolent despotism of the mission system and it was Indian labor which developed the missions into a successful operation.

Today, peppering the coastline and the inland area are ruins of these mission communities which evoke a unique California history of Indians and whites, of war and power, and of priests and heathens. Each mission still holds its own unique feature. The uncanny punctuality of the return of swallows to San Juan Capistrano on Saint

tions owe their knowledge of Indian culture to the few priests who took pains to record the intricacies of the Indians' languages and customs in several volumes of journals.

The self-reliant Indians were seduced into mission life by free and generous offers of food, colored beads, bright cloth and trinkets. But once baptized, they developed "a strange lethargy and inaction".

White diseases, such as measles and

<u>Left</u>, Father Junípero Serra in a late 18th-century portrait. <u>Above</u>, the interior of Mission San Michel Archangel looks much the same today as when it was built.

Joseph's Day (March 19) marks the annual *Fiesta de Las Golondrinas* (Feast of the Swallows). The San Gabriel Mission has six bells which have rung over the countryside for over half a century. The mission at Santa Barbara (also called the Queen of the Missions) boasts a white classic facade which reflects in a tranquil fountain. The Riverside mission marks the site where the first orange tree was planted in Southern California.

Detractors of the mission system condemn it as one which promoted outright slavery under the disguise of piety, and some blame it for the ultimate destruction of California's Indian population.

After three whole centuries of Spanish rule, Mexico broke away in 1821 and declared itself a republic on September 27. At about this time, secularization of the missions was sought by Spanish-Mexican settlers known as the *Californias*. Mexico City, beset by revolutionary turmoil, could only send a few governors and some ragtag soldiers north. The proud Franciscans refused allegiance to the revolutionary regime in Mexico, so they left the missions to return home to Spain. Thus, 8 million acres of mission land were frag-

50,000 acres (20,200 hectares). Indian slave labor became part of the plunder as did orange trees and grape vines.

The Secularization Acts: In 1834 Governor Figueroa issued the first of the Secularization Acts, which in theory gave lay administrators and Indian neophytes the right to ownership of the missions and their property. In practice, however, these acts were badly snubbed; secularization drove the Indians out into the world of poverty and helplessness. Like other slaves, they were psychologically ill-prepared

1822 MEXICAN RULE

mented into 800 privately owned ranches with some governors handing out land like after-dinner mints. Sold for as little as 23 cents per acre, the mission ranches were parcelled out to political favorites by the Mexican government. Orange orchards were cleared for firewood and herds were given to private hands. Even the influence of Hispanic Catholicism sank to a low ebb. Almost overnight, the "string of pearls" was transformed into a patchwork quilt of ranches.

Soldiers who had finished their time in the army often stayed on in California rather than return to Spain or Mexico. Under Mexican law, a *ranchero* could ask for as many as

to cope with freedom. Some returned to the hills, others indentured themselves as ranch hands or turned to drinking or gambling in the pueblos.

Quickly life changed to that of a frontier cattle range. Cattle raising in this part of the world made few demands on its owners. With no line fences to patrol and repair on the open range, and no need for vigilance because of branded stock, the *vaquero* had little work to pass his days. So he practiced feats of horsemanship to prove his masculinity and to impress the *señoritas*. His sports were violent, including calf branding, wild-horse roundups, bear hunts, cock and bullfights.

His entertainment included dances like the Spanish *fandango* and the Western waltz. His fiestas were fabulous; the host was generally bedecked in gold-braided clothes, dripping with silver.

The climate and the land were on the *rancheros'* side. Crops and game were plentiful. There were quail and hawks, eagles and turkey vultures, and the lordly California condor circled gracefully over the plains of tall mustard and wild grasses. Wildlife – badgers, coyotes, "jackass" rabbits and, in the mountains, grizzly bears, deer, gray wolves, mountain lions and wildcats – was in great supply. The weather remained temperate except for the occasional hot, dry, gale-

force wind the Indians called "wind of the evil spirits". The Spaniards called them *santanas*, a name which has become corrupted to Santa Ana winds today.

Of course, an occasional earthquake rumbled down the San Andreas Fault. The *rancheros* spent their energy rebuilding damaged *haciendas*, made from red-tile roofing set on white-painted adobe brick walls, but let the missions fall into ruins.

Left, a North Hollywood mural depicts the transition of California to Mexican sovereignty. **Above**, an 1842 portrait of Richard Dana, author of *Two Years Before the Mast*.

Restoration of the missions has only begun this century since they were declared historical landmarks by the state.

Author Richard Henry Dana, who came to California in 1835 to find his health at sea, called the *Californios* "an idle, thriftless people". Many *rancheros* made visits to the larger pueblos such as San Diego and brought syphilis back with them. Ranchos were lost during frequent visits to El Pueblo de Los Angeles' infamous "Nigger Valley", a cesspool of gambling and prostitution.

In his novel *Two Years Before the Mast*, Dana told of how cattle hides were thrown off the cliffs at Dana Point to the waiting ships below. These hides and tallow in 500-lb (227-kg) bags were the basic units of barter. The tanned hides skinned from three-year-old steers became rugs, blankets, curtains, sandals, chaps and even saddles. Rawhides were twisted into *reatas* (used for roping cattle) or were used to lash timbers together. Edible meat which did not hit the pot immediately was sun-dried as beef jerky or pickled for barter with trading ships. Curiously, milk was considered unhealthy and was never drunk. All fat became rendered into tallow; what wasn't traded was processed into candles and soap.

The Yankee trading ships which survived the precarious Straits of Magellan often stayed an entire year, working up and down the coast. They carried miniature department stores on board: gleaming copperware, framed mirrors, Irish linen, silk stockings, silver candlesticks, cashmere shawls and mahogany furniture. For many of the native-born, these were their first amenities of the civilized world.

A genteel contraband soon developed. To reduce import taxes, ships worked in pairs to transfer cargo from one to the other on the open seas. The partially emptied ship would then make port and submit to Customs inspection. With duties paid, it would rejoin its consort and reverse the transfer. Sometimes the Yankee traders unloaded cargoes in lonely coves and these were eventually smuggled ashore. Both sides fared well: the Yankee traders sailed south with full holds and the *rancheros* displayed their new finery with yet another fiesta.

The Mexican War: Official Washington soon became aware of this land of milk and honey on the Pacific coast. President Andrew

Jackson sent an emissary to Mexico City in the 1830s to buy California for $500,000. The plan failed. When James K. Polk took office in 1845 he pledged to acquire California by any means. He felt pressured by the English financial interests which plotted to exchange $26 million of defaulted Mexican bonds for the rich land of California.

The Bear... then Union: On May 13, 1846, President James Polk surprised no one by declaring war on Mexico. News of the war had not reached California by mid-June when a group of settlers stormed General Mariano Vallejo's Sonoma estate. Vallejo soothed the men with brandy and watched as they raised their hastily sewn Bear Flag over

Sonoma's Plaza. The Bear Flag Revolt is sanctified in California history, but for all its drama, it was immaterial. Within a few weeks Commodore John Sloat arrived to usher California into the Union. The Bear Flag is now the state flag of California.

Most of the fighting in the War of American Conquest took place in the south. The war in the north effectively ended on July 9, 1846, when 70 sailors and marines from the ship *Portsmouth* marched ashore in Yerba Buena village and raised the stars-and-stripes in the central plaza.

The bloodiest battle on California soil took place in the Valley of San Pasqual, near

Escondido. The Army of the West, commanded by General Stephen W. Kearney, fought a brief battle during which 18 Americans were killed.

Kearney's aide-de-camp was US naval officer Robert F. Stockton. Together they skirmished with Mexican-Californians at Paso de Bartolo on the San Gabriel River. The *Californios*, however, soon capitulated and California's participation in the Mexican War ended with the Treaty of Cahuenga.

The Treaty of Guadalupe Hidalgo, which came into force on July 4 (US Independence Day), 1848, ended the Mexican War. By this treaty, California became a territory of the United States of America. Through fierce negotiation, San Diego was saved from being on the south side of the Mexico-California boundary.

In 1850, California, the Bear Republic, became the 31st state of the Union.

Life on the *ranchos* flowed on with little change. Washington, DC, was even further away from California than Mexico City, so communication by land was slow. The *rancheros* had to depend on the Yankee trading ships. Cattle was still king. But a new word crept into the news – gold.

The Gold Rush: Gold was discovered in Placeritas Canyon, north of Mission San Fernando, in 1842. Francisco Lopez, rounding up stray horses, stopped to rest beneath an oak tree. He opened his knife to uproot some wild onions, and their roots came out attached to something bright in the sun – a nugget of gold.

Six years later, gold was discovered at Sutter's Mill near Sacramento in Northern California. Word spread to Easterners and the stampede began. What had been a single file of men trekking through the Sierras to California now became a torrent of gold-dazzled prospectors.

Rather than the solitary trapper, entire parties in covered wagons made their way west. When they encountered the sheer cliffs of the Sierra Nevada, they winched up the wagons or took them apart and lowered them down precipices. A time of change exploded its force upon the land.

Left, protrait of Gold Rush-era Chinese immigrant in traditional garb. **Right**, poster entices New Englanders to join the migration to California following the Civil War.

EMIGRATION TO
CALIFORNIA !

Do you want to go to California! If so, go and join the Company who intend going out the middle of March, or 1st of April next, under the charge of the California Emigration Society, in a first-rate Clipper Ship. The Society agreeing to find places for all those who wish it upon their arrival in San Francisco. The voyage will probably be made in a few months.— Price of passage will be in the vicinity of

ONE HUNDRED DOLLARS !
CHILDREN IN PROPORTION.

A number of families have already engaged passage. A suitable Female Nurse has been provided, who will take charge of Young Ladies and Children. Good Physicians, both male and female go in the Ship. It is hoped a large number of females will go, as Females are getting almost as good wages as males.

FEMALE NURSES get 25 dollars per week and board. SCHOOL TEACHERS 100 dollars per month. GARDNERS 60 dollars per month and board. LABORERS 4 to 5 dollars per day. BRICKLAYERS 6 dollars per day. HOUSEKEEPERS 40 dollars per month. FARMERS 5 dollars per day. SHOEMAKERS 4 dollars per day. Men and Women COOKS 40 to 60 dollars per month and board. MINERS are making from 3 to 12 dollars per day. FEMALE SERVANTS 30 to 50 dollars per month and board. Washing 3 dollars per dozen. MASONS 6 dollars per day. CARPENTERS 5 dollars per day. ENGINEERS 100 dollars per month, and as the quartz Crushing Mills are getting into operation all through the country, Engineers are very scarce. BLACKSMITHS 90 and 100 dollars per month and board.

The above prices are copied from late papers printed in San Francisco, which can be seen at my office. Having views of some 30 Cities throughout the State of California, I shall be happy to see all who will call at the office of the Society, 28 JOY'S BUILDING, WASHINGTON ST., BOSTON, and examine them. Parties residing out of the City, by enclosing a stamp and sending to the office, will receive a circular giving all the particulars of the voyage.

As Agents are wanted in every town and city of the New England States, Postmasters or Merchants acting as such will be allowed a certain commission on every person they get to join the Company. Good reference required. For further particulars correspond or call at the

SOCIETY'S OFFICE,
28 Joy's Building, Washington St., Boston, Mass.

Capt Sutter's account of the first discovery of the Gold.

"I was sitting one afternoon," said the Captain, "just after my siesta, engaged, by-the-bye, in writing a letter to a relation of mine at Lucern, when I was interrupted by Mr. Marshal, a gentleman with whom I had frequent business transactions—bursting hurriedly into the room. From the unusual agitation in his manner I imagined that something serious had occurred, and, as we involuntarily do in this part of the world, I at once glanced to see if my rifle was in its proper place. You should know that the mere appearance of Mr. Marshal at that moment in the Fort, was quite enough to surprise me, as he had but two days before left here to make some alterations in a mill for sawing pine planks, which he had just run up for me, some miles higher up the Americano. When he had recovered himself a little, he told me that, however great my surprise might be at his unexpected reappearance, it would be much greater when I heard the intelligence he had come to bring me. 'Intelligence,' he added, 'which if properly profited by, would put both of us in possession of unheard-of wealth—millions and millions of dollars, in fact.' I frankly own, when I heard this that I thought something had touched Marshall's brain, when suddenly all my misgivings were put an end to by his flinging on the table a handful of scales of pure virgin gold. I was fairly thunderstruck and asked him to explain what all this meant, when he went on to say, that according to my instructions, he had thrown the mill-wheel out of gear, to let the whole body of the water in the dam find a passage through the tail race, which was previously too narrow to allow the water to run off in sufficient quantity, whereby the wheel was prevented from efficiently performing its work. By this alteration the narrow channel was considerably enlarged, and a mass of sand & gravel carried off by the force of the torrent. Early in the morning after this took place, Mr. Marshal was walking along the left bank of the stream when he perceived something which he at first took for a piece of opal—a clear transparent stone, very common here—glittering on one of the spots laid bare by the sudden crumbling away of the bank. He paid no attention to this; but while he was giving directions to the workmen, having observed several similar glittering fragments, his curiosity was so far excited, that he stooped down & picked one of them up. 'Do you know,' said Mr. Marshal to me, 'I positively debated within myself two or three times whether I should take the trouble to bend my back to pick up one of the pieces, and had decided on not doing so when further on, another glittering morsel caught my eye—the largest of the pieces now before you. I condescended to pick it up, and to my astonishment found that it was a thin scale of what appears to be pure gold.' He then gathered some twenty or thirty pieces which on examination convinced him that his supposition were right. His first impression was, that this gold had been lost or buried there, by some early Indian tribe—perhaps some of those mysterious inhabitants of the west, of whom we have no account, but who dwelt on this continent centuries ago, and built those cities and temples, the ruins of which are scattered about these solitary wilds. On proceeding, however, to examine the neighbouring soil, he discovered that it was more or less auriferous. This at once decided him. He mounted his horse, and rode down to me as fast as it could carry him with the news.

At the conclusion of Mr. Marshal's account, and when I had convinced myself, from the specimens he had brought with him, that it was not exagerated, I felt as much excited as himself. I eagerly inquired if he had shown the gold to the workpeople at the mill and was glad to hear that he had not spoken to a single person about it. We agreed not to mention the circumstance to any one, and arranged to set off early the next day for the mill. On our arrival, just before sundown, we poked the sand about in various places, and before long succeeded in collecting between us more than an ounce of gold, mixed up with a good deal of sand. I stayed at Mr. Marshall's that night, and the next day we proceeded some little distance up the south Fork, and found that gold existed along the whole course, not only in the bed of the main stream, where the had subsided but in every little dried-up creek and ravine. Indeed I think it is more plentiful in these latter places, for I myself, with nothing more than a small knife, picked out from dry gorge, a little way up the mountain, a solid lump of gold which weighed nearly an ounce and a half.

Notwithstanding our precautions not to be observed, as soon we came back to the mill we noticed by the excitement of the working people that we had been dogged about, an to complet our disoppointment, some of the indians who had worked at the gold mine in the neighbourhood of la Paz cried out in showing to us some specimens picked up by himself, — *Oro! Oro — Oro!!!*

"THERE'S GOLD IN THEM THAR HILLS!"

James Marshall's world-shaking discovery took place in the millrace of a sawmill set by the American River in the Sierra Nevada foothills. History usually races by at this point, not stopping to ask just what a sawmill was doing beside an often-raging torrent in the mountains. That sawmill was one of the the screwier ideas of John Augustus Sutter – a man, one contemporary wrote, with a disastrous "mania for undertaking too much".

Born in Switzerland in 1803, Sutter arrived in San Francisco in 1839. Despite a disorderly career as a Swiss Army officer and dry-goods merchant, he somehow impressed Alta California's authorities enough to offer him the largest possible land grant, nearly 50,000 acres (about 20,000 hectares) of the Central Valley. Sutter named his grant "New Helvetia" and, using Indians as serf labor, set out to create a semi-independent barony.

Sutter's Fort, at what is now Sacramento, was often the first stop for bedraggled overlanders after their harrowing Sierra crossing. Sutter gloried in providing comfort and goods (at a price) to California's new settlers. He planted wheat and fruit orchards, bought out the Russians at Fort Ross, lent his aid to several of Northern California's jostling factions, and in 1847 decided to build the sawmill that was his ultimate undoing.

As John Bidwell, an astute early immigrant, wrote: "Rafting sawed lumber down the canyons of the American river (was such a) wild scheme that no other man than Sutter would have been so confiding and credulous to believe it possible."

Sutter had hired Marshall to oversee the mill's construction. (Today a recreation of the fabled mill stands at Colomba, 50-odd miles east of Sacramento.) On January 24, 1848, Marshall peered into the millrace and noticed a bit of shiny material, one of the millions of smithereens of gold that had been gaily tumbling down the streams of the Sierra for millennia.

Marshall took the nugget to Sutter. The two "applied every test of their ingenuity and the American Encyclopaedia", and decided that it was indeed gold. They raced back up to the sawmill, poked and panned awhile, and looked each other straight and clean in the eye. They had found the country of gold.

Sutter realized that New Helvetia would be overrun if word of the discovery leaked out prematurely. He swore his mill hands to secrecy. But Sutter's Fort was probably the worst place in California to keep a secret, and nuggets kept popping up in bars and stores at

A GOLD HUNTER ON HIS WAY TO CALIFORNIA, VIA S.ᵗ LOUIS.

the Fort and in the mission towns. John Bidwell wrote that "as a lumber enterprise, the mill was a failure, but as a gold discovery, it was a grand success." Sam Brannan shooed away the last scraps of silence. On May 12 he strolled down Montgomery Street in San Francisco, beaver hat cocked, a vial of gold dust held high, shouting "Gold! Gold! Gold on the American River!"

Gold fever: The Western world had been waiting for the myth to come to life for centuries. The Spanish had uprooted and discarded more than one civilization looking for the country of gold. The rest of the world had watched and waited and looked for itself.

Left, John Sutter's personal account of the discovery of gold at his sawmill. **Right**, an Eastern publisher's tongue-in-cheek view of a California-bound fortune seeker.

The myth had grown into a prophecy.

The news spread as rapidly as the times allowed. San Francisco was left nearly deserted, its shops stripped of axes, pans, tents, beans, soda crackers, picks and whatever else might conceivably be of use. Monterey, San Jose, all of Northern California's mission towns and farms joined in the scramble. Gold fever worked its way to Utah and Oregon, where "two-thirds of the able-bodied men were on their way to the diggings."

Ships in the Pacific spread the word to Peru, Chile, Hawaii and Australia. Lt. L. Loeser carried a "small chest… containing $3,000 worth of gold in lumps and scales" back to Washington, DC, where it was ex-

school-boy's map… The Sacramento River was reported as abounding in alligators… The general opinion was that it was a fearfully hot country and full of snakes."

Dodging snakes and alligators was a small price to pay for instant wealth. In the first three years of the Gold Rush, more than 200,000 men, a few women, and fewer children came to California in one of the greatest peaceful mass migrations in the history of the world.

The farm boys, sharpies, bored clerks and solid citizens who comprised this horde known as "The '49ers" were plucky and young – more than half were in their 20s. Almost all were male, though as always

hibited at the War Office, irradiating the Capital with cherry greed. On December 2, President Polk told Congress that the "extraordinary accounts" were true. A few days later the *New York Herald* summed it up: "The El Dorado of the old Spaniards is discovered at last."

Westward Ho!: In 1848, despite the ruckus of the Mexican-American War, California was still popularly thought of as somewhere tucked away behind the back of the beyond. Young Prentice Mulford of Sag Harbor, New Nork – who later became one of San Francisco's literary stars – remembered that "California was but a blotch of yellow on the

there were some bemused wives, indomitable cultural missionaries, and more than a few of those tough ladies who could turn a profit from the company of men. The '49ers needed all their pluck to survive the diggings, and before that the toilsome journey to California and its heady boom town of San Francisco.

About half of the '49ers chose the overland route to the gold country. Many were Eastern and Missouri Valley farmers who already owned the necessary wagons and stock. In April and May 1849, the jumping-off towns of St Joseph and Independence, Missouri, and Council Bluffs, Iowa, were choked with eager gold seekers. There they formed into caravans for the long, still-mysterious trek west. There were a number of routes, but most followed the shallow, weaving Platte River across Nebraska, their scouts calling back with news of the famous landmarks ahead – Courthouse Rocks, Chimney Rock, Scotts Bluff, Independence Rock, talismans of fortune to come.

The overlanders crossed the Rockies at South Pass near the forbidding Wind River Range in Wyoming, then dropped down to Salt Lake City. After reprovisioning at the Mormon capital, the worst part of the journey – the crossing of the Great Basin – began. Cholera was widespread. Indian attacks were

a constant fear. In some places waterholes were 30 to 40 miles apart. A broken axle, a sick animal, a lost trail could and often did mean bottomless disaster.

By the time the trains reached the eastern slope of the Sierra, what one chronicler had called "a mighty army" more often looked like a strung-out collection of stragglers. After the bitter dryness of the Humboldt Sink, the climb up the mountains began.

Left, **"Lift at the Mines" from a late 19th-century book. Pick-and-shovel work was hardly a romantic concept; neither was the perilous voyage around Cape Horn, <u>above</u>.**

Finally the crest was reached, and beyond it, after five or six months of work and heat and campfire dreams, the long view over the green western slope, down to the foothills and the country of gold itself.

The sea routes to California were simpler, sometimes shorter, and usually less exhausting. The quickest route was by way of the Isthmus of Panama, long before construction of the Panama Canal. Ships from the Eastern seaboard, crammed with gold seekers, sailed to the Atlantic port of Chagres, a "50-hut cesspool of matted reeds". From Chagres the '49ers made their way by canoe, foot and mule across the mosquito-infested and disease-drenched isthmus. (Their deeply rutted trail had been built centuries earlier by the Spanish, who used it to transport Peruvian gold to the Atlantic and back to Europe.) At the end of the trail lay "another tropical excrescence", the town of Panama. There the argonauts piled up, madly bidding for tickets on San Francisco-bound ships.

The Panama route took six to eight weeks. The voyage around Cape Horn was cheaper but took four to eight months, sometimes much longer. It was alternately boring and dangerous (between 1851 and 1853, 11 ships were lost at the icy cape); the rations were wormy and meager, the captains dictatorial, the quarters impacted with would be millionaires. But like the overlanders at their campfires, the Cape Horners sugared their voyage with dreams.

Those hundreds of thousands of reveries were fixed on the fabled Mother Lode, which ran for 120 miles (193 km) from north of Sutter's Mill to Mariposa in the south. Forty-niners worked the streams of the Klamath Mountains in the far north early on. Later, the southern deserts had their share of miners and boom towns. But the Mother Lode's wooden hills and deep valleys were the great centers of the raucous, short-lived argonaut civilization.

Gold Rush mining, especially in the early days before the streams were panned out, was a simple affair. The Mother Lode was owned by the federal government, and claims were limited to the ground a man and his fellows could actually work. Stockpiling of claims was thus impossible. Hiring a work force was unlikely, as there was little reason to make another man rich when one's own wealth-spouting claim was so easily got.

The Sierra streams did much of the miner's work for him. The rushing waters eroded the hillsides and sent placer gold (from dust to nugget size) rushing downstream. A miner crouched by the streambank, scooped up a panful of gravel, muttered, sighed, shifted, and turned his pan, letting the gold sink to the bottom as debris washed out. Later, sluices – in effect, pans made large – were built, holes were dug, and finally hydraulic mining took over. (It was banned in 1884 after causing dramatic ecological damage to the foothills.)

California was rushed into the Union on September 9, 1850. In November 1849, it had already formed a state government and drafted a constitution which guaranteed the

at dance halls, peering at nuggets, adding to the legend. The '49ers themselves knew they were part of a phenomenon. Their correspondence bristled with extravagances.

There was money to be wrung out of those hills. The problem lay in keeping it. In 1849, $10 million of gold was mined in California; the next year, four times that. In 1852, the pinnacle of the Rush, $80 million wound up in someone's pockets.

The men who started the Gold Rush, John Sutter and James Marshall, were only two of the many losers in the great game. Marshall ended his days in 1885 near the site of his discovery, broken-down, weepy, shaking his fist at fate. Sutter, whose barony was overrun

right to "enjoying and defending life and liberty, acquiring, possessing and protecting property, and pursuing and obtaining happiness", a typically Californian mix of the sublime and practical.

The Gold Rush was a world marvel. After all, the country of gold was a legend even before it was discovered, and once it was found it sold newspapers and books, rail, ship, coach and barge tickets, and enlivened imaginations in every corner of the globe. Authors like Alexandre Dumas, Mark Twain and Bret Harte spun romantic tales of life in the diggings. Countless reporters weaved their way through the Mother Lode, gaping

just as he'd feared, kept a brave front for some years. But history had swept him aside, too, and he died in 1880 after years of futile petitions to Congress for restitution.

As easy as it was to find, the Mother Lode's gold was easier to lose – to rapacious traders, in the gambling halls and bawdy-houses, to the simple unwisdom of young men. But for most it was a grand adventure. Many returned home sheepishly but full of stories for their grandchildren.

Old mine buildings and equipment, remnants of the Gold Rush era, persist in ghost towns like Bodie, east of the Sierras.

The Gold Rush's magic was nowhere more powerful than in San Francisco, immediately and forever after the capital of the country of gold. When Sam Brannan ambled down Montgomery Street with his vial of gold, the town's population was less than 1,000. By early 1850, when the madness was in full swing, upwards of 30,000 souls were in residence.

Bayard Taylor, a doughty reporter for the *New York Tribune*, witnessed the explosion of San Francisco into a "perpetual carnival". When Taylor arrived in September 1849, the town was still "a scattering of tents and canvas houses with a show of frame buildings on one or two streets". After four months in the diggings, he returned to find "an actual metropolis, displaying street after street of well-built edifices… lofty hotels, gaudy with verandahs and balconies were met with (everywhere), finished with home luxury and aristocratic restaurants presented daily their long bills of fare, rich with the choicest technicalities of Parisian cuisine."

Dollar eggs: For those who could afford it, the cuisine was indeed technical, but for most of the '49ers it was rough, ready and slightly less expensive. Eggs from the Farallone Islands sold for $1 apiece. Real-estate speculation was epidemic. As the city burst from the boundaries of Yerba Buena Cove, "water lots" sold for crazy prices on the expectation they could be made habitable with landfill. Much of today's downtown San Francisco is built on landfill.

Commodity speculation was a dangerous game. Whereas Sam Brannan might succeed in cornering the tea market Joshua Abraham Norton was wrecked trying to corner the rice market. Norton's ruin in 1853 scrambled his senses. After laying low for a few months, he put on a tatty uniform and proclaimed himself Emperor of the United States and Protector of Mexico. Emperor Norton I went on to enjoy a quarter-century reign as San Francisco's leading eccentric, a living reminder of the lunacy of the Gold Rush.

Vigilantes took the law into their own hands in the 1850s. Right, a graphic recreation of an 1856 execution.

None of California's new towns, much less San Francisco, were built with much care or foresight. Pre-Gold Rush street plans, based on tight grids, were expanded out from flat Yerba Buena Cove with a flick of pen on ruler, jauntily ignoring the city's hills – which is why San Francisco's streets barge up and down those hills, rather than gracefully following their contours. Most buildings were hasty wooden edifices, and between 1849 and 1851, six major fires ravaged San Francisco. Sacramento, smaller, marginally

quieter, also had its share of blazes.

Most of California's new tenants – fixed on their golden dreams – had little desire to pour the foundation for the orderly society that would surely follow the Gold Rush. The popular conception was that the foothills were crammed with gold. "Ages will not exhaust the supply," Bayard Taylor wrote.

In the end, the winners in the great money-scramble were those who took the time to sink roots by establishing businesses and buying land, taking advantage of the '49ers' disdain for tomorrow. So each fire was an opportunity for the arising bourgeoisie to build new, more solid buildings. Each boatload of grinning '49ers represented another batch of customers.

In 1851 the forces of social stability asserted their constitutional right to "acquire, possess and defend property" by warring against the criminal elements that feasted on California's plentiful lack of tranquility. In San Francisco, hoodlums (a word coined in late 19th-century San Francisco, by the way) had organized themselves into gangs like the Sydney Ducks and the Hounds. At least some of the city's fires were set by these gangs, in addition to routine robberies, beatings and generally ugly behavior.

Rise of the vigilantes: The robbery and beating in early 1851 of a merchant named

vigilante corps. Scores of California towns followed suit. California's first bout of vigilantism put a damper on crime for awhile. But within two years a resurgence of outlawry threatened the state's fragile social order.

In 1853 the Gold Rush began to wind down. Gold production dropped by $30 million. Real-estate values fell 20 to 30 percent. Immigration slowed to a trickle and merchants were cornered by massive over-supplies ordered during the heady days.

But San Francisco's growth had been phenomenal. At decade's end it had a population of 50,000, a level it had taken New York 190 years to reach, Boston 200, Philadelphia 120. California's capital had been in

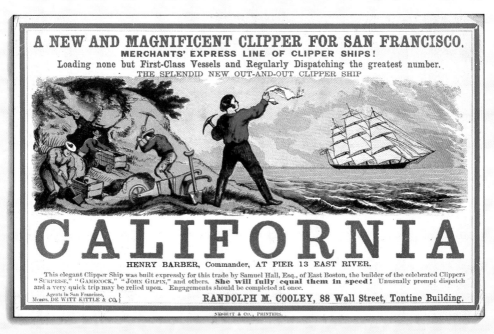

C.J. Jensen inflamed the righteous, especially Sam Brannan – a man who, according to historian Josiah Royce, was "always in love with shedding the blood of the wicked". Newspapers like the *Alta* brought up the specter of lynch law, and Brannan shouted that the time had come to bypass "the quibbles of the law, the insecurity of the prisons, and the laxity of those who pretend to administer justice". A Committee of Vigilance was formed; soon a Sydney Duck named John Jenkins was hanged for stealing a safe. (He dumped it in the Bay, but the absence of evidence didn't deter the vigilantes).

Within two weeks Sacramento had its own

Sacramento since 1854, but San Francisco presided without rival over a rapidly settling, coalescing state. Agriculture in the Central Valley had grown fantastically in response to the needs of the state's exploding population. In the decade of the 1850s, for instance, California's cattle herds grew from 262,000 to more than 3 million. Towns like Stockton, San Jose and Monterey were thriving as '49ers set up their shops and sank their roots.

Whatever chance California had of becoming placid, however, was swept away in 1859 by yet another torrent of riches flowing down the Sierra slope. This time it was silver, not gold, that geared up the rush.

The rush for silver: One of the most comfortless outposts of the Gold Rush had been centered around Nevada's Sun Mountain on the dry eastern slope of the Sierra near Lake Tahoe. There was a little gold up in the Virginia Range, enough for an occasional "$10 Gold Rush" as the crusty denizens ruefully put it. But eking a living out of the area's irritating bluish clay was wicked work. In June 1859 a sample of that "blue stuff" found its way to Melville Atwood, an assayist in Grass Valley. Atwood found an astounding $3,876 worth of silver in that sample of Sun Mountain ore.

At first it appeared that the Silver Rush would mimic the Gold Rush of a decade earlier. lionaires "expected to find masses of silver lying all about the ground". The problem for Twain and the thousands like him was that the silver was *in*, not *on*, the steep and rugged mountains. And getting it out was no matter of poking and panning.

The Silver Rush, it turned out, was a game for capitalists, men with the money to dig tunnels, buy claims, install the expensive machinery and mills that transformed the blue stuff into cash. They were men like William Ralston of the Bank of California in San Francisco, and the four legendary "Bonanza Kings", James Flood and William O'Brien – former saloon-keepers – and James Fair and John W. Mackay – old miners –

earlier. "Our towns are near depleted," wrote one spectator. "They look as languid as a consumptive girl. What has become of our sinewy and athletic fellow citizens? They are coursing through ravines and over mountaintops", looking for silver.

One of the athletic young men who rushed up to the Virginia Range was Mark Twain. In his marvelous book *Roughing It*, he describes how he and his fellow almost-millionaires

whose Consolidated Virginia regularly disgorged $6 million a month.

As usual, the treasures of the Comstock Lode (named for a gristle-brained old timer who, in traditional fashion, ended up broke) flowed downslope from the boomtown of Virginia City to San Francisco. By 1863, $40 million of silver had been wrestled out of the trembling tunnels in, around, and through Sun Mountain. Two thousand mining companies traded shares in San Francisco's Mining Exchange. Fortunes were made and lost in moments as rumors of bonanza or *borasca* (profitless rock) swept into town. At one time, more speculative money was wrapped up in Comstock mining shares than existed in real form on the whole Pacific Coast.

The Comstock lasted until the 1880s. The $400 million the Virginia Range yielded had plumped up California's economy. In San Francisco, Billy Ralston, the Comstock's greatest mine owner, had taken over from Sam Brannan as the city's top booster. (Sam by this time was going broke trying to make his resort at Calistoga into "The Saratoga of the West". He died, dollarless, in 1889.) Ralston poured his Comstock money into a myriad of grand schemes: he built the Palace, America's largest city hotel; he bought sugar refineries, lumber, stage and water companies; and as the 1860s drew to a close, he happily prepared for what he and his fellow plutocrats thought would be the capstone to the state's greatness – the long-awaited completion of the Transcontinental Railroad.

Advent of the railroad: Plans for a railroad linking the coasts had been floating around for many years. When the Civil War broke out Congress, intent upon securing California's place in the Union, at last stirred itself. In the winter of 1862, the Pacific Railroad Act granted vast tracts of Western land, low-interest financing and outright subsidies to two companies – the Central Pacific, building from Sacramento, and the Union Pacific, building from Omaha. As it happened, the Civil War largely bypassed California, but it nonetheless prompted the building of a railroad that brought unexpected havoc to the state.

The genius of the Central Pacific was a young engineer named Theodore Dehone Judah. Judah had built California's first railroad, the 22-mile Sacramento Valley line, in 1856. He spent years crafting the crucial route across the Sierra at Donner Pass. Unfortunately for Judah, the Central Pacific's other partners were uncommonly cunning and grabby men.

Charles Crocker, Mark Hopkins, Collis Huntington and Leland Stanford, who became known as "The Big Four", were Sacramento shopkeepers when they invested in Judah's scheme. Shortly after Congress dumped its largesse in their laps, they forced Judah out of the Central Pacific. He died, age 37, in 1863, still trying to wrest control from his former partners.

The Central Pacific made the Big Four almost insanely rich. The ex-dry goods merchants moved to San Francisco's Nob Hill and began a merry mansion-building jamboree. The government's haste to get the railroad built, and Stanford's political maneuvering, made the Central Pacific the virtual dictator of California politics for years. When Frank Norris wrote *The Octopus* in 1901, no one had to guess at the reference: the Southern Pacific (as it was renamed in 1884) had its tentacles in every corner of the state.

In the beginning, at least, carping at the Big Four's use of the railroad's treasury as a kind of private money preserve was a game for malcontents and socialists. In the mahogany boardrooms of San Francisco's

banks, on the editorial pages of its newspapers, in the overheated stock exchange, up and down Montgomery Street, the verdict was the same. The railroad would bring firm and fabulous prosperity to California.

The Golden Spike: In April 1868, five years after construction had begun on Sacramento's Front Street, the first Central Pacific train breached the Sierra at Donner Pass. (With typical cheek, the Big Four had convinced the government that the Sierra slope began a few miles outside of Sacramento, thereby netting millions in hardship allowances.) Once the historic rampart was crossed it was downhill work. On May 12, 1869, the Golden

Spike was driven at Promontory Point, Utah, and the coasts were linked.

"San Francisco Annexes the Union" read one San Francisco headline. But the rush of prosperity failed utterly to materialize. Only a few deep thinkers – none of them ensconced in boardrooms – had understood the financial calamity the railroad would bring.

One of the deepest thinkers of all was Henry George, a journeyman printer and passionate theorist. In 1868 George, whose idea of the Single Tax is still important in socialist thinking, outlined the catastrophe to come. In an article in the *Overland Monthly*, he predicted that California's immature factories would be undersold by the Eastern

George's prophecies began arriving with the first train. In San Francisco, real-estate dealing of $3.5 million a month fell to $1.5 million a month within a year. In the winter of 1869–70 a severe drought crippled the state's agriculture. Between 1873 and 1875 more than a quarter of a million immigrants came to California. Many were factory workers and few could find work. The "Terrible '70s" had arrived.

"The Terrible '70s": For William Chapman Ralston the 1870s were a calamity. As head of the Bank of California in San Francisco, he had presided over the endless boom mentality that was a legacy of the Gold Rush. He was, a friend said, a man "with a passionate,

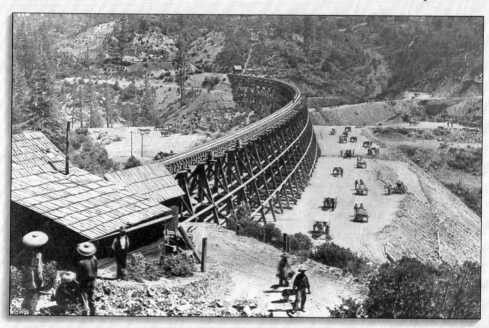

manufacturing colossus. He predicted that the Central Pacific's ownership of vast parcels of land along its right-of-way would drive prices of much-needed agricultural land shamefully high. George even saw the racial tensions that would result from the railroad's importation of thousands of Chinese laborers. "Crocker's Pets", as they were called, flooded the state's job market in the 1870s and became targets for bitter discontent.

Left, the domination of the railroad by "The Big Four" was a target of protest for the press. While they became very rich, Chinese laborers toiled for sparse wages, **above**.

almost pathetic love of California". In the mid '70s the full bloom of depression was on the state. On "Black Friday", April 26, 1875, a run on the Bank of California forced it to slam shut its huge oaken doors at Sansome and California streets. Driven into debt by Comstock mining losses and by the failure of the railroad to bring prosperity, Bill Ralston drowned the next day while taking his customary swim in the Bay.

Ralston's death signalled the end of California's booming affluence. Those hurt most by the great shrinkage of capital in the 1870s were the state's working people. During the Gold and Silver rushes California's laborers had enjoyed a rare freedom to move easily from job to job and to dictate working conditions. Now, however, with massive unemployment, unionization began to take hold. For the next 60 years California would suffer recurrent bouts of labor strife.

The depression was slow to disappear, but California was too rich to suffer permanently. In the next few decades it slowly built its industrial strength up to the point where it could compete with the East. After decades of depending on the land to deliver riches in the form of gold or silver, the state developed its agricultural lands as never before. In the Central Valley, wheat, rice and cotton became major cash crops. The splendid Napa

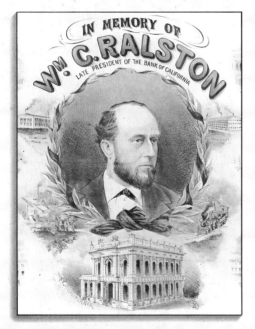

Valley began to produce fine wines in earnest in the late 1870s.

Orange orbs in the South: The thousands who jammed the trains destined for Los Angeles during the 1880s did not come here by chance. They knew why they had come – to seek out the golden avalanche of orange orchards. One photograph issued by the Chamber of Commerce was enough to convince the Easterners that these orchards existed in abundance in the Golden State, so they lost no time in coming. The photo showed an indelible image of snow-capped peaks, waving palms, and golden orbs amid dark-green leaves.

Sometime between 1873 and 1875, two or three orange trees were sent from the Department of Agriculture, Washington, DC, to Eliza and Luther Tibbetts in Riverside. The young trees had been budded from a seedless orange whose origin was Bahia, Brazil. The Tibbetts planted the trees, little knowing that a decade later navel oranges would alter the agricultural, economic and social patterns of the area. The Washington navel orange, as the seedless and sweet fruit was officially known, became (in the words of Charles F. Lummis) "not only a fruit but a romance".

Durable enough to survive long-distance shipping, this citrus fruit hit its prime by 1889 when more than 13,000 acres (5,260 hectares) of land in the six southern counties were devoted to its cultivation. Growers formed a marketing cooperative, the California Fruit Growers Exchange, famed for its ubiquitous trademark, Sunkist.

In a mere 18 months, Horace Greeley's "Go West, young man" philosophy became a reality. Many boomtowns took root and soon the population equalled that of the north.

This vast semitropical, often desert-like land reached its potential. Thousands of acres of good farmland sold by the railroads at low prices were planted with wheat, oranges, grapes, cotton, tea, tobacco and coffee. Irrigation converted vast tracts of this arid waste to fertile land bearing fruit and field crops. Agriculture, boosted by rail transportation, became the backbone of Southern California.

Meanwhile San Francisco's boomtown mentality may have taken a beating, but as the century wore on, its historic predilection for high living remained. Rudyard Kipling, visiting during the Gilded Age at the end of the century called it "a mad city, inhabited for the most part by perfectly insane people whose women are of a remarkable beauty." San Francisco's society had "a captivating rush and whirl. Recklessness is in the air".

The Gilded Age, with all its extravagance and corruption, continued right up to an April morning in 1906, after which nothing was ever the same again.

Left, low points of "The Terrible Seventies" include the death of financier William Ralston. **Right**, a turn-of-the-20th-century advertisement extols the virtues of Southern California.

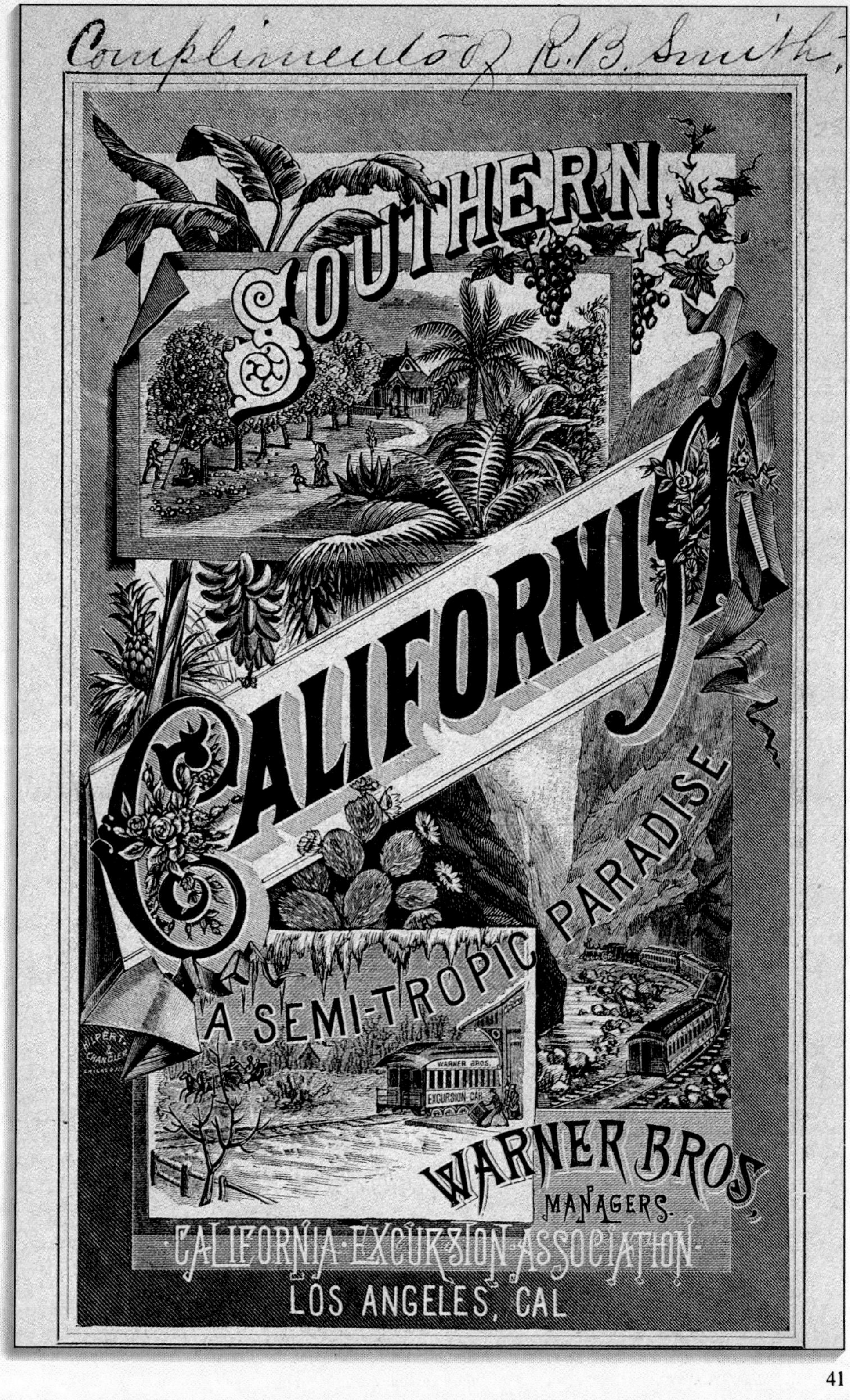

Compliments of R. B. Smith,
SOUTHERN
CALIFORNIA
A SEMI-TROPIC PARADISE
WARNER BROS.
EXCURSION-CAR
WARNER BROS,
MANAGERS.
·CALIFORNIA·EXCURSION·ASSOCIATION·
LOS ANGELES, CAL

Old San Franciscans talk about "The Fire of 1906", but it was an earthquake that started the fire that first shook Northern Californians from their beds at 5.12 a.m. on April 18, 1906. When the deadly San Andreas Fault lurched that morning it sent terrifying jolts through an area 210 miles (338 km) long and 30 miles (48 km) wide, from San Juan Bautista in the south to Fort Bragg in the north. Other towns like San Jose and Point Reyes Station near Drake's Bay suffered more from the initial shock than San Fran-

ered up what seemed important at the moment and trekked up the hills away from the firestorm. In Chinatown, women with bound feet were carried to safety. The streets were jammed with carts and carriages, and with dazed men and women carrying heirlooms and caged birds, old paintings and squawking children.

For three days and nights the fire raged. Three-quarters of San Francisco's homes, businesses and hotels were destroyed. From Oakland and Marin, from atop the city's

cisco. As it was, few lives were lost in the quake itself. Elaborate moldings crashed onto early morning streets, dishes fell, windows shattered, dogs barked, Enrico Caruso (appearing locally in *Carmen*) was scared voiceless, and San Francisco's new City Hall crumbled.

But as the city nervously started assessing the damage, a scourge of fires began in the Financial District. San Francisco was still a wooden city, and the fires quickly melded and began a sickening westward march. By mid-afternoon the Financial District was enveloped in flame. Billy Ralston's proud Palace Hotel was engulfed. Refugees gath-

hills, San Francisco appeared a single maw of flame. The fire's westward advance seemed inexorable. Mayor Schmitz and General Frederick Funston of the Presidio decided to halt the fire by dynamiting houses on the west side of Van Ness Avenue. Many (especially those whose Victorians were being blasted away) thought the dynamiting encouraged the fire. But a blessed shift in the wind ended the shouted debate, and the fire was driven back on itself.

In the end the destruction of San Francisco's hub was almost total. Buildings on Telegraph Hill were saved when they were draped with wine-soaked burlap. The Old Mint at

5th and Mission streets was rescued by heroic efforts of the Appraiser-General and his men. But when the fires at last burned out, more than half of the city's 400,000 residents were homeless. Some 28,000 buildings, four-fifths of San Francisco's property, had been destroyed. More than $400 million had gone up in smoke.

The Fire of 1906 was more horrifying than any before it, but San Francisco gathered up its Gold Rush spirit and immediately set to work rebuilding itself. For many months the city's parks were taken over by tent cities. In the unaffected areas all cooking was done in the streets while gas mains were carefully checked. Construction began, photographer

Street, the Wall Street of the West, were needed to process the money churned out by the state's industries, farms and banks. The Port of San Francisco was still one of the world's busiest. San Francisco's historic business of making business was unstoppable.

The rebirth of San Francisco after the Fire of 1906 ushered in an era of good feeling. In 1911 San Francisco elected a new mayor, James "Sunny Jim" Rolph, a shiny purveyor of good will and government-with-a-wink, an ideal complement to flush times.

Sunny Jim's reign encompassed some of San Francisco's giddiest times. There was, for instance, the Panama Pacific International Exposition, cranked up in 1915 to

Arnold Genthe wrote, "while the ruins were still smoking. On top of a heap of collapsed walls, a sign would announce: 'On this site will be erected a six-storey office building to be ready for occupancy in the fall.' "

San Francisco's renaissance was indeed plucky. It was also inevitable. The new, improved, taller buildings of Montgomery

Preceding pages: terrified San Franciscans watched helplessly as the fire of 1906 engulfed Sacramento Street. **Left**, the city appeared as a veritable wasteland on the day following the disaster, but that didn't dissuade hungry diners, **above**.

celebrate the city's rebirth. Still considered one of the greatest of the world's fairs, the Panama Pacific was built on 600 acres (244 hectares) of reclaimed land in what is now the Marina. The magnificent Tower of Jewels loomed over the fairgrounds while the Palaces of Agriculture, Industry and Education enlightened and thrilled millions of visitors. Today only one vestige of the flamboyant celebration remains. The Palace of Fine Arts, intended by its architect, Bernard Maybeck, to impart a certain "sadness modified by the feeling that beauty has a soothing influence", was saved from gradual decay by civic benefactors in the 1960s.

The 20th century brought about radical changes in the southern half of the state. Southern California mushroomed from an agricultural community to an industrial complex spurred on by the discovery of oil.

Edward L. Doheny's discovery of oil in 1892 in what is now the Westlake Park area made Los Angeles aware it was sitting on a fat reservoir of wealth. The "Salt Lake Field" in southwestern Los Angeles was developed, followed by fields in Huntington Beach, Santa Fe Springs and Signal Hill. Oil der-

Stanford right. He collected his money and this film sequence became history.

The movie industry: With its origins in the 5-cent peep show, the movie industry began in 1908. Everyone clamored for "flickers" and that brought an influx of self-made producers from the East to crank out one-reel Westerns and comedies. Filmmakers took advantage of the mild Californian weather for outdoor shooting. A special bonus was the geographical diversity of Southern California – mountains, deserts and ocean were all

ricks sprouted from the hills to the sea. Even Venice, constructed with canals rather than streets and sporting gondolas like its Italian counterpart, became an oil city. Fresno struck oil in 1899 and began steady oil refining as well as producing cotton, alfafa, potatoes and fruit.

Yet it was the film industry that shot Los Angeles to fame, and unwittingly, it was Leland Stanford who helped launch it. In 1878 Stanford wagered $25,000 that a galloping horse would at some time have all its four hooves off the ground. With a set of 24 cameras tripped a fraction of a second apart as the horse ran by, a photographer proved

within a day's drive, duplicating the entire world's scenery.

But for years directors could only shoot outdoors due to a lack of sophisticated photographic equipment. Even indoor scenes were shot outdoors in strong sunlight. The fields around Hollywood became filled with standing sets; an Arabic false front supplied the set for Douglas Fairbanks' *Thief of Bagdad*. From 1926, the Pickford-Fairbanks Studio immortalized such luminaries as actor Charlie Chaplin and directors D.W. Griffith and Cecil B. de Mille. Comedy became king. Mack Senett's Keystone Kops had the whole nation rolling in the aisles.

Before long, studios sprang up in Culver City and Universal City as well as Hollywood. The latter name, particularly, had by now become synonymous with the word "movies".

Silent movies accompanied by organ music gave way to the "talkies". Hundreds of movie houses sprang up. If a movie wasn't doing good box-office business, dishes were given away. Instant fortunes came to stars, directors and producers. Novelists earned more from film rights than from their original novels. Studios started instant fads, and shaped tastes and ideas the world over.

The watery war: Although the movies molded latter-day Southern California,

Mulholland, water bureau superintendent, explored the Owens Valley about 250 miles (400 km) northeast of Los Angeles. His bold plan was to construct a long aqueduct which would carry melted snow from the southern slopes of the Sierra Nevada to Los Angeles faucets.

In 1907 citizens had voted for two bond issues providing $24.5 million to build it. On its completion on November 5, 1913, the Los Angeles Aqueduct water gates opened. Some 30,000 Angelenos gathered near San Fernando to watch the first mountain waters cascading down the open aqueduct at the astonishing rate of 26 million gallons (98 million liters) a day.

without water it would have dried up. Since water that originated in the north had to supply the thirsty south, the state soon became divided into the "haves" and the "have-nots". Before 1913 Los Angeles depended on the Los Angeles River and local wells. The first settlers built a ditch, the *Zanja Madre*, to bring water to their fields. They also dug artesian wells.

Casting about for new sources of water to sustain the city's relentless growth, William

Left, a 1908 postcard pictured the new oil industry. **Above**, cast and crew held their breaths on an underwater film set of the 1920s.

The 233-mile (375-km) aqueduct has been supplemented by a conduit and today supplies 525 million gallons (nearly 2 billion liters) of water a day. All firmly believed this supply would take care of Southern California's thirst forever, but the city has been adding sources ever since. More water from the Parker Dam on the Arizona border arrived in 1941, but it cost the city a staggering $200 million. Electric power now comes mostly from Hoover Dam on the Colorado River about 206 miles away.

Even as water problems slowed to a trickle, the flood of newcomers to Southern California continued at a frightening rate.

World War II plunged California into a spasm of activity. Twenty-three million tons of war supplies and 1½ million men and women passed through the Golden Gate during the war's 46 months. The ports of San Francisco, Sausalito, Oakland, Vallejo and Alameda were busy 24 hours a day, building and repairing ships, loading supplies for the war machine. The federal government spent $3 billion on shipbuilding in the Bay Area. A dramatic new wave of immigration swept into the region as new factories needed new works – 100,000 at the Kaiser Yards in Richmond, 90,000 at Sausalito alone. Between 1941 and 1943 the number of wage earners in San Francisco almost tripled, an increase mirrored around the Bay. The federal government doled out $83 million in contracts to the California Institute of Technology (Cal Tech) alone. War jobs were generated everywhere. Even though 750,000 Californians left for stints in the service, the number of wage earners in California during the first half of the 1940s increased by nearly a million.

Following the war, the great suburban sprawl began in earnest as war workers and their families settled down to enjoy post-war prosperity. It was in large part the children of those families who were to play such a significant role in California's (and the nation's) disordered 1960s and 1970s.

As a new, almost instant society, California has always felt free to tinker with its fundament. Many of its newcomers, from the "Anglo hordes" of the 1840s to Sam Brannan's Latter-Day Saints to present-day arrivals, have come to the state to escape the burdens of conformity elsewhere. The great majority of Californians have always been settled, straight, and to one degree or another, God-fearing. But the anti-conformists – the colorful, sometimes crazy minority – have given California its name for verve and drive.

The beatniks: It was in San Francisco that the first stirrings of post-war protest and florid eccentricity were felt. While the

Pro-drug, anti-military protests are a reflection of the New Left and hippie movements which wielded great influence in the '60s.

American nation was settled into a prosperous torpor, the city's historically Italian North Beach area became the haunt of a loosely defined group of poets, writers, declaimers and pavement philosophers who became known as the beatniks (a word coined by San Francisco's famous newspaper columnist Herb Caen).

By today's standards the beatniks were rather bland. But in the 1950s they seemed titillating and somehow significant, a tempting combination for the nation's press. Latter-day Bayard Taylors ogled at their rambling poetry readings, sniffed at the light marijuana breezes drifting out of the North Beach coffee houses, and wondered if civilization could stand such a limpid assault.

As San Francisco novelist Herbert Gold has proudly written: "The beatnik begat the hippie and the hippie begat a life style that touches us in ways that extend from fashion and drugs and sexuality to politics and race and a sense of what America might be." The beatniks, it seems, mostly wanted America to go away. But it wouldn't, and before long "beat" had become a fashion and North Beach a tourist attraction.

The beats, though, had struck a nerve of dissatisfaction and alienation in America. Though it was never a coherent movement, it produced juice-stirring works like Allen Ginsberg's *Howl* and Jack Kerouac's *On the Road*. That inspired alienation gave rise to two parallel, dissimilar, but oddly congruent movements: the angry politics of the New Left and the woozy love fest of the hippies.

The first great protest of the protest-rich 1960s took place in San Francisco in the decade's first year. In mid-May, the House Un-American Activities Committee opened a series of hearings in City Hall. When hundreds of demonstrators met the Committee in the Rotunda, the police reacted furiously, turning water hoses and billy clubs on the crowds. Dozens of battered protesters were carted off to jail, but the angry shouts in City Hall were heard around the world.

The locus of dissent was the University of California at Berkeley. There the Free Speech Movement kept up a steady assault against racism, materialism and the stifling "multiversity" itself. As the war in Vietnam grew in horror, the New Left spread across America and the world, tilting at governments, bombing, marching, changing the way America looked at itself.

The hippies attacked their target with gentler weapons. While the New Left ranted at the evils of an affluent, smug, hypocritical society, the hippies tried to undermine that society with glimmering love and peace. In the mid-1960s, San Francisco became the center of the Hippie Revolution. The city was a natural refuge for the spacey idealists. It had, after all, been created by youthful myth-chasers. Many former beatniks like Ginsberg, Neal Cassady and Ken Kesey slid easily into the hippie style. The Haight-Ashbury neighborhood, which became the hippie encampment, was well-supplied with funky, cheap Victorians, and nearby Golden Gate Park was handy for roaming.

By 1967 the Haight was thronged with raggedy, long-haired young men and women. The movement reached its apogee in the massive Be-In that year and the celebrated Summer of Love the next. It was at the Be-In that Ginsberg first attempted to alter earthly consciousness by the mass chanting of the mantra *om*.

At first San Francisco was amused by the hippies. But as altogether too many sons and daughters of respected citizens took to stoned meandering, as the LSD hysteria took flight, cross-generational solicitude became scarce. Then, too, the hippies suffered as had the beatniks from their own outlandishness. Hippie became a world fashion.

Riots and social reform: Politically, many big names emerged out of California: Earl Warren, Chief Justice of the US Supreme Court; Presidents Richard Nixon and Ronald Reagan; and Governors Edmund G. Brown and Jerry Brown.

Blacks in Los Angeles had multiplied tenfold and were fed up with discriminatory employment and "unwritten" housing restrictions. On one desperately hot summer evening in 1965 the palm-shaded ghetto of Watts exploded. For six days the inner city boiled until the National Guard restored order.

The state's problems were just beginning. While Ronald Reagan was governor, the long-distance bussing of schoolchildren to achieve racial balance in schools infuriated blacks and whites. Militant Black Muslims demonstrated and two members of the Black Panthers organization died on the UCLA campus in demonstrations over the Black Studies program.

After the violence subsided, social reforms came by "working within the system". The first black lieutenant governor was Marvyn Dymally. March Fong Eu, a woman of Chinese ancestry, became Secretary of State. Thomas Bradley became the first black mayor of Los Angeles, Cesar Chavez, a Mexican-American, organized the farm workers in the upper agricultural valleys.

But the new generation of leaders that has since emerged in Southern California has its work cut out for it. Despite efforts to reform the system, some problems, especially those affecting the cities, seem to have worsened over the years. The recent explosion of gang violence in Los Angeles, for example, has focussed national attention on the seemingly intractable problem of urban poverty.

Gangs have been a part of Los Angeles life for more than 25 years, but gang rivalries have never been more vicious and have never taken so many innocent lives. The violence is being fueled by a billion-dollar trade in "crack", a cheap cocaine derivative that has become the drug of choice for an entire generation of young abusers.

Smog, smoke and spills: Californians have also started taking a serious look at their relentless exploitation of the environment. Abuse of the region's natural resources goes back for generations. Smog, created when the natural inversion layer in the Los Angeles basin traps industrial pollution and exhaust fumes, contributed to the quick decline of the citrus groves and damaged other crops.

Developers still pit their wits and legal expertise against the environmentalists. Yet these "eco-freaks" now have a vocal constituency. The Sierra Club has become caretaker of the wilderness; the Coastal Commission reviews all construction near the coastline; and all plans for major construction must be preceded by a federal environment impact report. Nuclear power plants at San Onofre and Mount Diablo (near San Francisco) also have strict legal controls. New voices are not only speaking; they are being heard.

Former President Ronald Reagan relaxes on his ranch near Santa Barbara.

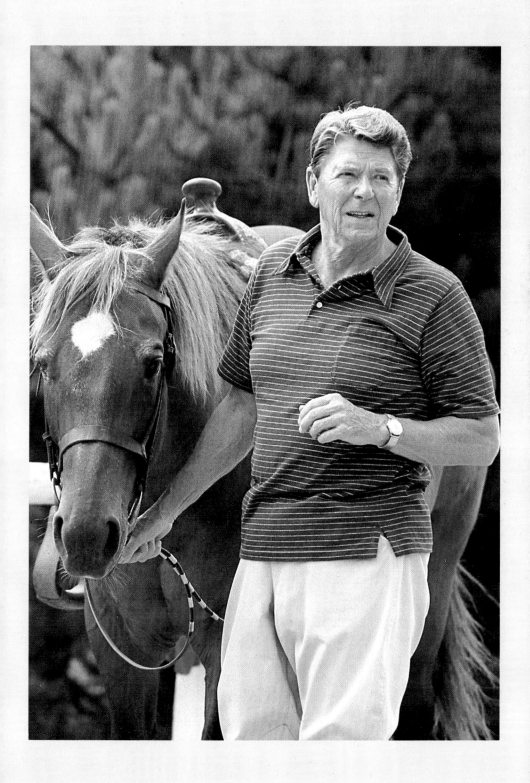

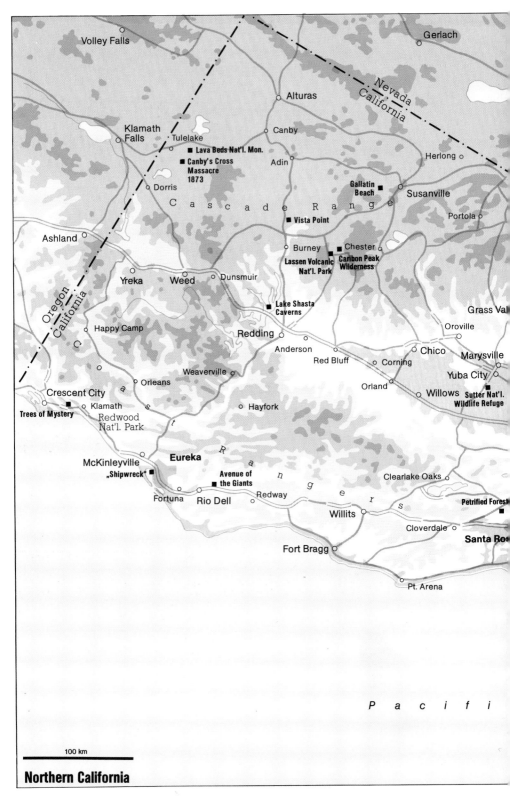

Volley Falls

Gerlach

Nevada
California

Alturas

Klamath
Falls
Tulelake
Canby

■ Lava Beds Nat'l. Mon.
■ Canby's Cross
Massacre
1873
Adin
Herlong

Dorris
Gallatin
Beach
Susanville

C a s c a d e   R a n g e
Portola

■ Vista Point

Ashland
Burney
Chester

Lassen Volcanic
Nat'l. Park
Caribon Peak
Wilderness

Yreka
Weed
Dunsmuir

Grass Val

Oroville

Happy Camp
■ Lake Shasta
Caverns

Redding
Chico
Marysville

Anderson
Yuba City

Weaverville
Red Bluff
Corning

Orleans
Orland
Willows
Sutter Nat'l.
Wildlife Refuge

Crescent City

Klamath
Hayfork

Trees of Mystery
Redwood
Nat'l. Park

R

Eureka
a

McKinleyville
n

„Shipwreck"
Avenue of
the Giants
Clearlake Oaks
g

Fortuna
Rio Dell
Redway
e
Petrified Forest

Willits
r

Santa Ro
s

Cloverdale

Fort Bragg

Pt. Arena

P   a   c   i   f   i

100 km

Northern California

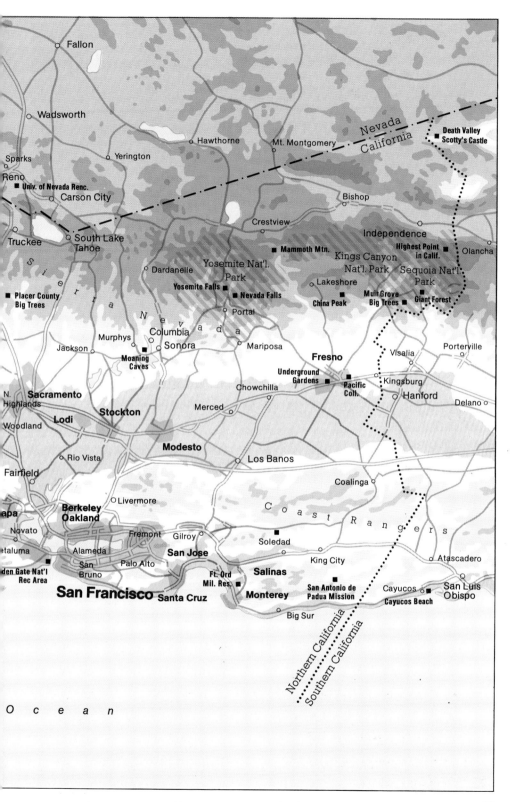

Okay, maybe there just isn't enough time. That's understandable. Northern California is not Paris or the Pyramids, compact and easy to explore. But don't let that get in the way. Make a little time; take a few chances. The upper half of California has more places than Gallo has grapes. The Golden Gate Bridge and Fisherman's Wharf and the Wine Country are nice, but they're not all there is.

Within the arbitrary boundaries this book has assigned to Northern California – the southern edge is an utterly imaginary line drawn north of San Luis Obispo and south of Paso Robles, over the mountains and through the central valley just south of Fresno, with a dip down to the southern tip of the Sierra then up to Lone Pine to the Nevada border – is more geographical and social variety than in any similar territory anywhere in the world.

There are the austere glacial cirques around Desolation Valley and the small peaceful tidepools on the Monterey Peninsula. There are the windswept meadows on the Mendocino coast and the hurried crush of San Francisco's Chinatown. There are rich bottomland and high desert plains, raging rivers and sweeping freeways, roller coasters and ski runs and lava caves and granite cliffs. And as if that wasn't enough, there is Yosemite, quite simply the most beautiful valley anywhere.

Travelers can be where the action is, or they can be utterly alone. They can drink the best wines made in America, eat the best seafood, take the best mud baths. They can ply the best golf courses, climb the highest mountain, see the oldest tree, or immerse themselves in the hottest hot tub.

Or they can just take a walk and discover things the authors of this book don't even know about.

Northern California, more than any other place in America, is an area where people live by choice. The climate is temperate, the vistas are extraordinary, the people friendly. Robert Louis Stevenson lived here for a while, and so did Ronald Reagan. Jack London spent most of his life here; Jack Kennedy went to school here. George Lucas lives here; so does Francis Ford Copolla. One city just to the east of San Francisco boasts more resident Nobel Prize winners than any other community in the world.

Certainly, this is a place worth exploring, a place with secrets worth discovering by foot, bicycle, bus, car, train or plane. But be forewarned: one visit may be all it takes to turn another visitor into a resident.

Preceding pages: State Highway 1, Big Sur. <u>Left</u>, Powell Street cablecars.

SAN FRANCISCO: CITY BY THE BAY

> Every man should be allowed to love two cities, his own and San Francisco.
> —*Gene Fowler, author, journalist and screenwriter (1890–1960)*

The United States has cities that trigger responses nearly as predictable as those in Pavlov's dogs. New York gains respect as a power place where the energy level always borders on overload. Cleveland is pitied because of its sad decline from regional eminence to municipal neediness. Some cities are amusing, like New Orleans; or dull, like Philadelphia. One, Los Angeles, defies comprehension because of its vast sprawl.

Only San Francisco wins visitors' love, straightaway and effortlessly. It is a pastel city for lovers and pleasure seekers, soft and feminine and Mediterranean in mood. Foghorns and bridges, cable cars and hills. Alcatraz and Fisherman's Wharf, Chinatown and North Beach – all invite feelings of fascination or enchantment. Scores of movies and television programs have made use of the remarkably beautiful natural setting.

San Francisco is comfortable with contradiction. It jealously preserves the past and delights in anachronism, yet rides the latest wave of fashion, whether in *haute couture* or computer chips. Haughty but humane, the city may fleece the tourist; but it maintained soup kitchens for the poor long before Reaganomics revived that custom elsewhere in the land. San Francisco is passionate about its views, but is always willing to lend a sympathetic ear to the latest corporation wanting to erect another high-rise slab.

San Francisco sits like a thumb at the end of a 32-mile (51-km) peninsular finger, surrounded by water on three sides and blessed by one of the world's great natural harbors. It is joined to the mainland by two of the acknowledged masterpieces of bridge design and construction, which blaze at night like strings of priceless jewels. In the daylight, San Francisco's profile of mighty towers and elegant hills looks from a distance like some place a prince would take a princess to live happily ever after.

Elegant and cosmopolitan, San Francisco is a sleek courtesan among the cities of the world, narcissistic and proud of it.

The sacred and the profane: Poll after poll acclaims San Francisco as the city Americans most like to visit, while 9 out of 10 people who come to the United States on foreign-exchange programs ask to be taken here. As a result, more than 3 million visitors a year come to the city and leave behind more than $1 billion annually, making tourism San Francisco's most profitable industry.

Certainly, there is no appetite, licit or otherwise, that need go ungratified in this sacred and profane queen city of the west, and no option that need go unexplored for lack of opportunity. With a population of 730,000 packed into 46.6 sq. miles (125 sq. km), San Francisco has a density of more than 15,000 people per square mile, and 10 times that

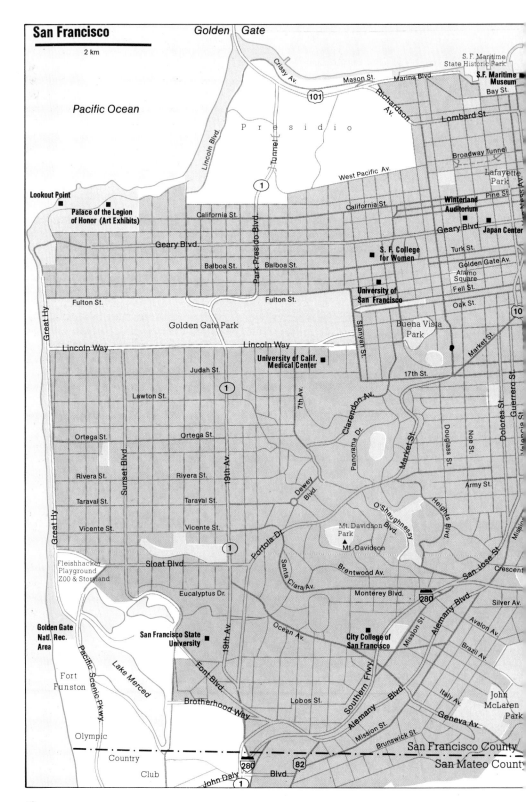

San Francisco

2 km

Golden Gate

Pacific Ocean

Presidio

Crissy Av.

Mason St.

Marina Blvd.

S.F. Maritime State Historic Park

S.F. Maritime Museum

Bay St.

Lombard St.

Broadway Tunnel

Lafayette Park

Lincoln Blvd

Richardson Av.

West Pacific Av.

Pine St.

Lookout Point

Palace of the Legion of Honor (Art Exhibits)

California St.

California St.

Winterland Auditorium

Japan Center

Geary Blvd.

Geary Blvd.

S. F. College for Women

Turk St.

Golden Gate Av.

Balboa St.

Balboa St.

Alamo Square

Fell St.

Fulton St.

Fulton St.

University of San Francisco

Oak St.

Great Hy

Golden Gate Park

Buena Vista Park

Stanyan St.

Lincoln Way

Lincoln Way

University of Calif. Medical Center

17th St.

Judah St.

Market St.

Guerrero St.

Lawton St.

7th Av.

Clarendon Av.

Panorama Dr.

Douglass St.

Noe St.

Dolores St.

Melancia St.

Ortega St.

Ortega St.

Rivera St.

Rivera St.

Sunset Blvd.

19th Av.

Dewey Blvd.

Army St.

Taraval St.

Taraval St.

O'Shaughnessy

Heights Blvd.

Vicente St.

Vicente St.

Mt. Davidson Park

Mt. Davidson

Portola Dr.

Missio

Fleishhacker Playground Zoo & Storyland

Sloat Blvd.

Santa Clara Av.

Brentwood Av.

San Jose St.

Crescent

Eucalyptus Dr.

Monterey Blvd.

280

Silver Av.

Golden Gate Natl. Rec. Area

Ocean Av.

City College of San Francisco

Mission St.

Alemany Blvd.

Avalon Av.

Brazil Av.

Great Hy

Pacific Scenic Pkwy.

Lake Merced

San Francisco State University

19th Av.

Font Blvd

Fort Funston

Lobos St.

Southern Frwy.

Alemany

Blvd.

Italy Av.

John McLaren Park

Brotherhood Way

Mission St.

Geneva Av.

Olympic

Brunswick St.

San Francisco County

Country

San Mateo County

Club

280

82

John Daly

Blvd.

1

62

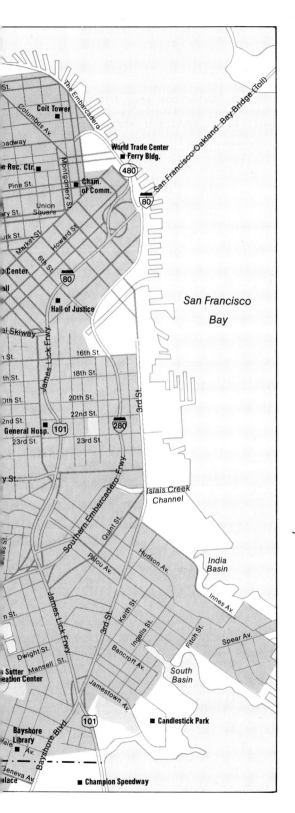

number in Chinatown. Elsewhere in the nine-county Bay Area (population: 5.5 million), the density averages 1,500 per square mile.

San Francisco is a city of neighborhoods as distinct and original as the people who live in them. Traveling from one to another is like watching a tightly edited movie. The character of each comes clearly into focus – different, and yet connected to the others by a common history.

Like all large cities, San Francisco accommodates the rich and the poor alike, and visitors are likely to see the same striking images of poverty and wealth as they see in the country's other urban centers.

Only a resident Dickens could do justice to the vast incongruities of this city. But unlike so many other places, social and economic diversity is embraced here. The boundaries between social classes are less clearly drawn than elsewhere. The promise of social mobility seems more tangible.

Of course, the vast majority of San Franciscans are middle-class. The people who fall within this broad category range from the ambitious young professionals who have invaded the city's fashionable districts to the immigrant families who run neighborhood businesses. More than other people, all San Franciscans – from the richest to the poorest, from the hushed precincts of Presidio Terrace to the run-down projects of Hunters Point – have a stake in their city. They are all an integral part of San Francisco's heritage.

An ethnic bouillabaisse: The residents of this charmed city, the nation's 13th largest, form a demographic bouillabaisse not found elsewhere on the North American continent. Although the descendants of early Italian, German and Irish families are still found in snug neighborhood enclaves, their numbers have been greatly diminished over the past couple of decades by the lure of suburbia with its cheaper and bigger houses. Their place has been filled by an influx of Asian and Hispanic people.

The city in recent years has become a mecca for Filipinos, the fastest growing minority, refugees from Southeast Asia; and both wealth and people from jittery Hong Kong. One consequence has been that the colorful 23 square blocks of Chinatown haven't been able to absorb the new arrivals. So they have spread their cultures west through the avenues into the formerly all-white Richmond and Sunset districts.

San Francisco is to an extraordinary degree a city for young singles. Between 1970 and 1980, the number of single persons 25 to 34 years of age jumped an astonishing 40 percent to more than 150,000. The traditional family was meanwhile decamping. During the same decade, the number of children below 18 in San Francisco dropped by 27 percent.

Many of the new singles were homosexuals fleeing hometown disapproval for San Francisco's famed easygoing tolerance. During the past 15 years, San Francisco's gays have emerged from a guilt-ridden existence "in the closet" to play a major role in the city's political, cultural and economic life. They have even been elected to the 11-member board of supervisors, which governs the city along with the mayor. The police department now actively recruits both gay men and women.

No one knows how many homosexuals live in the city. The most frequent estimate heard is 100,000, which would mean an improbable one in every seven residents.

The earthquake next time: Not everyone lives happily ever after in San Francisco. Alcoholism and the incidence of cirrhosis is greater in San Francisco than in any other major city. And the Golden Gate Bridge has been a magnet for the suicidal ever since it was completed in 1937. To date, more than 700 persons have jumped to their deaths from the span, most while facing the glittering city they believed had in some way failed them.

No one can predict when the next earthquake will come and lay waste to the great beauty of San Francisco as it did in 1906 and, most recently, in October of 1989. This last quake caused

Reflections in a Union Square boutique window.

millions of dollars of damage to the city (although most of the downtown remained intact) and cost over 60 people their lives. Although the 1989 earthquake is considered serious, it still isn't "the big one" Californians will someday have to face. People don't talk about it much, but the fear is always there, lying just below the surface like the treacherous San Andreas Fault itself.

It can be argued that this underlying tension is what gives San Francisco its special zest; that this may explain why it abandons itself so to self-indulgence. Tomorrow may never come, so why not live it up while you can? In San Francisco, having fun is what counts most.

Fun is easy to find in San Francisco, thanks to the happy accident of geography. Few cities reveal themselves as easily to the pedestrian. An unhurried 15-minute stroll will take one from the pinstriped heart of the financial district into Chinatown. The contrast in cultures is so sharp, one feels as though he should have had his passport stamped.

Union Square: Union Square is within easy walking distance of most of the city's hotels. Regarded during pioneer days as the city's geographical center, it was deeded to public use in 1850. It got its name a decade later from meetings held to demonstrate solidarity for the union of American states, then threatened by Southern secession.

Apart from the shaft supporting the winged statue commemorating Admiral George Dewey's naval victory over the Spanish in 1898, there is not much to be said for the square itself. Its main denizens are multitudes of pigeons and indigents seeking small contributions toward the purchase of potable fluids.

On the south of the square, facing Geary Street, are two major department stores – **Macy's** and the swanky **Nieman-Marcus**, featuring a glorious rotunda saved from its predecessor on the site. To the north, on Post Street, are the **Hyatt Union Square** hotel, its detailed fountain by sculptress Ruth Osawa demanding minute inspection; the distinguished **Bullock & Jones** store, purveyors of traditional men's clothing

Riding the rail in front of the Westin St Francis Hotel.

since 1853; and the posh **Saks Fifth Avenue** store.

Water always dashes against the seawall at the beginning of the 3½-mile (5½-km) **Golden Gate Promenade**. Joggers and romantics favor this bracing walk which gives a panoramic view of San Francisco, Alcatraz, Angel Island, the Marin shoreline and the East Bay.

Part of the promenade goes through **Crissy Field**, an airfield belonging to the 1,400-acre (567-hectare) **Presidio**. Established by the Spanish in 1776 and owned by the United States Army, the Presidio is the least warlike of any military installation. Only heaven ranks higher when servicemen and officers list their preferred posting. Lowly lieutenants occupy quarters with a view a millionaire would prize, and generals' housing is better situated than the home of San Francisco's resident billionaire, Gordon Getty, son of late oil tycoon J. Paul Getty. The Presidio's beautifully manicured grounds include stands of pine and eucalyptus, a museum, a hospital, a golf course, even a lake. The

spit-and-polish home of the Sixth Army, it is open to everyone except the people who live at the Soviet consulate on nearby Green Street, a third of whom are presumed to be spies.

Further down the promenade is the **Marina Green**, beloved by kite flyers, joggers and sunbathers. The big yachts moored in the harbor belong to the wealthy members of the **San Francisco Yacht Club**, whose handsome Spanish-style clubhouse looks out on the Bay.

The Plaster Palace: Across Marina Boulevard to the south is the classic rococo rotunda of the **Palace of Fine Arts**. It stands before a reflecting pond where ducks and swans glide. Designed by Bernard Maybeck, the Palace was originally built of plaster of paris for the Panama-Pacific Exhibition of 1915. It wasn't meant to last, but somehow it did. Not until 1967 was it strengthened and made permanent, thanks to the generosity of a millionaire who lived in the neighborhood. The Palace houses the **Exploratorium**, a museum with more than 500 exhibits to awaken even the most dormant interest in science. There is strong local opinion that this is the best science museum in the world.

The promenade continues past **Gas House Cove**, a middle-class yacht club, to **Fort Mason**, a former Army installation that has been turned over to the US Department of the Interior. The government administers the fort, part of the vast **Golden Gate National Recreation Area**, which extends north along the Marin County coast to include 20 miles (32 km) of beaches, timbered ridges and sylvan glades. Fort Mason has many interesting little nooks and crannies, ranging from **Green's** – a fine vegetarian restaurant run by Zen Buddhists – to museums, art galleries and the *S.S. Jeremiah O'Brien*, a lovingly restored World War II Liberty ship. It fires up its boilers once a year for a ceremonial tour of the Bay and can be visited most weekends.

Beyond Fort Mason is **Aquatic Park**, a terraced greensward that leads out to a small beach and curving municipal pier usually crowded with local fishermen. It includes the **National Maritime**

The Palace of Fine Arts.

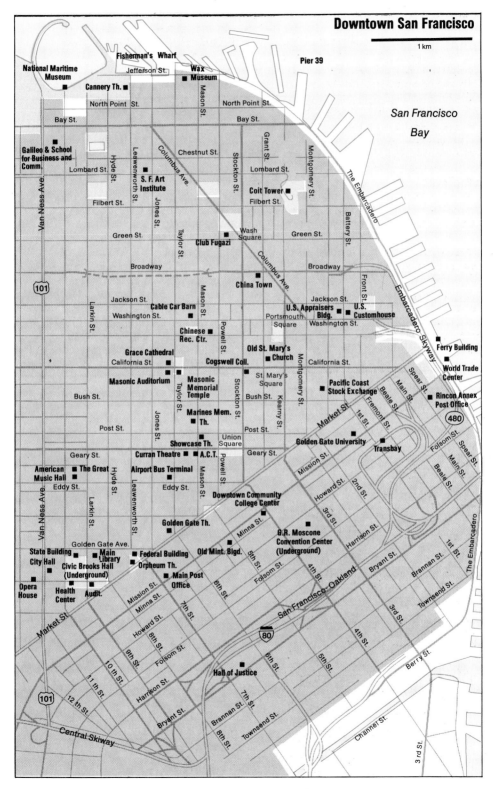

Downtown San Francisco

1 km

Fisherman's Wharf

Jefferson St.

Wax Museum

Pier 39

National Maritime Museum

Cannery Th.

North Point St.

North Point St.

Bay St.

Bay St.

San Francisco Bay

Mason St.

Galileo & School for Business and Comm.

Chestnut St.

Grant St.

Lombard St.

Lombard St.

Hyde St.

Leavenworth St.

Columbus Ave.

Stockton St.

Montgomery St.

S. F. Art Institute

Filbert St.

Coit Tower

Filbert St.

Jones St.

Battery St.

Green St.

Taylor St.

Wash Square

Green St.

Club Fugazi

Columbus Ave

Broadway

Broadway

101

Larkin St.

Mason St.

China Town

Jackson St.

Cable Car Barn

Washington St.

Jackson St.

Front St.

U.S. Appraisers Bldg.

Portsmouth Square

U.S. Customhouse

Washington St.

Chinese Rec. Ctr.

Powell St.

Ferry Building

Grace Cathedral

California St.

Cogswell Coll.

Old St. Mary's Church

California St.

World Trade Center

Masonic Auditorium

Taylor St.

Masonic Memorial Temple

Stockton St.

St. Mary's Square

Kearny St.

Montgomery St.

Pacific Coast Stock Exchange

Spear St.

Main St.

Rincon Annex Post Office

480

Bush St.

Bush St.

Beale St.

Fremont St.

Folsom St.

Spear St.

Marines Mem. Th.

Jones St.

Post St.

Post St.

Union Square

Showcase Th.

A.C.T.

Market St.

Powell St.

Golden Gate University

Transbay

Geary St.

Curran Theatre

Geary St.

Mission St.

1st St.

Main St.

American Music Hall

The Great

Hyde St.

Airport Bus Terminal

Mason St.

Howard St.

2nd St.

Beale St.

Eddy St.

Leavenworth St.

Eddy St.

Downtown Community College Center

3rd St.

Harrison St.

The Embarcadero

Van Ness Ave.

Larkin St.

Golden Gate Th.

Minna St.

G.R. Moscone Convention Center (Underground)

Golden Gate Ave.

State Building

Main Library

Federal Building

Old Mint. Bldg.

5th St.

4th St.

Brannan St.

1st St.

City Hall

Civic Brooks Hall (Underground)

Orpheum Th.

Folsom St.

San Francisco–Oakland

Bryant St.

Townsend St.

Opera House

Health Center

Audit.

Main Post Office

6th St.

Mission St.

7th St.

Minna St.

Howard St.

8th St.

Folsom St.

80

4th St.

5th St.

3rd St.

Market St.

9th St.

10th St.

101

11th St.

12th St.

Harrison St.

Hall of Justice

6th St.

7th St.

Berry St.

The Embarcadero

Central Skiway

Bryant St.

Brannan St.

8th St.

Townsend St.

Channel St.

3rd St.

Museum, which has all kinds of natural displays and photographs, and is adjacent to the Hyde Street Pier, where the museum's floating displays are docked. These include a sidewheel ferry and three schooners that carried freight in the days of sailing.

Across the street from Aquatic Park is the fanciful **Ghirardelli Square**, a superb example of putting the past to work in the present. Ghirardelli Square was built as a wool mill during the Civil War era and later become a chocolate factory. When the chocolate business moved elsewhere, it could easily have been torn down to make way for something modern. But William Matson Roth, a financier with a keen aesthetic sense, saw the possibilities for rebirth. Over a five-year period, starting in 1962, it was transformed into a brilliant showcase for retail shops, restaurants, bookstores and bars. There is usually some free entertainment going on somewhere in the Square, likely including tomfoolery by mimes, who are nearly as common locally as gulls.

Down the street east of the Square, across from a cable-car turnaround, is a durable attraction – the **Buena Vista Cafe**. The owners make so much money selling Irish coffees to locals, who stand elbow-to-elbow with tourists at the bar, one wonders why they bother serving food. But those lucky enough to get a table are glad they do. This is not primarily one of the body shops where singles gather to swap telephone numbers, but many a romance has had its start here.

Fisherman's Wharf: Tourism surveys claim **Fisherman's Wharf** is what 84 percent of all San Francisco visitors have come to see. Although the fishing boats look like parts of a quaint set designed in the Walt Disney studios, they are actual working vessels that put out before dawn to fish the abundant waters outside the Golden Gate. The catch they bring back often determines the "special of the day" at the numerous restaurants clustered around the wharf. Italians historically skippered and manned the boats and also ran the res-

Jogging along Marina Green below Pacific Heights.

taurants. A glance at the names of the restaurants – **Sabella's, Tarantino's, Alioto's** – indicates that not much has changed.

Chances are Fisherman's Wharf will be where visitors have their first encounter with one of the city's proudest legends, its crusty sourdough bread. It is quite unlike anything found elsewhere. Natives swear the secret ingredients rolls in with the fog, working a mysterious influence on the bacteria in the sourdough starter. The best way to enjoy this bread is with sweet butter, Dungeness crab and a crisp Chablis.

The Wharf has catered to generations of tourists and knows how to do it with skill. At sidewalk concessions, strollers can watch crabs being steamed and can buy shrimp or crab cocktails as take-away treats. There are numerous shops selling low-budget souvenir items for friends and relatives who are not excessively encumbered by good taste. There is also an assortment of carnival midway-type attractions on Jefferson Street.

The **Wax Museum** presents nearly 300 wax mannequins in costumes that sometimes bear a passing resemblance to those of the great people in history they purport to represent. **Ripley's Believe It or Not! Museum** assembles under one roof a collection of some 2,000 peculiar things once belonging to the late cartoonist Robert Ripley. The **Guinness Museum of World Records** offers a gallery of biggest, smallest, fastest, slowest and other such pacesetters from the pages of the Irish brewer's best-seller.

A short walk east, **Pier 39** is a popular tourist attraction. This 45-acre collection of shops, arcades, fast-food restaurants and other diversions reproduces a cutesy past that no one in San Francisco remembers. Why, the critics asked, have they reproduced a turn-of-the-19th-century Cape Cod whaling village? The only thing authentic at Pier 39 is the **Eagle Cafe**, a waterfront fixture favored for decades by fishermen and longshoremen before it was moved intact from its original site a couple of blocks away.

Ghirardelli Square.

The tall masts and rigging at water's edge nearer to the main Wharf belong to the graceful Scottish-built clipper **Balclutha**, a 265-foot (81-meter) beauty open to the public. It put to sea in 1886 and made many voyages around Cape Horn. Two piers away is one of the Wharf's newest draws, the **Pampanito**, a World War II submarine whose narrow passageways may awaken claustrophobia. The yellow choppers taking off at intervals near the *Balclutha* belong to **Commodore Helicopters**. The price is steep, but the ride they offer around Alcatraz is unforgettable.

Flying over the Bay is fun, but skimming across its waters is even better. For those with the time and money, chartering a sailboat is the best way to go. For those with less time and money, hopping aboard a big tour boat is nearly as good. **Red and White Fleet** at Pier 41 and **Gold Coast Cruises** at Pier 45 offer regular trips. They have snack and liquid bars on board. The usual route takes passengers out along the Marina Green and under the Golden Gate Bridge before heading back for a circuit past Angel Island, Alcatraz and the Bay Bridge.

Alcatraz Island: Another tour boat outfit, the **Blue and Gold Fleet**, has headquarters at Pier 39 east of Fisherman's Wharf. There is a colorful rivalry between Blue and Gold and Pier 41's Red and White, sometimes manifested in the maneuvering that goes on between the boats off **Alcatraz.** Each tries to sail close to the island to give its passengers the best view.

The island's famous prison, however, is falling apart. Its steel bars are being eaten away by salt air and its pastel buildings are slowly giving way to the ravages of time. What is it about ruins that make them so appealing?

In the case of Alcatraz, part of the explanation lies in its location. Just over a mile offshore of San Francisco, it is windswept and scoured by swift tides. When it was first sighted in 1775 by Spanish Lieutenant Juan Manuel de Ayala, the only occupants were pelicans so Ayala named it *Isla de los Alcatraces*, or the Island of Pelicans.

Its strategic location in the Bay obviously suited it to military purposes and it was garrisoned with soldiers in the 1850s. Because escape from the island was a remote possibility, renegade servicemen were incarcerated on Alcatraz, to be followed by Apaches taken prisoner in Arizona during the 1870s Indian wars and prisoners from the Spanish-American War.

Alcatraz evolved into a federal prison that housed such case-hardened criminals as Mafia leader Al Capone and the notorious Machine Gun Kelley. Those few desperate inmates who managed to escape their cells in bids for freedom perished in the frigid waters surrounding the island.

Empty cells: The prison was finally closed in 1963 when the costs of repairing the constant ravages of wind and weather grew too great. Since then, proposals have surfaced from time to time to put the island to some sort of use, but all have come to nothing. A band of American Indians occupied the island for an 18-month period in the 1970s to dramatize their differences with the Bureau of Indian Affairs, but they were only too glad to finally leave.

So the prison buildings crumble away bit by bit as people increasingly think the best think to do with Alcatraz is just to leave it as it is, a symbol of "man's inhumanity to man". Park rangers give one-hour guided tours of those parts of the island safe to traverse, including a peek at some of the cell blocks. Ferries leave from Pier 41. Warm clothing is essential.

The Golden Gate: When sailing under the **Golden Gate Bridge**, it is interesting to consider that at one time there was a respectable body of engineering opinion that held it would be impossible to build a span at this point because of the depth of the water (318 feet/97 meters, at the deepest point) and the powerful tidal rush in and out. The city authorized the first studies in 1918, but not until 35 years later was the first shovelful of earth turned under the gaze of master engineer Joseph B. Strauss, no relation to the Waltz King. Four years later, it was finished at a cost of

Picking out dinner at Fisherman's Wharf.

$35 million and the lives of 11 construction workers.

The bridge is 7 miles (11 km) long, including its freeway approaches. The suspension section alone is 6,450 feet (2,320 meters) long. The towers stand 746 feet (228 meters) above the water, and the span is 220 feet (67 meters) above the water at low tide. There are two piers supporting it, the biggest of which extends 100 feet (31 meters) below the water. They poured 693,000 cubic yards (520,000 cubic meters) of concrete and used more than 100,000 tons of steel in its construction. There are 80,000 miles (128,700 km) of cable helping to support it. Crews are continually sandblasting rust off the bridge and repainting it using 10,000 gallons (38,000 liters) of orange paint a year. More than 17 million south-bound cars cross the bridge each year, paying a toll to do so. (Nobody counts the northbound cars because no toll is collected from them.) The bridge was built so sturdily that it has been closed only three times due to high winds.

North Beach nightclubs: Broadway is the heart of the city's nightclub district, a stretch tawdry enough for the most jaded tastes. On weekend nights, the streets are thronged with people who come to ogle the hookers and be lured into dark joints by cold-eyed barkers with smiles as dazzling as real zircons. Inside, these patrons sip liquor-flavored water sold at larcenous prices and watch naked ("totally nude" is the preferred usage on street posters) women dance in a manner meant to seem erotic.

But there is an undeniable excitement to the street. The neon lights are bright and live music blares from inside many clubs. There are also some nice restaurants and a variety of wonderful coffee shops where midnight snackers can sip expresso or *caffe latte*, fork down pastry, and eavesdrop on some first-rate conversation at neighboring tables. This area, known as **North Beach**, has always been congenial to writers, artists and other deep thinkers. At the same time, it has retained the flavor of an old-fashioned Italian neighborhood whose

Waterfront transport, Pier 39.

dual anchors are the **Church of Saints Peter and Paul** on grassy **Washington Square** and the little working men's bars where elderly Italians sip red wine and consider the affairs of the day.

The outside tables at **Enrico's** on Broadway are a good place from which to study the passing scene. Many interesting local characters and homegrown celebrities drop by at night, including entertainers from up and down the street who are taking their breaks between shows. The man in the beret is the excitable owner, Enrico Banducci. The sizeable bartender is named Lucky and no prudent man would dream of giving him any trouble.

Most people find a visit to **Finocchio's** fun – it's one of the world's best drag shows. There are four shows a night and busloads of tourists from all over the world troop in to gape and rub their eyes. Indeed, it is hard to believe at first that all those beautiful entertainers are men – until they yank their wigs off.

A few steps away is the **Condor Club**, where a waitress named Carol Doda

peeled to the waist one night in 1964 and ushered in the topless boom. The venerable Doda used to descend nightly from the ceiling atop a piano. She was clad only in a G-string, showing her debt to silicone technology.

Those with their hair dyed magenta, or who perhaps have a nostril pierced with a safety pin, fit right in with the punk-rock crowd that lines up outside the **Mabuhay Gardens** on Broadway to catch the first show at 11 o'clock nightly. Talk about schizophrenia: this is a staid Filipino restaurant by day.

A word of warning – parking is near impossible in North Beach at night, and police are very strict on illegally parked vehicles. It is best to walk or take a taxi.

The **Washington Square Bar and Grill** is a hangout for lawyers, politicians, writers and others who make their livings from words. Rugby experience is helpful in getting a drink from the small crowded bar. Another favorite North Beach haunt of the wordsmiths is the **City Lights** bookstore in Columbus Street. For some 30 years it has been operated by poet Lawrence Ferlinghetti, one of the literary lights of the 1950s beat era. Across the alley is **Vesuvio's,** a wonderfully atmospheric bar where intellectuals in rimless glasses sip aperitifs and think long thoughts. And nearby, on Columbus, is the **Tosca Cafe**, where off-duty cops and society swells play pool and listen to opera records on the jukebox.

Above North Beach, at the end of Lombard Street, is **Telegraph Hill**. The *moderne* tiara crowning the hill is **Coit Tower**, built in 1934 by Mrs Lillie Coit in memory of San Francisco's heroic corps of firefighters.

Chinatown: Standing on the corner of Broadway and Columbus Avenue, surrounded by the glitter and sleaze of North Beach, one is near enough to the Grant Avenue entrance of exotic **Chinatown** to hear the clacking of *mahjong* tiles. If Chinatown were the only attraction San Francisco had to offer visitors, it would still be worth the trip.

San Francisco's Chinatown is the biggest Chinatown outside of Asia, and

the steady influx of immigrants keeps it growing. Its streets are narrow, crowded and alive with color and movement. It extends for eight blocks, far enough to make visitors feel after a time that they might be walking the teeming, traffic-choked streets of Hong Kong or Shanghai. Mysterious alleys abound. Tiny cluttered herb shops offer powders and poultices promising everything from rheumatism relief to the restoration of sexual powers.

In Chinatown's dozens of hole-in-the-wall shops, one can buy anything from cheap trinkets to exquisite screens and massive hand-carved furniture costing thousands of dollars. Silken clothing, hand-painted vases, paper lanterns, rattan furniture, and many other Asian articles are for sale.

Some of the world's finest Chinese restaurants can be found in this quarter. It would be supreme folly for visitors not to take advantage and have at least one meal here. **Johnny Kan's** and the **Empress of China** are the best known of the fancy restaurants, but there are any number of obscure restaurants and tiny cafes where diners can sit down with the Chinese locals and eat well and cheaply.

Veteran gastronomes have been known to cry out in ecstasy after a meal of *dim sum*. These delicious pastries, filled with meat, chicken, shrimp or vegetables, are a favorite Chinatown lunch. Waitresses push them from table to table on carts like peddlers. Diners select the dishes they want; the number of empty dishes on the table at the end of a meal determines the charge. Best bets for *dim sum* are the **Tung Fong, Hong Kong Tea House** and **Asia Garden**, all on Pacific Avenue, and **Louie's** on Grant Avenue. Those who like friendly insults with their food can climb the stairs and thread their way through the kitchen at **Sam Wo's**, where Edsel Ford Song will oblige them.

Intriguing though it is, Grant Avenue should not be the sole focus of Chinatown exploration. Grant is the face Chinatown wears for tourists. One block over is Stockton Street, where the real business of life is carried on. Tiny

Chinese women, ancient enough to have had their feet bound many decades ago, totter on shopping errands. Old men smoke cigarettes and read Chinese-language newspapers. Bright-eyed children chatter on their way to or from school. Crates of fresh produce and meat are unloaded from double-parked trucks as staccato bursts of Chinese dialect are exchanged.

The **Chinese Cultural Center** in the Holiday Inn on Kearny Street is worth a visit. It offers art shows, entertainment and guided tours.

Theater district: It's only a couple of blocks west from Union Square to San Francisco's **theater district**, located around Geary Street. The 1,768-seat **Curran Theater** and the 1,300-seat **Geary Theater** stand side by side. The Geary is the home of the American Conservatory Theater, one of the nation's best repertory companies. The Curran offers some of the biggest hits from New York's Broadway. Incidentally, San Francisco also has more than 50 cinemas offering everything from the raunchiest hardcore pornography to the artiest and most obscure foreign-language import.

Other theaters in the general area are the 800-seat **Theater on the Square**, 450 Post Street, and the experimental **One Act Theater**, 430 Mason Street. A little further afield is the **Golden Gate Theater** at 25 Taylor Street. This ornate 2,400-seat theater, formerly a movie house, hosts out-of-town musicals.

Continuing west on Geary, it's eight blocks from Union Square to Van Ness Avenue, a broad north-south thoroughfare with a planter strip in the middle. This is one of the city's main arteries serving as the gateway (via Lombard Street) to points north across the Golden Gate Bridge.

The Civic Center: Abutting Van Ness at McAllister Street is **City Hall**, one of the most beautiful public buildings in the United States. It was designed by Arthur Brown, an architect so young and so unknown that he figured he might as well shoot for the moon in the early 20th-century competition to select the building design. To his surprise, Brown

Grant Avenue, Chinatown.

and his partner, John Bakewell, won with a design that called for the lavish use of costly marble and a dome patterned after St Peter's Cathedral in Rome.

Built in 1914, City Hall is honeycombed with municipal offices and both civil and criminal courts. The full effect of the building is best felt from its Polk Street entrance, which faces a plaza. The magnificent stairway inside leads to the second-floor Board of Supervisors chambers. This is the building in which Supervisor Dan White shot Mayor George Moscone in 1978 for refusing to reappoint him to the seat White had resigned. White then shot gay Supervisor Harvey Milk for smirking at him. After White was convicted of manslaughter and given a wrist-slapping sentence, howling mobs descended on City Hall and were only narrowly prevented from breaking in.

Across the plaza from City Hall is the stately main branch of the **Public Library**, built in 1916. The south end of the plaza is occupied by the **Civic Auditorium** (1913) and the north side by a **State Office Building** (1926). Together, they present an appearance of order and harmony. This comprises San Francisco's Civic Center. The brutal federal building standing behind the state building on Golden Gate Avenue is a reminder of how badly the Civic Center could have turned out had it been planned less carefully.

Opposite City Hall on Van Ness Avenue are a series of distinguished buildings. The **Veterans Auditorium Building** (1932) at the corner of Van Ness and McAllister Streets houses the 915-seat **Herbst Auditorium** and the **San Francisco Museum of Modern Art**. The latter includes works by such 20th-century masters as Picasso and Matisse as well as noted American artists. Next to it is the 3,535-seat **Opera House** (1932), one of the world's greatest. It has a summer opera festival and a regular season running from September to December. The opera company, which draws the foremost artists of the day to its stage, shares quarters with the highly **Interior of City Hall.**

regarded San Francisco Ballet. Across the street from the Opera House is the lavish 2,958-seat **Louise M. Davies Symphony Hall**, completed in 1980.

Davies Hall is the new home of the San Francisco Symphony, which some critics feel has improved so much in recent years that it is ready to break into the elite circle occupied by the New York, Philadelphia, Boston, Cleveland and Los Angeles orchestras. Davies Hall has greatly increased the city's cultural capacity, permitting longer opera and symphony seasons and a separate ballet season.

The symphony offers special attractions like "Mostly Mozart" and "All-Beethoven" festivals, a Summer Pops Concert where music lovers can bring picnics, and Sunday afternoon summer concerts at Sigmund Stern Memorial Grove south of Golden Gate Park.

Davies Hall has triggered quite a boom in the Civic Center area. Expensive condominium buildings are rising to the north, hotels are being smartened up, and excellent restaurants like the **Hayes Street Grill** are opening. The **Opera Plaza** complex, where apartments begin at around $240,000 is a good example of the quality. It has a street-level bar with a European flavor. Its **Modesto Lanzone** cafe, like its sister restaurant in Ghirardelli Square, draws raves over its lighter-than-air pasta.

The **Richmond district**, fogbound much of the summer, is an area of orderly streets, tidy homes and manicured lawns. These allow it to blend well into the neighboring **Sunset district**, which is equally middle class and conservative. One can easily become lost in this grid of streets, so the best thing drivers can do is to follow the signs that guide them along the city's 49-mile (79-km) **Scenic Drive.**

The drive snakes past the **Cliff House**, which overlooks the Pacific Ocean and peers down upon barking seals clinging wetly to the rocks below. This is worth a stop, as generations of San Franciscans have testified since 1863. The present Cliff House is the fifth to have been built here. Its predecessors have all burned down or suffered some other tragedy.

North of Cliff House is verdant **Lincoln Park**, whose 270 acres (109 hectares) include an 18-hole municipal golf course and the handsome French-style **California Palace of the Legion of Honor**. The palace is really a fine museum. At the entrance is one of five existing bronze casts of Rodin's famous statue, "The Thinker". The museum also has 18th-century paintings and tapestries as well as works by impressionists like Monet, Renoir and Degas. Also within the palace is the **Achenbach Foundation for Graphic Arts**, the largest collection of prints and drawings in western America.

Golden Gate Park: South from the Cliff House, the Scenic Drive leads past the pounding surf of **Ocean Beach** (too dangerous for swimming) into **Golden Gate Park**, one of the great urban parks in the world. It is 3 miles long and half a mile wide, and consists of groves of redwoods, eucalyptus, pine and countless varieties of other trees from all over the world. It is dotted with lakes, grassy meadows and sunlit dells. There can be

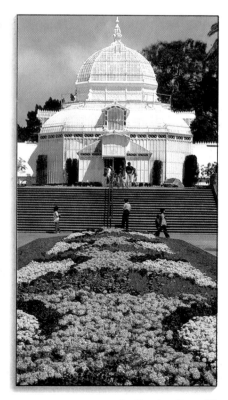

thousands of people within its borders, but Golden Gate Park is so large that one can easily find solitary tranquility in a misty forest grove or by a peaceful pond. More than a century ago, the park was painstakingly reclaimed from sand dunes through the herculean efforts of a crusty Scottish landscape architect named John McLaren. Park superintendent for 55 years, McLaren so disliked statuary that he shrouded all human likeness in dense vegetation. Most park statues remain "lost" today.

The park has many varied attractions. There are baseball and soccer fields, horseback riding trails, tennis courts, bowling and horseshoe pitching areas, flycasting ponds, even a polo field. Visitors can rent bicycles to tour the park from any of a number of adjacent shops, as well as roller skates from vendors who keep their stock in the back of trucks. Part of John F. Kennedy Drive, which runs through the park, is closed off on Sundays so that skaters can strut their stuff. Some of their routines are quite spectacular.

The park has feasts for the mind as well as the eyes. The **California Academy of Sciences** comprises three museums in one. The natural history section incorporates displays of anthropology and ethnology with dioramas of North American and African animals. The **Morrison Planetarium** has a whiz-bang laser light show about our tiny, undistinguished corner of the universe under its 65-foot (20-meter) dome. The **Steinhart Aquarium** has nearly 16,000 specimens of marine and shore life on display in its 190 tanks. In addition to a gang of appealing warm water penguins, the Aquarium also features a simulated swamp and doughnut-shaped "fish roundabout". The Steinhart's latest attractions include a first-hand look at the intricate pattern of sea life around a living coral reef, and the fierce anatomy of a frozen great white shark.

Across the Museum Concourse, past the Music Concourse where Sunday afternoon concerts are given, is the **M.H. De Young Memorial Museum**. Blockbuster traveling exhibits are presented here, but even without these shows, the De Young – which opened in 1921 – is the city's best museum. Its collection includes Renaissance and Medieval paintings and tapestries, sculpture and suits of armor, African and Polynesian galleries.

An adjunct of the De Young is the **Asian Art Museum**, donated to the city by the late Avery Brundage, the iron-willed millionaire who dominated the international Olympic movement for half a century. The Brundage collection has some 10,000 items, making it the largest of its kind outside the Orient. It includes precious jades, ceramics, sculptures, bronzes, vases, figurines and a host of other examples of Chinese and other Asian art, some dating back 3,500 years. Brundage bought his pieces during his global travels, paying top dollar at a time when there was little Western interest in Asian art.

South of the museums is **Stow Lake**, a pleasant body of water where sporty types can rent rowboats or pedal boats and work up a sweat before quenching their thirst with a beer at the snack bar.

All set to sail that model at a pond in Golden Gate Park, by remote control, of course.

The island in the middle of the lake is called Strawberry Hill.

The **Conservatory of Flowers**, half a mile east of Stow Lake, was built in 1878, modeled after the Palm House at London's Kew Gardens. It was shipped piece by piece around Cape Horn from Dublin. It has permanent displays of many plants and features spectacular seasonal displays of blooms.

The **Japanese Tea Garden**, built in 1894, is a harmonious blend of architecture, landscaping and pools. It was here, many years ago, that fortune cookies were invented. The custom spread to Chinatown, then traveled throughout the Chinese food industry in the Western world. The garden was disassembled during World War II, then restored to its former grace when the threat of wartime vandalism had passed.

Stanyan Street borders the eastern edge of the park and intersects with **Haight Street**, one of the world's most famous thoroughfares in the 1960s. That was when long hair, tie-dyed fabrics, hallucinogens and a belief in the power of love and peace persuaded a generation of alienated young people that they could create an alternative lifestyle.

They were called "hippies". They openly smoked marijuana, took up forms of Eastern mysticism, declined to be sent overseas to fight in foreign wars, and otherwise were a thorn in the sides of their elders, who sometimes sent police in riot gear to the middle of the Haight-Ashbury district to clean it up. Haight Street was once so gaudy and bizarre that tour buses ran up and down it with their windows full of goggle-eyed tourists. Like most such radical departures from the social norm, the hippie experiment fell victim to time and fashion. Hippies now maintain only tenuous footholds in rural communes of Mendocino County and the Santa Cruz Mountains. Haight-Ashbury itself has returned to a quiet existence as a faintly down-at-the-heels neighborhood.

The financial district: From Union Square, the most interesting approach to the **financial district** is by foot down Post Street. An elegant series of shops

Left, Victorian houses, Hyde Street. Right, the Transamerica Pyramid and Columbus Tower on Columbus Avenue.

includes the **Alfred Dunhill of London** smokeshop on the corner of Stockton Street; **Gump's**, famous for its crystal and jade and *objets d'art*; **Eddie Bauer**, the outdoors clothier and outfitter; **Shreve & Co.**, jewelers; **Gucci**, maker of costly footwear and other leather goods; and **Brooks Brothers**, the classy conservative tailor to those with button-down tastes.

The financial district is roughly bounded by Kearny Street on the west; Washington Street, a quaint neighborhood of tasteful antique shops, and interior decorator showrooms, on the north; and Market Street on the southeast. After the Bank of America colossus, which is so tall its top sometimes disappears in the fog, the most distinctive building is the **Transamerica Pyramid** on Montgomery Street. At first, a lot of people were appalled by its, well, unorthodox appearance. But now almost everyone has come to like it for the architectural eccentric it is.

In the nearby $300 million **Embarcadero Convention Center** is the **Hyatt Regency Hotel**, which boasts a spectacular 20-story atrium lobby. This is the sort of newcomer that has elbowed the venerable **Sheraton Palace Hotel**, a few blocks further west on Market Street, from the ranks of the city's premier hotels. The Palace, opened in 1875, is San Francisco's oldest luxury hotel. Its 150-foot Palm Garden, with its leaded-glass dome roof bathing diners in light, remains as striking as ever. The Pied Piper bar with its beautiful Maxfield Parrish mural is a fine place to have a drink. Seven American presidents have stayed here, from Ulysses S. Grant to Franklin Roosevelt. One of those presidents, Warren G. Harding, died at the Palace in 1923 while still in office.

Market Street is a thoroughfare of contrasts. In the financial district, it's comfortably interesting. But it turns seedy down toward 5th Street, and stays that way for four blocks before beginning to revive. It finally ends at the multi-intersection that includes 24th and Castro streets, one of the busy hubs of gay action. Broad, tree-lined and well-lit at night, it has all the elements needed to become one of the world's great avenues. The city even spent millions of dollars building a tunnel beneath Market Street to eliminate the clutter of streetcars. But somehow the street has never achieved its potential.

South of Market: South of Union Square, Powell Street passes near the eastern fringe of the **Tenderloin district**, a neighborhood of sleazy bars, porn parlors and residential hotels where the poor are ruthlessly exploited by the owners and their agents. Drag queens traipse coquettishly, drug dealers sell their stepped-on cocaine and sugared heroin, hookers beckon, and street-wise Vietnamese children offer bags of garlic to passersby. It's a good area to avoid after nightfall.

When people talk about "**South of Market**", they refer to the hodgepodge of businesses and run-down residences that once ran to China Basin and the waterfront. Once an exclusively industrial neighborhood, South of Market – or "**So-Ma**", as many call it now – is one of the hottest locations in the city.

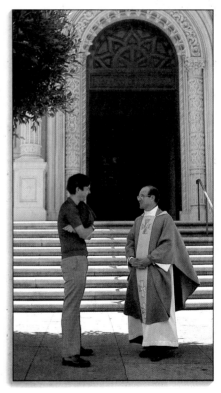

In addition to the **Moscone Convention Center**, a 6-acre exhibition hall that accommodates 30,000 people, South of Market boasts some of the city's hippest nightclubs, galleries, cafes and theaters.

Most of the action in SoMa is located on Harrison and Folsom streets. The **Oasis** offers rock-and-roll, an outdoor deck and a swimming pool on the roof. The **DNA Lounge** has new wave and occasional jazz, a comfortable loft, plenty of neon, and "cigarette girls" toting trays of smokes and lollipops. The ultra-hip might prefer clubs like the **Billboard Cafe**, which features political art created by local talent, or **Club DV8**, which offers performance art and alternate music in what appears to be a Roman temple. The **Stud**, which attracts a predominantly gay crowd, is a little more hardcore. The **Paradise** offers live blues, pop and assorted performance artists, and **Milestones** has quickly become one of the city's best places to catch live jazz. There are several restaurants in the SoMa district too.

Among the trendiest are **Max's Diner** and **Cafe SoMa.**

For the more conservative traveler, SoMa is also the home of the **Old Mint**, which was built in 1874 and managed to survive the earthquake of 1906.

Latinos and gays: Mission Street heads due south into the heart of the **Mission district**, San Francisco's great melting pot of Latin American cultures. **Mission Dolores** (Dolores Avenue near 16th Street) was founded less than a week before the American Declaration of Independence was signed in 1776, and its 4-foot adobe walls still form what is the oldest building in San Francisco. The graves of many of the city's earliest pioneers, and thousands of native Costonoan Indians, can be found in the mission cemetery.

The Mission district oozes Hispanic culture. Red-tile roofs predominate on public buildings, palms and utilitarian shops line the streets, and restaurants offer the gamut of Latin-American cuisine – from Mexican to Chilean, Cuban to Salvadorean.

Market Street and the Financial District.

The macho Latino culture sometimes clashes with the neighboring gay culture of **Noe Valley**. The concentration of gays here and around the **Duboce Triangle** is so great it is said a homosexual can lead a full life and never come in contact with a heterosexual. He can do his banking at a gay bank, buy his croissants at a gay bakery, have his television fixed by a gay technician, get his teeth capped by a gay dentist, and so forth.

The busy promiscuity that once characterized the gay scene in San Francisco has been chilled by the onset of AIDS. But the restaurants are still crowded, the bars are still hopping, and the sidewalks are still filled with shoppers.

Much the same can be said for nearby **Union Street**. By day, Union Street is a chic stretch of boutiques, antique stores, gourmet shops, delicatessens and classy restaurants. At night, the singles bars are the main attraction where the young, hip and beautiful go in search of each other.

A note from sports desk: Sports fans flock to famed **Candlestick Park** on a rocky promontory at the southeast corner of the city. The San Francisco '49ers football team, winners of the 1982, 1984 and 1988 Super Bowl symbolic of American football supremacy, and the San Francisco Giants baseball team both make their homes in this stadium. Up to 60,000 spectators can be accommodated.

Not far to the west, amidst the look-alike suburban homes of **Daly City**, the **Cow Palace** has hosted everything from rock concerts and basketball games to livestock shows. Seating capacity at this arena is 14,300.

Every visitor takes a different memory away from San Francisco. There is the street that drops off steeply toward the whitecapped bay, where sailboats heel before the wind. There is the fog drifting through the Golden Gate, blurring the bridge's sparkling lights. There are the savory dishes that magically blend to make the perfect meal. There is the simple fun of a cable-car ride.

Indeed, San Francisco – the city that may be gone tomorrow – has mastered the good life.

San Francisco Giants baseball at Candlestick Park.

THE PENINSULA: HIGH-TECH LIVING

The Peninsula is a 55-mile (89-km) swath of high hills, tall trees and beautiful estates, located between the Pacific Ocean and San Francisco Bay. To its north is San Francisco city. At its southern end lies the sprawl of the **Silicon Valley**. There, the highlands of the Peninsula glide head-on into the newly affluent, high-technology communities of Los Altos, Sunnyvale, Santa Clara and San Jose. Sales by Silicon Valley firms set records in the 1980s and the $100,000-plus suburban homes spread like a heat rash across the ample flatlands.

The style of the Peninsula is sophisticated and current. Six thousand residents have doctorate degrees, and Stanford University is the hub of much academic and cultural activity. Mixed with the high-mindedness, however, is a great deal of new money (millionaires made from scratch are as common as tennis courts) and old (San Mateo is one of the four wealthiest counties in California, with a blue-book list of locals including the Hearsts, the Crosbys and the Caspar Weinbergers).

Stanford University: A farm – a blue-blooded horse ranch – is exactly what **Stanford University** was a little over a century ago when Leland Stanford and photographer Muybridge began their experiments. Today, it is the cultural heartbeat of the Peninsula. It is located in the northwestern corner of **Palo Alto**, a comely city of 57,000 known for its environmental policies and praised as one of the "model little cities of the world".

When Stanford first proposed his plan for a private university in the 1880s, the response ranged from curious surprise to outright criticism, with one East Coast academician claiming that there was as much need for a new university in the West as there was for "an asylum for decayed sea captains in Switzerland". But a Yale of the West it became. Today it is an acclaimed center for the study of science, engineering and medicine.

The Memorial Church, Stanford University.

84

More than 10 Nobel laureates are among its 1,200 faculty members as well as 75 members of the National Academy of Science and three Pulitzer Prize winners.

Architecturally, Stanford's handsome, rough-hewn sandstone buildings are Romanesque in style, though the red-tiled roofs, the burnt adobe color of the stone, and the wide arches give the university a Spanish mission look. The effect is one of uncluttered calm.

Stanford lacks the greenery associated with Ivy League schools on the East Coast. The entrance, along Palm Drive (off University Avenue via US Highway 101), is rather bleak but meant to reflect the landscape of the West.

The exception to the overall prosaic quality of the university is **Memorial Church**, which dominates the **Inner Quad**, or central courtyard. It is resplendent in stained glass and richly colored murals, with a domed ceiling.

Seals and thrills: The most scenic route in the Peninsula is State Highway 1, winding from **Pacifica**, a west San Francisco suburb, to Santa Cruz in the south. Though less dramatic than the cliffside reaches of the Monterey Peninsula, this leg of State 1 is an enchanting day's drive, boasting two vintage lighthouses – **Pigeon Point** near Pescadero (west of San Jose), the second tallest lighthouse in the United States; and **Montara** in the north, where a youth hostel is open in a nearby building.

A special coastal spot is **Año Nuevo State Park**, 20 miles (32 km) north of Santa Cruz near the San Mateo-Santa Cruz county line. Here, whiskered and roly-poly elephant seal pups are born in January, when entire seal families are visible from lookout points along the beachfront. The seal families are so popular with sightseers that the beach often gets crowded. It is best to call Año Nuevo State Reserve after October 1 for information and reservations.

San Jose was the first pueblo to be founded in Northern California by the Spanish, in 1777. Until 1956, the San Jose area was providing America with half its supply of prunes. But the orchards of three decades ago have now sprouted condominiums and industrial parks. Today, San Jose is the fourth largest city in California with a population approaching 700,000.

San Jose is a busy, fast-paced city, with several major hotels, nightclubs and no fewer than 100 shopping centers. Sightseeing is minimal in metropolitan San Jose, although three major wineries are located within the city limits and all offer free tours and tastings – **Almaden, Mirassou,** and **Turgeon and Lohr.**

For entertainment of a more eccentric bent there is the red-roofed, sprawling, touristy but nonetheless fascinating **Winchester Mystery House** in downtown San Jose. It was built in convoluted stages by Sara L. Winchester, who inherited the fortune of her father-in-law, the famed gun manufacturer. Sarah was a spiritualist who believed that she would live as long as she kept adding to her house. Sixteen carpenters worked on the mansion for 36 years, adding stairways that lead to nowhere and doors without rooms.

The spiritual realm is also the basis for the **Rosicrucian Egyptian Museum** and planetarium. A recreated walk-in tomb of 2,000 BC and the West Coast's largest collection of Egyptian, Babylonian and Assyrian artifacts are contained within the building, which draws a half-million visitors annually.

For youngsters in particular, the most exciting attraction in the San Jose area is **Marriott's Great America**, located off the Bayshore Freeway near **Sunnyvale**. A theme park drawing upon five venues of old America (Hometown Square, Orleans Place, Yankee Harbor, Yukon Territory, and Midwest Livestock Exposition and County Fair), it has live stage shows, arcades, snack bars and gift shops. But it is perhaps best known for its wild rides like "The Demon", a scary roller coaster, and "The Edge", a frightening 2½-second fall.

New attractions include Skyhawk and Rip Roaring Rapids. The Hot Ice skating arena hosts a regular series of ice shows choreographed by the director of Ice Capades, and the newly constructed Imax theater features films produced especially for its stunning 90-foot screen.

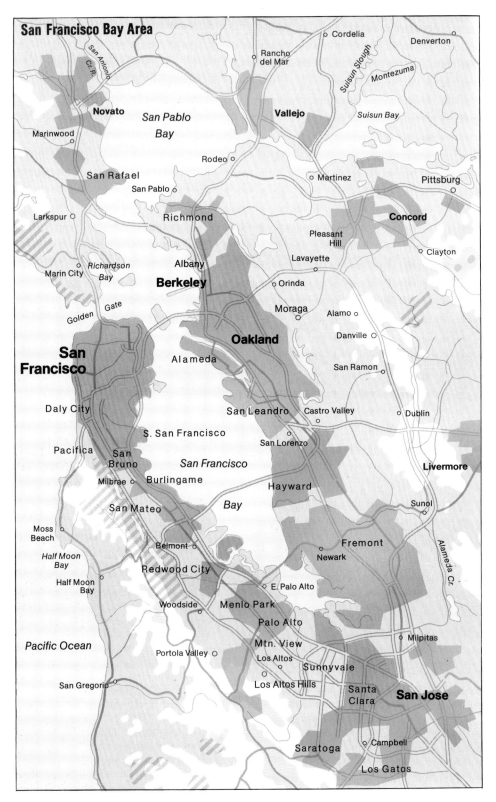

San Francisco Bay Area

Novato
San Pablo Bay
Marinwood
San Antonio Cr. R.
Cordelia
Rancho del Mar
Denverton
Suisun Slough
Montezuma
Vallejo
Suisun Bay
Rodeo
San Rafael
San Pablo
Martinez
Pittsburg
Larkspur
Richmond
Concord
Pleasant Hill
Clayton
Richardson Bay
Albany
Lavayette
Marin City
Berkeley
Orinda
Golden Gate
Moraga
Alamo
Danville
Oakland
San Ramon
San Francisco
Alameda
Daly City
San Leandro
Castro Valley
Dublin
S. San Francisco
San Lorenzo
Pacifica
San Bruno
San Francisco
Livermore
Milbrae
Burlingame
Hayward
Sunol
San Mateo
Bay
Moss Beach
Belmont
Fremont
Half Moon Bay
Newark
Redwood City
Alameda Cr.
Half Moon Bay
Woodside
E. Palo Alto
Menlo Park
Pacific Ocean
Portola Valley
Palo Alto
Milpitas
Mtn. View
Los Altos
San Gregorio
Sunnyvale
Los Altos Hills
Santa Clara
San Jose
Saratoga
Campbell
Los Gatos

OAKLAND AND THE EAST BAY

"The Mysterious East Bay" is San Francisco columnist Herb Caen's condescending name for the wilds of Alameda and Contra Costa counties, the butt of a thousand San Francisco in-jokes. Beleaguered, bush-league **Oakland** can never seem to live down Gertrude Stein's infamous quip, "When you get there, there is no there, there." And **Berkeley** is still "Berserkeley" to those who remember the student unrest of the 1960s.

Yet snotty San Francisco sighs nostalgically for the shipping business the Port of Oakland – now the second largest container port in the world – has long since wooed away. Once-shabby Oakland is very much a city on the way up, pouring millions of dollars into urban redevelopment. And Berkeley, though still lovably quirky, is now a hotbed of student "rest": the University of California has metamorphosed into Preppy Heaven.

Socially, Oakland may be one of the most interesting cities in the country; block by block, it is certainly among the best integrated. Its population is 47 percent black, 38 percent white, most of the rest Asian and Hispanic. The city owes much of its new vitality to the black capitalists who have taken over the city's political life in recent years. The city council is dominated by black members. In 1977, Lionel Wilson, Oakland's first black mayor, was elected with the help of the radical Black Panther Party (now defunct) and the Democratic left. But once elected, Wilson was quick to form alliances with much more moderate political elements. Mayor Wilson recently announced his intention to run for an unprecedented fourth term.

Lakes and other landmarks: Oakland's most obvious landmarks are the **Tribune Building**, with its distinctive tower; the **Oakland City Hall**, with its wedding cake cupola; and, in the hills above the city, the five-towered, white granite **Mormon Temple**. Also visible from the Nimitz Freeway, for those driving toward the airport, is the **Oakland-Alameda County Coliseum Complex**, former home of the Oakland (now LA) Raiders football team and current home of the city's beloved baseball As. And there's a natural landmark – **Lake Merritt**, a salt-water tidal lake in the center of the city. Visitors can skim across the lake in a replica of an old-time paddlewheeler and then take the kids to **Children's Fairyland** at **Lakeside Park**, 7 acres of nursery-rhyme fantasies with live animals as part of the scenery.

Within walking distance of the lake are two wonderfully contrasting architectural delights – the **Oakland Museum** at 1000 Oak Street and the **Paramount Theater** at 2025 Broadway. The museum is a modern stunner, built on three levels. The Hall of California Ecology, devoted to natural sciences, is on the first level; the Cowell Hall of California History is on the second; and the Gallery of California Art occupies the third. For devotees of art deco, the Paramount, designed by Timothy Pflueger, is a treat.

A patriotic oarswoman on Lake Merritt, Oakland.

Oakland's version of Fisherman's Wharf is the tediously pedestrian **Jack London Square** and **Jack London Village**. The author of *The Sea Wolf* and *Call of the Wild* might not be impressed were he alive to see it. Here are the overpriced restaurants, the T-shirt shops, the ever-so-adorable souvenir emporiums found in tourist traps anywhere. At least there is a view of the Oakland estuary. The **First and Last Chance Saloon** where London himself (an Oakland native) used to belly up, and a log cabin he is supposed to have occupied in the Klondike, are the main attractions.

Berkeley bizarre: The mighty **University of California** is now spread over nine campuses throughout the state. It is considered one of the greatest universities in the world, outranking all other American universities in number of Nobel laureates. But it began as a humble prep school operating out of a former fandango house in Oakland. It was then called Contra Costa Academy and at one point, with only three students enrolled, its housekeeping staff got so worried about their paychecks they set up a tavern right in the academy.

The school's founder, the Reverend Henry Durant, quickly closed the tavern and recruited more students. He had 50 by 1855. The school acquired a charter as the College of California and eventually merged with the state's not-yet-organized university at its current site north of Oakland. In 1866 the new college town was named for Bishop George Berkeley, an 18th-century Irish philosopher who had written a poem that caught the fancy of a member of the naming committee – a poem about a new golden age of learning in America.

When the city of Berkeley incorporated in 1878, it had a population of only 2,000, but the town grew very fast as the university developed and as thousands of San Franciscans moved to the East Bay after the earthquake and fire of 1906. However, it was the Free Speech Movement of 1964 that put it on the map, for better or worse.

The issue was an administrative order limiting partisan political activities on

White-shirted defenders haul down the ball carrier in a college football game at UC Berkeley.

campus. But the movement's real importance was in kicking off the snowballing campus rebellions of the '60s. For several years thereafter the campus was a smoldering center of protest and politics. It ignited again in 1969, when students once more took to the streets to stop the university's expansion in an area they wanted to preserve as a "People's Park". They won, after a fashion, though the violence led to the death of an onlooker. After the People's Park incident, things cooled down.

Though the students are once again bent over their textbooks, Berkeley is still a carnival of quixotic politics. In local elections, slates of liberals face slates of ultra-liberals, happily splitting hairs over rent control, traffic control and tobacco control. Berkeley was one of the earliest cities to adopt an anti-smoking ordinance and its anti-auto regulations are not to be believed. In fact, driving in Berkeley can be an adventure without a map, for traffic barriers to discourage cars in residential neighborhoods can turn the bewildered out-of-towner into a rat in a maze. The best plan is to keep to the main streets, or "arterials" – or better yet, simply to park and walk in the university area.

On the approach to Berkeley, two buildings catch one's eye. On a hillside toward the south is a fairy-tale white palace. That's the **Claremont Resort Hotel**, finished just before the Panama Pacific Exposition of 1915. The other landmark is a tall, thin, pointed structure, the university's belltower. Its official name is **Sather Tower**, but it's known to all simply as the "Campanile" because it's modeled after St Mark's Campanile in Venice, Italy.

To get the feel of Berkeley at its liveliest, the visitor should walk down Telegraph Avenue from Dwight Way to the University. Here students, townspeople and "street people" pick their way between rows of shops and street vendors offering jewelry, pottery, plants and tie-dyed everything. On a good day, the atmosphere is rather like that of an Asian bazaar.

A refreshing afternoon at the Claremont Hotel in the Oakland hills.

MARIN: HOT TUBS AND WILDERNESS

Marin County has a reputation at least in the Bay Area, as the mecca of hot-tub hedonism. The stereotypical Marin resident is newly affluent (having made his money in computer software or video tapes), cosmopolitan, artsy and politically liberal. On the dark side, he is intellectually shallow, narcissistic and self-indulgent, often found in his lush backyard glade soaking in his tub and imbibing a bone-dry Chardonnay or some other mild hallucinogen. His hauntingly beautiful female counterpart is golden-limbed and sun-buttered, to be found reading her tarot cards over bean-curd soup, behind the stained glass windows of her redwood cottage.

This stereotype has some validity, as a visitor may discover if he listens in on a couple of Marinites conversing in Psychobabble:

"Martha isn't centered yet, but our dyad is processing through her ego block with some pre-orgasmic body work," says one.

"I can resonate to that," replies the other.

But this should not dissuade the eavesdropper from his visit. The residents may sometimes be a bit phony and self-centered but they can also be friendly and amusing, and while they do guard their habitats and privacy, they often throw open their homes and hot tubs to the gentle visitor who uses the right approach.

Aside from its inhabitants, Marin County has a panoply of good bars, restaurants, public baths and other amusements that are democratic in the sense that social status is determined strictly on the basis of good cash and credit cards.

What is generally less known about Marin, even locally, is that the county offers some of the premier outdoor experiences in Northern California. Right on the northern lip of a metropolitan area of some 5 million inhabitants are tens of thousands of acres of pristine coastline, unspoiled redwood groves and mountain meadows, untrammeled by development and looking pretty much as they did on Day One. This green belt offers an outstanding opportunity for hikers and nature lovers, as well as those following a lighter regimen of hot tubs, massage and good food.

With the lighter regimen in mind, the first stop for most Marin visitors is **Sausalito** (a corruption of the Spanish *saucelito*, meaning "little willow"). The waterside shops, the warrens of pricey boutiques, and the houses perched behind them on a steep slope draw inevitable comparisons to Mediterranean *villes* of the Riviera. The main drag, Bridgeway, is thronged on most weekends. The atmosphere is casual. It's usually easy to make new friends.

Mount Tamalpais: Mount Tamalpais is a hiker's nirvana. This mountain, often called the "Sleeping Maiden" because of several voluptuous bumps on her ridgeline, contains 30 miles (48 km) of trails within 6,000 acres (2,430 hectares) and many more miles of hiking in the contiguous watershed lands.

Left, free and easy houseboat living in Sausalito harbor. **Right**, the scene on Sausalito's quaint Bridgeway.

On Mount Tam's lower elevations, often shrouded in fog, are stands of virgin redwood. Above, the mountain's chaparral-covered high slopes jut proudly into the sunshine, overlooking San Francisco Bay and the Pacific.

One of the redwood stands at the base of Mount Tam is not only dark and quiet; it is world renowned. This is the **Muir Woods National Monument**. At the turn of the 20th century, a not-very-farsighted Marin water district planned to condemn a property called Redwood Canyon, cut the timber on it, and with the profits build a dam and reservoir. This scheme so appalled one wealthy Marinite named William Kent that he peeled off a layer of his own bankroll to buy the land. Then, using the provisions of a then-obscure federal law, he deeded the redwood stand to the government as a national monument. President Theodore Roosevelt thought the woods should be named after their benefactor, but Kent modestly declined, giving the honor instead to his old friend, Sierra trekker and naturalist John Muir.

Thus Muir Woods, almost 300 acres (120 hectares) of unrivaled arboreal beauty, came into the public domain. Here the mighty sequoias grow to 200 feet (61 meters) in height, 16 feet (5 meters) in diameter, and live to 1,000 years in age. About 1 million visitors a year amble through these rows of giants. Energetic walkers can leave the crowds behind by heading up the steep slope of Mount Tam on the **Ben Johnson Trail**, through deeply shaded glens rife with ferns and mushrooms, past ever-changing groves of bay, tan oaks, madrona and nutmeg.

Marin Headlands: Beyond Mount Tam, Marin County's green belt extends some 50 miles (80 km) to the distant tip of Point Reyes National Seashore. The coastal country, known as the **Marin Headlands**, offers so many possibilities for walkers that – according to veteran hiker and outdoor writer Margaret Patterson Doss – they could not be exhausted in a lifetime.

Muir and Stinson beaches, at the foot of Mount Tamalpais, are popular among

Nude beach, Marin County coast.

anglers hoping to hook surf perch and rockfish, and among birdwatchers who want to spy such out-of-the-way creatures as the sooty shearwater, brown pelican, Western grebe, killdeer and millet. When the fog pulls back, the beaches also attract sunbathers. They get crowded only when sweltering inland weather drives tract-home lemmings toward the sea.

Windswept Point Reyes: Point Reyes is a triangular peninsula separated from the rest of the world by the main fissure line of the San Andreas Fault. Geologists say the fault is prying Point Reyes gradually northeast at an average rate of 2 inches (5 cm) a year. The epicenter of the 1906 San Francisco earthquake was a half-mile from where the main park headquarters now stand on Bear Valley Road. On **Earthquake Trail**, visitors can see where the quake moved one stone fence 15 feet (4½ meters).

To get to the park headquarters and most of the trailheads in the National Seashore, drivers go up State 1 past the town of Olema to Bear Valley Road.

The park is open only to those who are willing to walk or ride a horse. The terrain is varied; much of it is steep. Gloomy forests suddenly open on sweeping meadows. The coast is rockbound with occasional pocket beaches. From atop wind-whipped **Mount Wittenburg** there is another beautiful view. There are three overnight campgrounds in the park.

At the tip of the Point Reyes promontory perches a **lighthouse** which warns ships away from the treacherous coast. One of the foggiest places in Marin County it usually has no view at all. When there is a view, it is a good place from which to spot migrating whales.

On the northern edge of the national seashore, Pierce Point Road meanders around to several beaches – **Abbott's**, **Kehoe**, and the most ruggedly dramatic, **McClure's**. These beaches are not recommended for swimming because of the danger of sharks, undertow and rip tides. **Drake's Beach**, on the southern side, is somewhat protected from winds.

Horses, <u>left</u>, and water birds, <u>right</u>, find homes at Point Reyes National Seashore.

THE CALIFORNIA WINE COUNTRY

Standing on the summit of **Mount St Helena**, which dominates the Wine Country counties of Napa, Sonoma, Mendocino and Lake, a vast panorama stretches for mile after mile below one's feet.

There are the Napa Valley's emerald vineyards, crystal Lake Berryessa, Sonoma Valley and Jack London's beloved Valley of the Moon, where oak trees dot grassy hills the color of champagne. To the west, the vast Santa Rosa Plain unfurls until cut off by Sebastopol's apple orchards and the redwood groves of the Russian River. The river's great horseshoe bend tacks up to the Alexander Valley's vineyards. Northward, the burgundy-hued Mendocino ridges guard the inland valleys from cool sea breezes. To the east, the sun glints off the waters of Clear Lake. San Francisco lies south.

Little old winemakers: Father Jose Altimira, founder of the Mission San Francisco de Solano at Sonoma, and General Vallejo, who colonized Sonoma and Napa counties with land grants to his relatives and friends, dabbled in winemaking. But it was Count Agoston Haraszthy who pushed Sonoma into wine stardom. Haraszthy, a flamboyant Hungarian political refugee, began Buena Vista, California's oldest commercial winery, in 1857. He trekked across Europe to cull wine-grape cuttings for California's growers. Ever restless, Haraszthy migrated to Nicaragua, where he was later eaten by alligators.

Charles Krug, a German political exile and protege of Haraszthy, started the Napa Valley's first commercial winery in 1861. By the 1880s, Napa and Sonoma valley wines were winning medals in Europe.

The long night of Prohibition almost – but not quite – destroyed the wineries. Following repeal of Prohibition in 1933, Beaulieu Vineyard's Georges de Latour, the Mondavi family and others began resurrecting the wine industry.

In the 1960s, a wine boom began as large corporations marketed vintage-dated varietal wines at reasonable prices, and small, privately owned wineries produced more expensive estate-bottled wines at higher costs. Old-time winemaking families were joined by oil barons, engineers, doctors and actors who revitalized old wineries and opened new ones. By the US bicentennial celebration of 1976, Napa wines were beating French vintages in European tastings.

Strikingly modern wineries – Robert Mondavi, Sterling, Sonoma Vineyards – arose beside century-old stone ones. Creative spirits traded urban strife for country calm and started restaurants, country inns, small "organic" produce farms or shops selling hand-made furniture and pottery.

Crushing and fermenting: In the spring, the vineyards glow yellow with wild mustard blooms; the grape leaves appear in April. In dusty summer, the vines leaf out with insignificant grape flowers. Dry, moderately warm weather is needed for grapes to mature properly.

Autumn brings the grape harvest,

Preceding pages: vineyards surround a Napa Valley homestead. **Left,** Alexander Valley grape pickers bring in the harvest. **Right,** a winemaker works in his cellars.

when the air hangs heavy with the scent of crushed fruit. Grape leaves turn scarlet, gold and purple, creating miniature forests of fall colors. Winter rains between November and March provide the dormancy grape vines need. Vines are pruned to force remaining branches to yield more fruit. One vine can produce one-third of a case of wine.

Wines begin at the crusher, where the juice is freed from the grapes. Red wines are born when the grape skin and pulp go into the fermenting tank, where yeast is added to convert sugar to alcohol and carbon dioxide. Grape skins are pressed to extract more juice, then the reds are aged in stainless steel or wooden tanks. The wine is clarified, then aged further before bottling.

White wines are made from the fermentation of the juice alone, drawn off from the grapes immediately after crushing. Yeast is added, and fermentation occurs in stainless steel tanks. Leaving the yeast creates dry wines; stopping yeast action makes sweeter wines. Champagne, or sparkling wine,

begins the same way, then undergoes a second fermentation. The carbon dioxide is trapped within the bottle, hence the bubbles.

Vintages mean less in California than in Europe, thanks to the state's relatively benign climate. For red wine varieties – Cabernet Sauvignon, Pinot Noir, Zinfandel – 1974, 1978, 1980, 1984 and 1985 were good years. For white wine varieties – Chardonnay, Chenin Blanc, Riesling – 1975, 1977, 1980, 1984, 1986 and 1987 were good years.

Winery visits should be limited to three a day. Most wineries are open between 10 a.m. and 4 p.m. daily. It is a good idea to try a tour (usually 1½ hour) and tasting at a large winery, coupled with tasting-room stops at smaller wineries. Many wineries are open by appointment only; for a full list, oenophiles can send a self-addressed, stamped envelope for "California's Wine Wonderland" Wine Institute, 165 Post Street, San Francisco, CA 94108.

For those who want to romp across the Wine Country in a Mercedes or

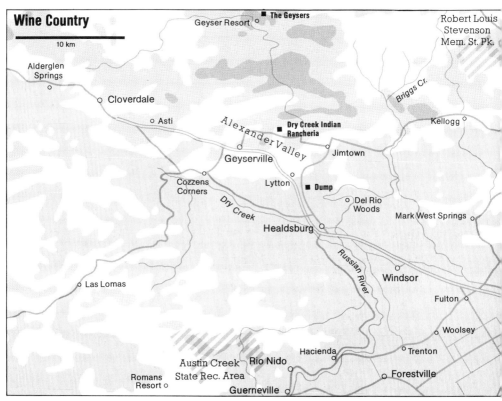

Wine Country

10 km

The Geysers
Geyser Resort
Robert Louis Stevenson Mem. St. Pk.

Alderglen Springs

Cloverdale

Asti

Briggs Cr.

Alexander Valley

Dry Creek Indian Rancheria

Kellogg

Geyserville

Jimtown

Cozzens Corners

Lytton

Dump

Dry Creek

Del Rio Woods

Mark West Springs

Healdsburg

Russian River

Las Lomas

Windsor

Fulton

Woolsey

Hacienda

Trenton

Austin Creek State Rec. Area

Rio Nido

Romans Resort

Forestville

Guerneville

doubled-decked London-style bus, imbibe at private sippings, or dine with a favorite vintner, wine-touring services such as California Wine Tours, Sonoma-California Touring or Wine Tours International are available.

Napa County: The **Napa Valley** (*nàpa* means "plenty" in the local Indian dialect) is compact – wineries, delis, restaurants and country inns lie close together. Although rural, the country's mix of San Francisco socialites, titled Europeans, semi-retired Hollywood screen-writers and producers gives Napa County a genteel, if sometimes slick, aura.

A 30-mile (48-km) thrust of flatland between the pine-forested **Mayacamas Mountains** and the buff-colored **Howell Mountains**, the Napa Valley is pinched off in the north by Mount St Helena. The valley evokes an ordered, European air, with expanses of vineyards broken by farmhouses, stone wineries and a series of towns spaced along State Highway 29, "**The Great Wine Way**". Strict land-control measures have kept valley development confined to the towns and the freeway south of Yountville, but have also escalated land prices.

The Wine Country begins in earnest at **Yountville**, for the vineyards abut the village's historic, renovated brick and stone buildings. Yountville's city-park picnic stop is across from George Yount's grave at the pioneer cemetery. He got his 11,000-acre (4,450-hectare) Mexican land grant for roofing General Vallejo's Petaluma Adobe, surely one of history's best contracting deals.

Domaine Chandon Winery, next to the California Veterans Home, is French throughout; in deference to Gallic sensibilities, the champagne is called sparkling wine. The winery, owned by Moet and Chandon, makes sparkling wine in the *methode champenoise*; that is, it is fermented in the same bottle from which it is poured.

Adventurers can take an early morning hot-air balloon sweep above the vineyards, followed by a champagne picnic. Most flights leave from Yountville. A one-hour flight costs $95 to

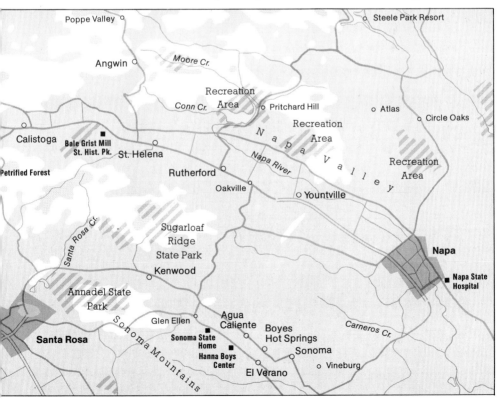

$110 per person. Four balloon companies operate in the valley; among them is **Adventures Aloft** (Vintage 1870 complex), which has bicycle and moped rentals, too.

The 40 wineries of St Helena: St Helena, the Wine Country's capital, is noted for its 40 wineries, historic stone buildings, picnic parks, chic shops, pricey restaurants, country inns and low crime rate. The **Silverado Museum** is stuffed with Robert Louis Stevenson memorabilia – first editions of his work and souvenirs of his global jaunts.

South of town, the **Martini Winery**, run by one of the valley's oldest wine-making clans, offers reasonably priced wines (Cabernet Sauvignon to sherry) in an unpretentious setting. Wine and soap mix at **Spring Mountain Vineyards**, planted in the hill country west of St Helena. CBS' *Falcon Crest* soap opera is filmed at the winery's **Miravalle** mansion, built in 1885 by playboy Tiburcio Parrott.

A trinity of giant wineries – **Beringer, Christian Brothers** and **Charles Krug** – lie north of St Helena. Jacob and Frederick Beringer started their winery in 1876, modeling the Rhine House (1883) after their ancestral estate in Mainz, Germany. They dug limestone caves for aging wine. Today's winery, owned by Nestlé (yes, the chocolate people) features Fumé Blanc and Cabernet Sauvignon in the mansion tasting room, spacious lawns and a regal row of elms fronting the winery.

Christian Brothers' Greystone building was the world's largest stone winery when erected in 1889 by mining magnate William Bourn. This white-elephant winery changed hands frequently until the Christian Brothers, a Catholic educational order, bought it in 1950. The tour is informal, the tasting room elegant.

Founding father Charles Krug sired Napa's wine industry when he lugged a cider press from Sonoma to squeeze grapes. Today's winery building dates from 1874. Owners Peter Mondavi and sons have an informative, traditional tour, with tastings of Krug and C.K. Mondavi label wines, including

Beringer Brothers Winery, St Helena: below, the Rhine House...

100

Cabernet Sauvignon and Chenin Blanc. Krug's August Moon Concerts present classic productions on the lawn.

Two miles north of St Helena is **Freemark Abbey**, a winery, restaurant and shopping place. There's no abbey here; the name is an amalgamation of the owners' names. The once-a-day tours are small, a welcome change from larger wineries. The better wines include Chardonnay, Cabernet Sauvignon and Edelwein, a late-harvest Johannisberg Riesling. At the nearby **Hurd Beesway Candle Factory**, visitors can watch candle-making in progress.

Three miles north of St Helena is the **Bale Grist Mill State Historic Park**. The mill, built in 1846 by Dr Edward Bale (General Vallejo's physician and Krug's father-in-law), recalls the days when the Napa Valley was planted chiefly in wheat, Bale's *Rancho Carne Humana* ("Ranch of Human Flesh") was named when Bale misunderstood the Indian words for the area.

Two champagne cellars, **Hanns Kornell** and **Schramsberg**, are close to

Bothe-Napa Valley State Park. Kornell, a refugee from Nazi Germany, resurrected a historic stone winery to make his German-style *methode champenoise* champagnes. His speciality is Sehr Troken, a dry variety. Tours are excellent. Schramsberg, open by appointment, is almost unchanged from the day when Jacob Schram invited Robert Louis Stevenson into the cool champagne cellars to taste 18 different vintages of wine.

Sterling Vineyards – part-Greek monastery, part-fantasy – reigns over the upper valley atop a knoll. For a fee, a tram whisks visitors 300 feet (91 meters) up for a self-guided tour. The tram fee is applicable toward purchase of Cabernet Sauvignon, Sauvignon Blanc and other wines.

The Silverado Trail: The **Silverado Trail** parallels State 29 between Napa and Calistoga, then joins with the highway as the route into Lake County's resort and wine region. Built as the road from Mount St Helena's cinnabar mines to Napa's river docks, today's Silverado Trail is an elevated, two-lane road above the valley floor offering motorists and bicyclists vistas, uncrowded wineries (most with picnic tables) and hidden valleys in the Howell Mountains.

A popular stop is **Rutherford Hill Winery**, an ark-like structure with picnic grounds and Chardonnay, Cabernet Sauvignon and Zinfandel wines. **Stag's Leap**, a rocky promontory where a 16-point Roosevelt elk plunged to its death, overlooks **Stag's Leap Wine Cellars** and **Clos du Val Wine Company**. Stag's Leap winemaker Warren Winiarski made the French jump when his 1973 Cabernet Sauvignon took first place over Bordeaux wines in a 1976 European judging.

The tragedy-ridden Berryessa family lost sons and soil in the Mexican War; today their Napa county land grant is a warm-water nirvana. **Lake Berryessa** can be reached via State 128 from St Helena or State 121 from Napa. Fishermen can pull in trout, bass and catfish aboard a rented houseboat. Sailors, waterskiers, campers and swimmers have their choice of seven resorts around

...and wine tasting.

this lake, which has more shoreline than Lake Tahoe.

New, bold and friendly, **Lake County's** visitor-seeking wineries are scattered along State 29 as it wraps around **Clear Lake**, California's largest natural lake. (Lake Tahoe lies partly in Nevada.) Besides producing Cabernet Sauvignon, Zinfandel and Sauvignon Blanc grapes, Lake County is famous for Bartlett pears and walnuts.

The first stop for travelers northbound from Napa County is **Guenoc Winery**, on Butts Canyon Road near **Middletown**. This reborn winery once was owned by British actress Lillie Langtry, companion to the Prince of Wales, later King Edward VII. Langtry started the winery to gain California residency for a divorce to marry a lover housed on a nearby ranch.

Kelseyvill's orchard country surrounds **Konocti Winery**, where one can imbibe Cabernet Sauvignon or Johannisberg Riesling while toe-tapping to bluegrass music on Sunday afternoons. Konocti puts on a Fall Harvest Festival every October.

Clear Lake's alpine, sun-warmed waters attract bass and catfish fishermen, waterskiers, boaters and swimmers. Resorts ring the lake; or campers can pitch a tent in **Clear Lake State Park** at the foot of conical **Mount Konocti**, an extinct volcano.

Sonoma County: Sonoma consists of many places. It is a patchwork of country roads, towns, orchards, ridges and hills. US 101, the Wine Country's only freeway, traverses the north-south length of **Sonoma County**, entering the county near **Petaluma**. There, travelers can pick up Camembert or Brie at the **Marin French Cheese Factory** or see General Vallejo's **Petaluma Adobe**, the state's grandest *hacienda*. The freeway runs through Santa Rosa, Healdsburg (gateway to the Alexander, Dry Creek and Russian River valleys), and Cloverdale on the Mendocino County border.

The **Sonoma Valley** is steeped in wine, literary and political history. *Sonoma* is a Patwin Indian word meaning "land of Chief Nose" after an Indian leader with a prominent proboscis.

Vallejo romanticized it as the "Valley of the Moon", and author Jack London took up the call with a book of the same title about frazzled urbanites rejuvenated by clean country living. State 12 runs the length of the valley, passing through the towns of Sonoma and Kenwood. Glen Ellen, Jack London's old haunt, lies off State 12.

Father Altimira founded California's last mission, **San Francisco de Solano**, in 1823. Vallejo set up the town in 1835, making **Sonoma** the northernmost outpost of a Catholic, Spanish-speaking realm that, at its peak, extended all the way to the tip of South America.

It briefly became a republic after the Bear Flag Revolt in 1846, when Americans stormed Vallejo's home. Haraszthy's winemaking innovations at **Buena Vista Winery** a decade later forced Californians to recognize the state's vinicultural potential.

The **Sonoma Plaza**, largest in California, today dominates the town. Several restored adobes and the **Sonoma State Historic Park** – Mission San Francisco de Solano, the **Sonoma Barracks** and Vallejo's home – ring the Plaza and nearby streets.

Sandwiched among this history are enough culinary stops to put the town on the Weight Watchers hit list. Jack cheese, California's only native cheese, can be sampled at the **Sonoma Cheese Factory**, a good picnic supply stop. **Vella Cheese Company** is just off the Plaza, while the scent of sourdough bread lures passers-by inside the **Sonoma French Bakery.**

Two blocks from the Plaza stand **Sebastiani Vineyards**, some dating from mission days; Sam Sebastiani is the third generation to run them. East of Sonoma, **Hacienda Wine Cellars** and Buena Vista Winery are both connected with Haraszthy. Tickets are available at the winery for Buena Vista's summer classical concerts.

The Gundlach and Bundschu families have been involved in winemaking for over 125 year; **Gundlach-Bundschu Wine Cellars'** Zinfandel, Cabernet Sauvignon and Merlot are especially good.

Nearby, the super-expensive, beautifully decorated **Sonoma Mission Inn and Spa** offers elegant exercise and tasty meals.

Also worth a visit is Jack London's cottage, where he wrote many of his 51 books, the ruins of his arson-destroyed **Wolf House**, his grave, and the museum of memorabilia inside his widow's home are part of the **Jack London State Historic Park**. The surroundings, high in the **Sonoma Mountains**, form an invigorating mixture of history, picnicking spots and hiking trails. The **Glen Ellen** exit off State 12 leads to the park.

The **Valley of the Moon Winery** occupies part of Senator George Hearst's 19th-century vineyards. Today those vineyards produce a fine Zinfandel. **Grand Cru Vineyards**, a tucked-away winery born during the wine boom of the 1960s and '70s, has picnic sites plus fine Gewurztraminer and Chenin Blanc.

Near Glen Ellen is **Beltane Ranch**, today a bed-and-breakfast inn. It was once owned by Mammy Pleasant, a former slave who held sway in 19th-

century San Francisco with voodoo and anti-racist activities.

North on State 12, visitors come to two wineries in **Kenwood,** and an old resort town with outdoor mineral-spring pools at **Morton's Warm Springs**. **Kenwood Winery** features Zinfandel, Cabernet Sauvignon and Chenin Blanc. Chardonnay lovers head for **Chateau St Jean** with its pseudo-medieval tower and fine Johannisberg Riesling.

Famed botanist Luther Burbank picked **Santa Rosa** as "the chosen spot of all the earth" to create his plant experiments. He developed more than 800 new plants, including many fruits, vegetables and flowers, yet relished few of them except asparagus. Visitors can tour his home (in summer) and gardens (all year) in the heart of Santa Rosa.

Santa Rosa's trinity of adjoining parks form a 5,000-acre (12,000-hectare) urban oasis with a children's amusement park and lake in **Howarth Park**; camping, picnicking and boating in **Spring Lake Park**, and hiking and equestrian trails in **Annadel State Park**.

Bicyclists relax by the Silverado Trail.

SACRAMENTO,
THE STATE CAPITAL

No one should get the idea that Sacramento is a city.

There are more than 1 million people living in and around Sacramento, but it's still not a city, at least not in the sense that San Francisco is. In fact, when Sacramentans talk about going to "the city", they mean San Francisco.

No, Sacramento is the ultimate cow town, a nice, big, prosperous, comfortable, tree-shaded cow town.

To anyone who has driven out of San Francisco on a 55°F (13°C) summer day and stopped in 85°F (29°C) Sacramento, it seems a blazing furnace. But all in all, Sacramento's summer is pleasant. Humidity is low, it seldom rains, and the prevailing wind is a marine breeze from the San Francisco Bay that cools the nights. Its most unpleasant weather is winter fog, which can block out the sun for days or weeks on end, leaving the thermometer stuck at 42°F (6°C).

Left, the State Capitol.

Sacramento started out as John Sutter's New Helvetia Colony. Sutter, a German Swiss, had the dream of founding an independent state in the wilderness between Oregon and Mexican California.

The colony thrived until January 1848, when James Marshall walked into the fort with his gold find from Sutter's sawmill in the hills to the east. Sutter's workers left for the goldfields, squatters grabbed his land, and Sutter died in 1880 in Washington, DC, attempting to defend his land titles.

What emerged from the Gold Rush was Sacramento. It became the state capital in 1845 after San Jose, Vallejo and Benicia all had a brief reign. Since then, technology and fashion have left their marks, but a rather distinct image of old Sacramento can still be detected beneath the town's modern veneer.

A visit to Sacramento should start at the beautifully restored **Capitol** building which is surrounded by 40-acre (16-hectare) **Capital Park**. This manicured arboretum has a vast collection of California flora and examples of plants from every climate and continent on Earth. It is especially popular for brown-bag lunches; the parade of passersby include everyone from briefly clad, headset-wearing roller skaters and homeless people to state officials and office workers. The blue-gray squirrels are cute to a fault and shameless beggars.

The Pony Express remembered: Other "don't-miss" attractions include the **Old Governor's Mansion** (15th and H streets), **Sutter's Fort** (between 26th, 28th, K and L streets) and the **Indian Museum** on the fort grounds. There is a bronze plaque at 29th and B streets next to an insulation company yard, marking the point where Sutter first came ashore to found his colony.

Visitors will find **Old Sacramento** along the west end riverfront, where the old Pony Express and Transcontinental Railroad stations have been restored. The **California State Railroad Museum** and Old Sacramento State Historic Park are also well worth a visit, as is the gracious **Crocker Art Museum** on 2nd and O streets.

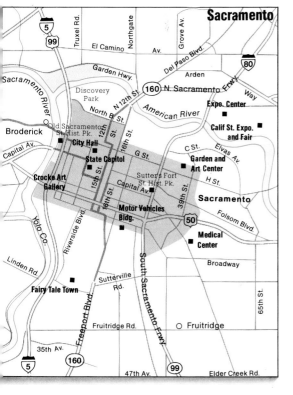

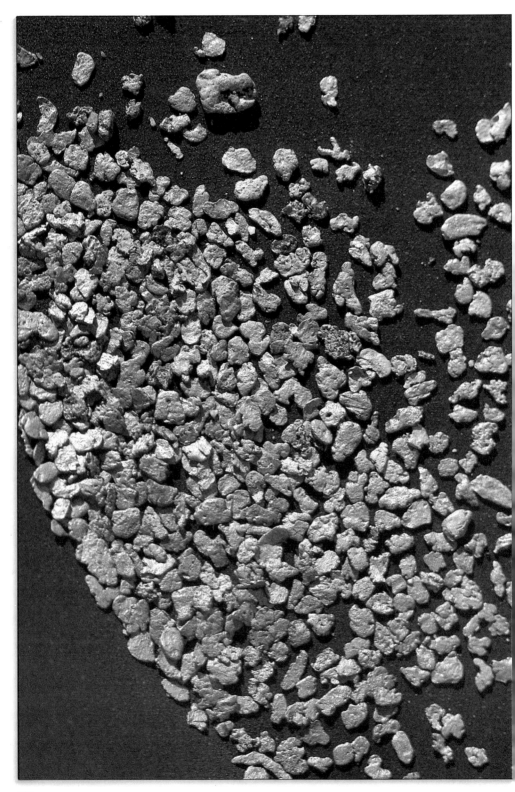

EXPLORING THE GOLD COUNTRY

There may have been an end to the Gold Rush, but it was not because they ran out of gold.

No, they merely ran out of the gold that was lying around on top of the ground. As the holes got deeper and more dangerous, the work got harder, slower and more expensive, until finally it was no longer cost-efficient to dig.

Geologists say there is at least as much gold in the Mother Lode today as was taken out in the previous century. Latter-day gold miners say the 7 million pounds that the old-timers got was only 10 percent of the wealth nature deposited there. Either way, there is a good deal left – and quite a few people are looking for it. There is something inexplicably compelling about gold, and the same holds true for the Gold Country.

There is also another gold rush going on, from Mariposa to Nevada City – real estate. Travelers on State Highway 49, the Gold Country's major arterial, are likely to see more real-estate signs than ghost towns. The modern miner is competing for land with the housing developer rather than with the claim jumper.

In the lowest of the Gold Country foothills, spring begins as early as March. The roadsides from the Central Valley towns of Sacramento, Stockton and Fresno are crowded with wild mustard, an edible plant that adds tang to a salad and which covers the beef-cattle grazing land with miles of yellow blossoms. In the spring months, a succession of wildflowers moves up the hills and turns entire mountainsides blue and purple with lupine and brodiaea. There are larkspur and popcorn flowers, purple vetch and baby blue eyes, and the maroon of the red bud, a flowering bush. In the canyon of the Merced around Metzler's, there are times in the spring when fresh, new, unnamed waterfalls appear every few hundred yards. The waterfalls last until native California poppies bloom, usually in June.

Sonora, named for the Mexican state from which many of its first '49ers came, is a city again, one that may be losing a struggle with the real-estate developers. The edges of town are now built up with strings of small shopping centers. Beyond are the homes on one-acre lots that burden the community's water and sewage facilities and pack its streets until traffic stops. But all this development has happened because Sonora is beautiful… and it still has an enjoyable downtown. The **Gunn House**, a private home now operated as an inn, is highly recommended.

The Mother Lode and jumping frogs: In the 1870s there was a pocket mine at the north end of Sonora where the operators found a vein of nearly pure gold and recovered, they say, $160,000 worth of gold in one day. It was part of *La Veta Madre*, "The Mother Lode", from which the legends sprang. It is the kind of story that keeps miners at work, back there in the dark tunnels.

The real treasure of Tuolumne County these days is **Columbia**. Just a few minutes north of Sonora and just off State 49, this old town has been restored as a state park and is as good a place as can be found to learn about the Mother Lode. For those who have traveled in the eastern United States, Columbia can be compared to Williamsburg, Virginia, another restored historical town.

Columbia once had a population of 15,000, 50 saloons, competing daily newspapers and at least one church. Nearly $90 million in gold was mined there over 20 years. Much of restored Columbia is closed to automobiles, but the quiet majesty of the town makes it worth parking and walking. There are shops, theaters, a museum, and best of all, the splendid **Columbia City Hotel**, open for meals and overnight lodging. The hotel is operated as a laboratory for local junior-college students of hotel management. Around Columbia, as in many of the Gold Country towns, there are several rock or gold shops whose proprietors may be willing to show visitors where to look for gold and perhaps even teach them how to mine.

Back on State 49, still headed north, a sign indicates the summit of **Jackass Hill**. It is named for the animals so

What the miners came for: gold nuggets.

central to gold prospecting, and it is the place where Mark Twain lived in 1864. The Twain cabin has been reconstructed around the original hearth. During the time Twain lived in the cabin, he heard and wrote what is possibly his most famous yarn, "The Celebrated Jumping Frog of Calaveras County". The actual jumping frogs were supposed to have been a bit north in **Angels Camp** – and they still are.

Angels Camp still harbors the **Angels Hotel**, where Twain is said to have heard the frog story. Better yet, each May the community holds a frog-jumping contest that attracts thousands of people to the area – so many, in fact, that the only way to actually see a jumping frog is to enter one's own in the contest. Any frog more than 4 inches (10 cm) in length is eligible. The wiser course may be to avoid Angels Camp during the week of the frogs. Twain would have.

Black Bart and Kit Carson: From the Angels Camp area, a detour leads up into the mountains to **Murphys**, a Gold Rush period town that is enough off the track to be a natural museum. The **Mercer Caverns**, well worth a visit, are in this area. Farther up State 4 is **Calaveras Big Trees State Park**, a magnificent stand of sequoias.

San Andreas is another town whose present is a triumph of development interests, but whose past is alive with romantic echoes. Black Bart, a real stagecoach bandit, was tried here in 1883 for some of the 28 robberies he allegedly committed. Bart was a San Franciscan with expensive tastes and little income. So he instituted a series of polite, bloodless robberies of the gold-laden stages in the Mother Lode. His shotgun was always unloaded and no one was ever hurt. Nevertheless, he served six years in San Quentin prison. Then he disappeared.

In good weather, the drive from San Andreas to **West Point** on the Mountain Ranch and Railroad Flat roads is beautiful. West Point was so named because it marked the end of Kit Carson's attempt to cross the Sierras. Now it has

Once a Gold Rush boom-town, the Columbia of today has been fully restored for tourism.

just a few hundred residents and a historical marker.

In recent years there have been attempts to reopen some of the 500 old mine shafts around West Point. A few of these shafts now crush ore and even welcome visitors. Those who stand in the mouth of a mine shaft, even in midsummer, can see their breath condensing in the cold air seeping up from thousands of feet beneath the ground. Modern techniques of deep-rock mining differ very little from those used by the '49ers. In fact, the gold pan and sluice boxes being used by weekend miners are essentially the same tools used 100 years ago.

From West Point, travelers can loop back west to **Mokelumne Hill**, a town once so rich in gold that its claims were limited to 16 sq. feet (about 1.5 sq. meters). According to legend, the lust for wealth ran so high that there was a murder a week here for more than four months. On a more benign note, Mokelumne Hill is the site of the founding of the **E Clampus Vitus Society**, a group devoted to good deeds and good times. The Society is still around and active, and generally has an entry in any parade or fair in the Gold Country.

From Sutter Creek to Grass Valley, about 75 miles (121 km), the countryside surrounding State 49 is mostly a commuter suburb of Sacramento. There are big Safeway supermarkets, rush-hour traffic and cable television. In fact, in the Auburn area and again around Grass Valley, State 49 suddenly and inexplicably becomes a freeway. Nonetheless, there are many things to do and see along the way.

Placerville Gold: Poor Red's in **Eldorado**, a town just south of Placerville, has a reputation for barbecued ribs and chicken. It's a plain place with prices to match. **Apple Hill**, just above Placerville on US Highway 50, has made a cooperative business of marketing apples. In fall, the whole countryside smells of cider. Bushels of fruit sell for about $10.

Placerville itself was once called Hangtown because of the chosen method of execution. It was the nexus of wagon,

19th-century mining techniques.

mail, Pony Express and telegraph routes and consequently was a busy and exciting place.

Placerville may be the only town in America with its own gold mine. The **Gold Bug Mine**, north of town, is in a public park and is open for inspection.

North of Placerville on State 49 is **Coloma**, the birthplace of the Gold Rush. There is a state historic park now at the spot where in 1848 John Marshall found the yellow metal that made California. He was building a waterway for John Sutter's lumber mill when he was distracted by something glittering in the water. The state has reconstructed the mill, though not exactly at the same place, since the **American River** has changed its course in the past century.

For those who don't want to spend all their time meditating on history, Coloma is a pleasant place for a raft trip. A number of companies offer one-day and longer trips down the American River.

Auburn, at the junction of State 49 and Interstate 80, is so much a part of the Sacramento economy today that there is a proposal to link the communities with a light rail commuter service.

The **Placer County Museum** in Auburn is counted as one of the best in the mountains, with collections of native Indian materials as well as gold-mining paraphernalia. Nearby is the colorful and unusual **Firehouse.**

Auburn is a good place to jump off for a visit to Lake Tahoe (up I-80) with a return via State 20 near **Emigrant Gap**. State 20, the old Tahoe-Pacific Highway, is one of California's great drives. It rejoins State 49 in the Nevada City-Grass Valley area.

Grass Valley was the center of the deep mines, and there are several splendid places to get a sense of what they were like. Some of them, including the **North Star**, have shafts that go hundreds of feet below sea level. The shafts are now closed and flooded. The **Nevada County Museum** in the town of Grass Valley is a good one. The **Empire Mine State Park**, east of town, is the site of a mine that produced $100 million worth of gold before it closed in the mid-20th century.

Grass Valley is now the center of high-technology industry, most notably the manufacture of equipment for television broadcasting, and is once again a name recognized around the world.

Nevada City north: Nevada City is as quaint as Grass Valley is up-to-date. It is the kind of place that attracted city people early. They busily converted the old factories and miners' stores into restaurants, museums, antique stores and theaters. There are a couple of pleasant bars – **McGee's** and **Cireno's** among them – and the **National Hotel** still puts up overnight visitors in rooms tastefully furnished with antiques.

Ten miles (16 km) north of Nevada City there is a large state park at the old **Malakoff Diggings**, a place that generated one of the very earliest pieces of environmental legislation. Visitors to the Malakoff mine can see the effects of hydraulic mining, a method of gold extraction in which high-powered streams of water are directed from cannons at the side of the mountain. This method was effective, but it devastated the mountain, and waterways were clogged with mud as far as San Francisco Bay. The technique was banned in 1884 but the scars, only slightly healed by time, are still awesome.

It's an hour's drive from Nevada City to **Downieville**, a fitting end to a tour of the Gold Country. The country here is higher, cooler and much less crowded than further south. From **Camptonville**, midway along the route from Nevada City, the lovely **Henness Pass Road** veers off into the mountains. In good weather, it is a lovely side trip. There are a number of campgrounds a few miles toward the pass.

Downieville itself is almost as perfect as a picture, a tiny remote place hemmed in by steep hillsides, with a population of not more than 500. There are however, a few places to eat or stay the night.

The real Gold Country is fading fast, a victim of developers and the unyielding ravages of the years. Like the glittering nuggets themselves, the real Gold Country is hard to find – but it's certainly worth seeking.

An old miner reflects on days of what-might-have-been.

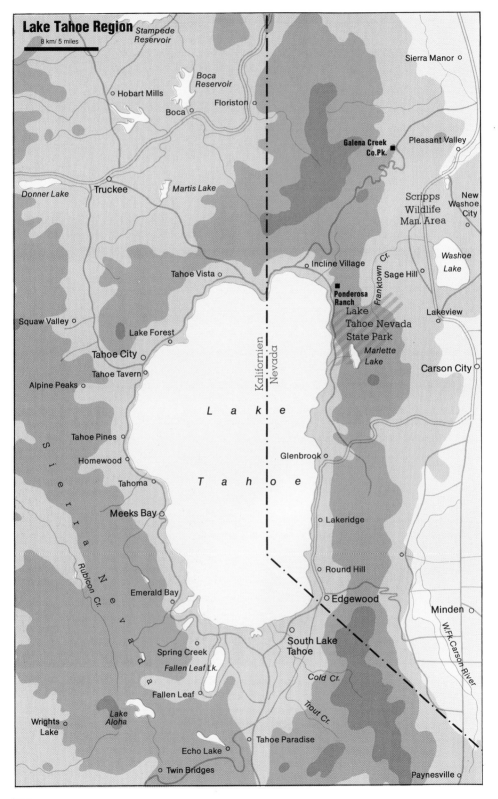

Lake Tahoe Region

8 km/ 5 miles

Stampede Reservoir
Sierra Manor
Boca Reservoir
Hobart Mills
Floriston
Boca
Galena Creek Co.Pk.
Pleasant Valley
Scripps Wildlife Man. Area
New Washoe City
Donner Lake
Truckee
Martis Lake
Washoe Lake
Incline Village
Tahoe Vista
Sage Hill
Ponderosa Ranch
Squaw Valley
Lake Forest
Lake Tahoe Nevada State Park
Lakeview
Tahoe City
Tahoe Tavern
Marlette Lake
Carson City
Alpine Peaks
Kalifornien
Nevada
Lake
Tahoe Pines
Homewood
Tahoma
Glenbrook
Sierra Nevada
Tahoe
Meeks Bay
Lakeridge
Rubicon Cr.
Round Hill
Emerald Bay
Edgewood
Minden
Spring Creek
South Lake Tahoe
Fallen Leaf Lk.
Cold Cr.
Fallen Leaf
W.Fk. Carson River
Lake Aloha
Wrights Lake
Trout Cr.
Echo Lake
Tahoe Paradise
Twin Bridges
Paynesville

LAKE TAHOE: THE NO. 1 RESORT

Mark Twain called it a "noble sheet of blue water lifted 6,308 feet above the level of the sea", but that's because he came for the scenery rather than a late-night show at a cocktail lounge.

Actually, when Twain wrote those words about **Lake Tahoe** in *Roughing it* (1872), the horse was the preferred way to make the trip, and the lake was as pure and sparkling as the silver being dug out of the nearby Comstock Lode.

These days Lake Tahoe's blue waters are sometimes green with algae and its blue skies brown with smog. Many tourists seem more intent on the indoor attractions (roulette wheels and craps tables) than outdoor ones (sun, water and winter snow). No fewer than three McDonald's perch on its shores, keeping company with hundreds of other fast-food outlets, motels, condominiums, video arcades and, at last count, two miniature golf courses.

Nonetheless, Lake Tahoe – a 200-mile (320-km) drive from San Francisco – is still the place city folks usually mean when they speak of going to the mountains for the weekend. Only a few miles from the furious bustle of the Nevada casinos are wilderness, hiking trails, hidden lakeshore caves, snow-covered backroads ideal for cross-country skiing and quiet beaches that look much the same as when Twain dug a toe into them.

Legalized gambling, among the lake's biggest attractions, is also among its biggest problems. One-third of the lake lies in the state of Nevada, the only place in the United States (outside of Atlantic City, New Jersey) where casino gambling is legal. High-rise casinos – looking more at home in San Francisco's financial district than in the beautiful Sierras – are a main cause of the growing traffic jams, smog, noise, lake pollution and sewage problems.

The rush to the slush: Recreation is the lifeblood of the lake and in winter that means downhill skiing. On Friday nights,

the weekend exodus from the Bay Area begins. Tens of thousands of cars with skis strapped on their roofs like sections of picket fences stream up I-80 or US 50 toward the lake. They bring tire chains that they don't know how to install, sunscreen lotion that they forget to apply, and pairs of gloves of which they will invariably lose one. Many will return home with plaster casts, courtesy of their own recklessness and the dozens of orthopedic doctors whose offices are conveniently located at the base of the slopes.

The largest ski areas are **Squaw Valley**, at the northwest side of the lake, and **Heavenly Valley**, on the south side. Each has more than two dozen ski lifts and terrain to satisfy skiers of every ability, including novices. These days, skiers need to bring with them as much money as gamblers – the price of a daily ticket at the major resorts was, at last count, $32. All resorts have stores at which skis can be bought or rented, as well as ski schools and instructors.

Heavenly Valley is the favorite ski

Preceding pages: skier glides down the slopes of Heavenly Valley.
Right, a one-armed bandit at a South Lake Tahoe casino.

area for those who like to duck into the casinos at night, as it is located at **South Lake Tahoe**, the busiest part of the lake and just across the state line from Nevada. For all their commotion, the casinos can actually come in handy for skiers in the evening – most offer all-you-can-eat buffet dinners for $5 or so, to lure customers to the gambling tables. The preferred buffet is to be found at **Harrah's**, followed by those at **Caesar's Tahoe**, the **High Sierra** and **Harvey's** hotels. There's no law, however, that says a person can't just visit the dining room, eat his fill after a tough day of skiing, and depart with his fortune still in his pocket.

But most skiers prefer the northern half of the lakeshore on the California side, particularly the area around Tahoe City. It's quieter, cleaner and the selection of ski areas is better. In addition to Squaw Valley, skiers can choose **Alpine Meadows, Sugar Bowl, Boreal Ridge** and **Northstar**. The latter caters particularly to families – its gentler slopes keep most of the show-offs away.

Boreal, perched on the edge of four-lane I-80, is perhaps the easiest to reach. Sugar Bowl is the matriarch, having been around longest. Alpine Meadows is preferred by experienced skiers, as the runs rated "expert" make up 40 percent of the terrain – the highest percentage in the Sierras.

Cross-country skiing, which is more like a hike in the woods than a flight down a mountainside, is attracting more people each year. The skis are longer and narrower, the uphill stretches can make the legs ache, but the silence and solitude are blessed.

Summertime exploits: In the summer, camping, swimming, fishing, hiking and boating take over, and none of them requires a parka. Marinas at South Lake Tahoe and **Zephyr Cove**, Nevada, offer daily cruises aboard large vessels, including an authentic paddlewheel steamer. A daytime cruise on the *M.S. Dixie*, departing from Zephyr Cove, costs $17 and takes 2½ hours; evening cruises include dinner or cocktails and cost more. The new boat on the block is

Lunch on the ski hill, Alpine Meadows.

the 140-foot (43-meter) *Tahoe Queen*, an authentic steam paddlewheeler that can carry 500 passengers. Both boats cruise through spectacular **Emerald Bay State Park**, an isolated, tree-lined wilderness tucked into the southwest corner.

Hikers and backpackers usually head for **Desolation Wilderness**, a lake-studded area west of Emerald Bay. Nearby is the **El Dorado National Forest** Visitor Center, offering orientation programs and guided walks. A wilderness permit must be obtained for backpacking in Desolation Wilderness – it's a popular place that frequently fills to capacity in summer. The **Granite Peak** area is also good for backpacking, and Emerald Bay, **D.L. Bliss** and **Sugar Pine Point** state parks are excellent for short walks and picnics.

On any summer weekend, joggers and bicyclists take to the roads ringing the lake. The 75-mile (121-km) circle makes a strenuous one-day bike ride or a leisurely two-day trip.

Getting to Lake Tahoe is easy and, thanks to the many casinos seeking to lure fresh blood from the Bay Area, inexpensive. The drive from San Francisco takes 4–5 hours in good weather and light traffic. Chains should always be carried in winter, and drivers should be prepared to either lie on their backs in roadside slush to put them on, or to pay $10 to hire one of the "chain monkeys" who cluster on the side of the road.

A cheaper way to the lake is by bus. Buses run all day throughout the Bay Area to the pleasure domes at South Lake Tahoe, offering substantial rebates on the bus fare to passengers once inside the casino. There are also frequent flights to airports at South Lake Tahoe and **Reno**, Nevada.

Probably the most spectacular way to get to the lake is on Amtrak's daily cross-country train, the *California Zephyr*, which leaves Oakland shortly before noon and arrives in Truckee in time for dinner. The train follows the same trans-Sierra route carved in the 1860s, and the view from the windows of the lounge car is unforgettable.

Tranquil boating on Emerald Bay.

YOSEMITE AND THE HIGH SIERRA

When plans were being made for Queen Elizabeth II's state visit to California in 1983, the monarch insisted on a three-day vacation stopover. Not Palm Springs. Not Santa Barbara. Not the Napa Valley wine country. What she wanted most of all, she told her advisors, was to see **Yosemite Valley**.

For the waterfalls. Nowhere else in the world are there so many big falls in such a small area, including 2,425-foot (739-meter) **Yosemite Falls**, the highest in North America. When Ice Age glaciers scoured out 8-mile (13-km) long, mile-wide Yosemite Valley they left behind several smaller hanging valleys on either side, high but not dry, conduits for free-leaping torrents whose very names suggest their variety: **Ribbon, Bridalveil, Silver Strand, Staircase, Sentinel, Lehamite, Vernal, Nevada, Illilouette**.

For the rocks. "Great is granite," wrote New England clergyman Thomas Starr King in 1878, "and Yosemite is its prophet." As the prehistoric ice flows melted and retreated they exposed the colossal building blocks of the Sierra Nevada, shaped and polished into scenery on a grand scale – **El Capitan, Cathedral Rock, Three Brothers, Royal Arches, Half Dome, Clouds Rest**. In the daredevil world of technical rock climbing, from Austria to Australia, there is only one true mecca, Yosemite Valley.

And for all the rest, the meadows and forests and wildflowers, the birds and deer and bears, the myriad conjunctions of animate and inanimate that make the Valley, in writer Edward Abbey's words, "A place where a man should count himself lucky to make one pilgrimage in a lifetime. A holy place."

From Indians to autos: A holy place is exactly what Yosemite (say "yo-seh-mih-tee") Valley was to its original inhabitants, the Ahwahneechee Indians. Because of Yosemite's isolation, the tribe managed to keep its mountain paradise a secret from whites until 1851, a full year after California attained statehood, when the US Cavalry arrived and herded the Ahwahneechees across the Sierras to a barren reservation near Mono Lake.

As with much of the American West, subjugation of the Indians paved the way for settlement. During the decade following its "discovery", Yosemite Valley was fenced, farmed and logged by homesteaders. Visitors, drawn in increasing numbers by newspaper and magazine accounts of Yosemite's marvels, were appalled to find cow pastures instead of mountain meadows. In 1864, public pressure on the California legislature resulted in the Yosemite Grant, the first attempt in the nation's history to preserve a natural scenic area from commercial exploitation.

There are many who will argue today that the attempt has failed. With thousands of hotel rooms and campground sites, restaurants, supermarkets, liquor stores, gift shops and even a jail, Yosemite Valley has become the textbook example of overdeveloped park-

land. In a controversial, decade-long planning effort, the US National Park Service spent millions of dollars trying to determine what to do about degradation of the Yosemite environment; the principal recommendation, elimination of the private auto from the Valley, seems unlikely to be implemented before the year 2000, if ever.

In the meantime, roads in the east end of the Valley near **Mirror Lake** have been restricted to shuttle buses, bicycles and pedestrians. A convoluted one-way traffic pattern almost everywhere else makes driving a truly masochistic experience, especially in summer.

Luckily, visitors can park their cars in one of the Valley's large parking lots and make use of the free shuttle buses. Because Yosemite Valley is so flat and compact, nearly all its biggest attractions are most easily seen by combining shuttle-bus rides with short walks on well-maintained trails. Visitors can also arrange guided horseback trips through the Valley stables, near **Curry Village** (the first large developed area on the Yosemite loop road). Bicycles may be rented at Curry Village and **Yosemite Lodge**, and several bikeways make two-wheeled travel by far the most efficient choice of locomotion for visitors and residents alike.

Unless one has only a few hours to spare, it's a mistake to simply ride the shuttle-bus loop and assume all the high spots have been hit. In most cases, bus stops are merely staging area for exploration of nearby meadows, waterfalls and historic sites.

Lodging runs the gamut from inexpensive cabins at Curry Village to the palatial suite atop the **Ahwahnee Hotel**, with Yosemite Lodge occupying middle ground.

Yosemite by the seasons: In summer, Yosemite Valley's singular concentration of natural beauty has its far less felicitous human analogue, complete with overcrowded campgrounds, traffic jams and hour-long waits in cafeteria lines. Although the Valley comprises only 8 sq. miles (21 sq. km) of the park's 1,189-sq.-mile (3,080-sq.-km) area, it plays host to more than 90 percent of all Yosemite's overnight visitors. The surest way of seeing Half Dome without an enveloping wreath of smog is during the off-season, September to May.

Autumn brings a rich gold to the leaves of the Valley's oak trees, and the sun's lowering angle etches the granite domes and spires into sharper relief. Nights are cool, mornings apple-crisp. It's a good time to focus binoculars on rock climbers, lured back to Yosemite's great walls by mild daytime temperatures. Autumn also brings herds of wild deer, migrating through the Valley en route to winter forage in the Sierra foothills. An early-morning stroller may not see another soul on his way through a meadow in October, but chances are excellent he'll see at least half a dozen deer, bounding fleet and silent through the golden grass like dancers.

Yosemite Valley is emptiest in winter, when most of the action shifts to the ski resort of **Badger Pass**, 21 miles (34 km) away and 3,000 feet (900 meters) higher. Badger's gentle pine-fringed slopes offer few challenges for accom-

Yosemite Falls.

plished skiers, but prove ideal for family groups and novice-to-intermediate skiers who don't mind the 45-minute commute by car or bus from the Valley. In the Valley, the Yosemite Mountaineering School at Curry Village offers instruction in nordic (cross-country) skiing, as well as beginning and advanced rock climbing, and an outdoor ice-skating rink boasts views of Glacier Point, Half Dome, and the frozen remnants of Yosemite Falls.

Spring is the favorite season of many Yosemite residents. Wildflowers carpet the meadows, and the roar of wild water resounds throughout the Valley. The force of the runoff is such that most of the waterfalls are unapproachable; gale-force winds and drenching spray enliven the normally placid one-quarter mile walk from Yosemite Lodge to the base of Yosemite Falls. But on full moon nights, the deluge is well worth braving for tantalizing glimpses of rare lunar spray bows. Popularly called "moonbows", these ethereal silver arches shimmer softly with the colors of the spectrum and reach heights of 200 feet (60 meters), only to dissolve into formless mist with a puff of wind.

Seeing Yosemite when the crowds have gone home is the best way to experience the sublime tranquility that inspired the words of John Muir and the photographs of Ansel Adams. But even on the Fourth of July there are several routes of escape from the Instamatic Army. To the south, State Highway 41 climbs 9.3 miles (15 km) to **Chinquapin** junction, where a 15.5-mile (24.9-km) paved road departs for **Glacier Point**. From this famed viewpoint, 3,200 feet (975 meters) above the floor of Yosemite Valley, the entire park comes into unforgettable stomach-clutching focus. Directly below, the meadows, forest and waterfalls of the Valley appear in dollhouse scale, dwarfed by the awesome verticality of the huge northside cliffs and domes. No less compelling is the 80-mile (129-km) vista to the east and south, a panorama of lakes, canyons, waterfalls and the rugged peaks of Yosemite's High Sierra. Close at

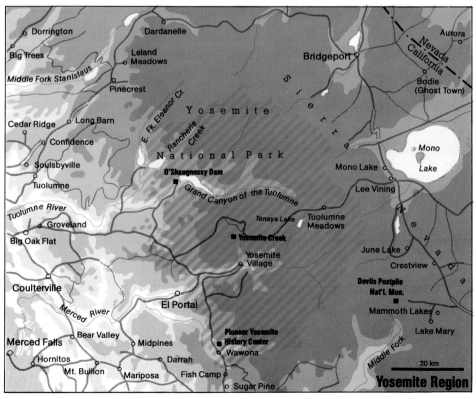

hand are the granite steps of the **Giant's Staircase**, where Vernal and Nevada falls drop the raging waters of the **Merced River** 320 and 594 feet (98 and 181 meters) respectively.

From Glacier Point, Half Dome is the most prominent landmark, a great solitary stone thumb thrusting skyward. Park rangers are accustomed to one question more than any other: what became of Half Dome's other half? The surprising answer is that the dome never had another half of solid rock, only slabs of granite on the sheer north face that were peeled away like onionskin by advancing glaciers during the Ice Age. At the height of glaciation, 250,000 years ago, Glacier Point itself lay under 700 feet (213 meters) of ice, and interpretive markers explain how the 2,000-foot (610-meter) thick Merced and Tenaya glaciers ground down from the high country to merge near Half Dome and quarry out Yosemite Valley. The mighty glacier filled the Valley to its brim, and extended down the Merced canyon to **El Portal**, 15 miles (24 km) to the west.

Mariposa and Tuolomne: Five miles (8 km) south of Wawona, just inside the park's southern boundary, a short side road leads to the **Mariposa Grove** of giant sequoias, a 250-acre (101-hectare) preserve containing more than 500 mammoth redwood trees. It was here that John Muir slept under the stars alongside President Theodore Roosevelt, and persuaded the chief executive that the ancient forest should be added to the infant Yosemite National Park. The Mariposa Grove's largest tree, the **Grizzly Giant**, is at least 3,800 years old, with a height of 200 feet (61 meters) and a girth of 94.2 feet (28.7 meters). The best way to experience the big trees is to walk: leave the pavement and wander at random among trees that were already giants when Christ walked the Holy Land.

If Wawona and the Mariposa Grove are Yosemite's Black Forest, **Tuolumne Meadows** is its Switzerland. Reached by an hour's drive north from the Valley on the scenic **Tioga Road**, and situated at 8,600 feet (2,620 meters) above sea

Lambert Dome and the Tuolumne River, Tioga Road.

level, Tuolumne is the gateway to an alpine wilderness encompassing, in John Muir's words:

> …innumerable lakes and waterfalls, and smooth silky lawns; the noblest forests, the loftiest granite domes, the deepest ice-sculptured canyons, the brightest crystalline pavement, and snowy mountains soaring into the sky twelve and thirteen thousand feet arrayed in open ranks and spiry pinnacled groups partially separated by tremendous canyons and amphitheatres; gardens on their sunny brows, avalanches thundering down their long white slopes.

Perhaps not surprisingly, familiarity with such an array of natural wonders is not gained easily. The only way to see the more remote areas of the Tuolumne backcountry is to hike, with all creature comforts carried in a backpack that may tip the scales at 50 lbs (23 kg) or more. A less arduous alternative, at least on some of the smoother trails, is to arrange a horsepacking trip through the Tuolumne stables, run by Yosemite Park & Curry Company.

Tuolumne is also the site of **Tuolumne Meadows Lodge**, central star in the summer constellation of high Sierra Camps. Arranged roughly in a circle, about 9 miles (14½ km) apart, these six permanent tent camps provide lodging, meals and hot showers to hikers and horsepackers on the High Sierra Loop trail. Elevations of the camps vary from 7,150 feet (2,180 meters) to 10,300 feet (3,140 meters), and a night of acclimatization in Tuolumne is recommended before departure. In a typical year, camps are open from June 14 through September 1, with advance reservations essential. Wilderness permits, available free of charge at park ranger stations and visitor centers, are required for *all* overnight trips in the Yosemite backcountry.

Sequoia and Kings Canyon: It is tempting to dismiss **Sequoia** and **Kings Canyon** national parks as Yosemite without Yosemite Valley. Judging from park visitation figures, many California travelers do just that. In any given year, 2.5 million visitors converge on Yosemite; the comparable figure for Sequoia/Kings Canyon is barely 400,000. (Although Sequoia and Kings Canyon parks were established separately, their adjoining areas are administered as one unit.) Even though 7,000-foot (2,130-meter) deep Kings Canyon exceeds Yosemite Valley in sheer vertical relief, and the sequoia forests of the southern park are larger and more numerous than Yosemite's groves, the absence of waterfalls and striking rock formations make them pale alongside their more celebrated northern cousin. The result is a national park bereft of the most common national park headaches – traffic jams, over-crowding and crime – reason enough for solitude-seeking vacationers to beat a path to the entry station.

Much more so than Yosemite, Sequoia/Kings Canyon is a wilderness park, with only two developed areas near its western boundaries. The backcountry extends east across the west

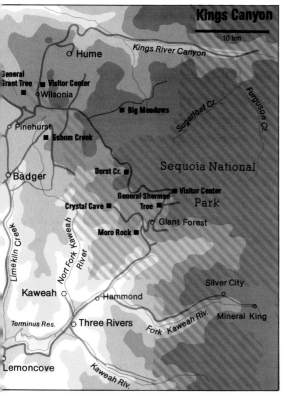

slopes of the Sierras as far as the crest of the range, encompassing the headwaters of the Kern and San Joaquin rivers and the highest Sierra summits, including Mount Whitney. Ironically, a majority of the park's mountain trails are most easily reached from trailheads out of Lone Pine, Big Pine and Bishop on the Sierra's east side, a 250-mile (400-km) drive from park headquarters near **Three Rivers**. As in Yosemite, wilderness permits are required for overnight backcountry camping.

The most scenic approach to the Kings Canyon section of the park, State 180, begins in the sprawling agricultural city of **Fresno**. A 52-mile (84-km) drive through the Sierra foothills leads to the **General Grant Grove**, a stand of massive 3,000-year-old sequoias notable for the wide-open parkland around their bases.

Thirty-eight miles (61 km) past the Grant Grove (where campground sites are available by advance reservation), State 180 drops into Kings Canyon at **Cedar Grove**. In contrast to Yosemite Valley, this gaping chasm is V- rather than U-shaped; the smaller flow of the **Kings River** has yet to deposit enough alluvium to level out the canyon's floor. Cedar Grove offers idyllic camping and fishing alongside the placid waters of the Kings, and rustic lodging is also available. Two trailheads lead north and east toward the High Sierra, but the 6,500-foot (1,980-meter) climbs on south-facing (and sun-broiled) slopes are only for the fit and experienced.

After backtracking to Grant Grove, visitors can proceed into the park's Sequoia section by following State 198 south for 28 miles (45 km) to **Giant Forest**. A short nature trail here leads to the **General Sherman Tree**, believed to be the earth's largest living thing. California's coastal redwood (*sequoia sempervirens*) are taller than the Sierra subspecies (*sequoia gigantea*), but in terms of girth and overall volume the mountain redwoods come out on top.

Hotel rooms, restaurants, a grocery store and a visitor center make Giant Forest the closest approximation of an urban center Sequoia/Kings Canyon has

to offer. Three campgrounds lie a few miles farther south on State 198. The road continues southward past good camping and boating at **Lake Kaweah**, and drops back into the San Joaquin Valley at **Visalia**, 50 miles (80 km) from the park boundary

The Eastern Sierra: Approached from the west, through the foothills of the Gold Country and on into Yosemite or Sequoia/Kings Canyon, the Sierra Nevada begins gently. Low, rolling hills studded with oak trees give way to higher hills blanketed with pines, which in turn give way to an accelerating crescendo of granite domes, spires and ridges, culminating in the 13,000- and 14,000-foot (4,000-meter) peaks of the crest.

But there is nothing gradual about the Sierra when approached from the east, up US 395 from Southern California. On the east side, the mountains of the crest drop precipitously nearly 10,000 vertical feet (3,000 meters) in the space of a few miles, a single great front nearly 200 miles (320 km) long. From **Walker Pass** at the southern end of the range to **Tioga Pass** on the eastern Yosemite boundary, not a single highway cleaves the scarp, the longest contiguous roadless area in the United States outside Alaska.

Owens Valley: Driving north from Los Angeles, the dramatic scenery begins on the shores of **Owens Dry Lake**, near the hamlet of **Olancha.** To the left, the tawny, unforested peaks of the southern Sierrras rise abruptly, cresting in granite pinnacles 12,000 feet (3,650 meters) high. To the right, across the wide, shimmering lake bed, the softer, more rounded contours of the somewhat lower **Inyo Range** dissolve into black and purple foothills. These are the portals of **Owens Valley**, deepest in America, "The Land of Little Rain". The vegetation here is hardy desert flora – scrub oak, mesquite, sagebrush. Owens Valley and the Inyos receive less than 10 inches of rain yearly.

Just past the northern end of the lake bed, 21 miles (34 km) north of Olancha, State 136 departs east for Death Valley. Located at the junction is the **Interagency Visitor Center** which dis-

Backpacker dwarfed by natural giants, Kings Canyon.

penses maps, information and wilderness permits for the extensive public lands under federal jurisdiction. In winter, the center is a mandatory stop for the latest word on campground closures and road conditions. In the busy summer season, rangers will steer travelers to campgrounds with spaces still available. Unlike the national park camping areas on the west side of the Sierras, many east-side campgrounds do not accept advance reservations, and first come, first served is the order of the day.

Mount Whitney: On a patio outside the Visitor Center building, telescopes are trained on the summit of **Mount Whitney**, at 14,495 feet (4,418 meters) the highest mountain in the United States outside Alaska. A trail leads to the very top of Whitney where portable latrines have been set up to cope with the tide of visitors. It's a strenuous three-day hike (two up, one down), but no technical skills are required, and thousands make the trip every summer. The most difficult part of the journey in fact, can prove to be getting a reservation: many Whitney trail permits are snapped up a year in advance. For reservations, which are free of charge, write Inyo National Forest, Mount Whitney Ranger District, Lone Pine, CA 93545.

Skiers and devils: North of Crowley Lake, a 2-mile (3 km) road leads to **Mammoth Lakes**, the largest downhill ski resort in America. In winter, Mammoth is where Los Angeles goes skiing, and it is not uncommon to share lift lines with 20,000 other powder hounds. On the plus side, Mammoth offers gourmet dining (at **Roget's** and **La Boulangerie**), wine and cheese shops.

A summer (not winter) attraction is **Devils Postpile National Monument**, a 30-minute drive west of Mammoth Lakes into the Sierras. About 630,000 years ago, dark molten lava poured through Mammoth Pass and flowed into the deep canyon of the middle fork of the San Joaquin River, where it cooled, solidified and cracked into astonishingly uniform vertical columns. Successive glaciation scraped and polished the tops of the columns into a smooth, tile-like

Alpine panorama greets a descending Mount Whitney climber.

surface. Today, the abrupt geometric pickets of Devils Postpile (80 feet/24 m high, ¼-mile/0.4 km long) offer mute testimony to the power of the twin forces that shaped the entire Sierras – fire and ice. Limited camping is available in summer at **Agnew Meadows** (just before the monument boundary on State 203) and **Red's Meadows** (just after the boundary).

At **Deadman Summit**, north of June Mountain, US 395 begins a long descent into Mono Basin, once the site of an inland sea and today the focal point of an ongoing controversy over Los Angeles' appropriation of eastern Sierra water. **Mono Lake**, the last remnant of that sea, is the oldest continuously existing body of water in North America, and islands near the lake's northern shore are breeding grounds for 90 percent of the world's California seagulls. Eerie calcified rock formations on the shoreline are called *tufa* and examples are preserved at **Moon Lake State Tufa Reserve**.

From May until November, or until the first winter snow falls, the town of **Lee Vining** on Mono Lake's western shore is the east entry to Yosemite National Park, via 9,991-foot (3,045-meter) Tioga Pass. From Lee Vining, Tuolumne Meadows is a 45-minute drive away; it takes at least two hours to reach Yosemite Valley. Campgrounds are spaced every 15 miles (24 km) or so, and unlike the rest of the park's sites, are *not* reservable in advance.

North of Mono Lake, the Sierra crest begins to lower, although "lower" in this case still means snowy summits 11,000 feet (3,350 meters) high. Eleven and a half miles (18½ km) north of Lee Vining, a graded side road leads 13 miles (21 km) to **Bodie State Historic Park**, which offers both an excellent view of the northern Sierras and a fascinating glimpse into the life of a '49ers' boomtown. Once the wildest camp in the West, Bodie was home to a ragtag collection of miners and confidence men who made silver fortunes by day and squandered them by night in opium dens, saloons and bawdy houses.

Calcified rocks rise from Mono Lake, the oldest body of water in North America.

VALLEY OF THE SAN JOAQUIN

The San Joaquin Valley is California's neglected middle child. Stuck between the brash, self-indulgent coast and the awe-inspiring Sierras, the valley suffers the kind of image problem more associated with the American Midwest than the Golden State. Not to be confused with the source of Moon Zappa's musical parody "Valley Girl" (the San Fernando), or even with John Steinbeck's austere collection *The Long Valley* (the Salinas), the San Joaquin endures on its own terms.

Though its name is often mistakenly applied to California's entire Central Valley, the San Joaquin comprises just the southern two-thirds of that 450-mile (720-km) long, 50-mile (80-km) wide basin. It follows the course of the **San Joaquin River**, flowing south to north, to the Sacramento-San Joaquin Delta, where both rivers empty into San Francisco Bay.

Mostly flat and treeless, the valley doesn't at first appear to offer much in the way of attractions. It is experienced by most travelers as something to be passed through quickly on the way to somewhere else. Even the Queen of England got a taste of the valley experience on her California vacation. Interstate 5, running the length of the valley, is the main link between Los Angeles and the Bay Area, and the east-west routes to Lake Tahoe and the Sierras all cross the valley. So the valley can only sell itself by virtue of being in the middle of it all. Fresno, for instance, boasts of being the only community in the United States within an hour and a half of three national parks (Yosemite, Sequoia and Kings Canyon).

The San Joaquin *is* known for some unpleasant natural phenomena. Valley fever – a little-known respiratory illness – is spread when strong winds stir up the spores of a fungus indigenous to the arid soil in parts of the valley. And in December and January, dense "tule fog" blankets the area for days at a time, making driving hazardous.

But its second-class status bothers San Joaquin Valley residents very little. The business of the valley is farming, and it succeeds at that like few other spots on earth. The nearby Gold Country mining claims were abandoned long ago, but the valley is still enjoying general prosperity. It has become one of the fastest growing areas in the state.

Heaven for farmers: Agriculture, after all, is California's biggest industry, and more than half of its $14 billion a year in farm goods is produced in the San Joaquin. Fresno County alone accounts for some $2 billion of that, making it the No. 1 farming county in America. The valley's alluvial soil, covering more than a million irrigated acres (400,000 hectares), supports some of the most productive farming in the world. And beneath the soil are deposits of oil and natural gas. Major crops include cotton, grapes, tomatoes, corn, fruit and nuts.

Recently, as population has grown, valley cities have experienced a boom as commercial and manufacturing centers. But it's still the fields, orchards,

Left, San Benito County cattle ranch. Right, time for a snack at the Fresno County Fair.

canneries and processing plants that sustain the area. Employment in the valley is more closely tied to rainfall than to the vagaries of the economy.

It is the abundance of that most precious of the state's resources – water – that keeps things going and makes the San Joaquin Valley a recreational as well as an agricultural heartland. Aside from the Sacramento River Delta and the mammoth irrigation projects it supports, several of California's great rivers flow through the area – the San Joaquin, the **Stanislaus**, the **Tuolumne**, the **Merced**, the **Kings**, and further south, the **Kern**. Most are renowned for outstanding, and occasionally terrifying, stretches of whitewater rafting.

It doesn't take long to see that the valley is the lifeline of California. An hour out of San Francisco going eastward, I-580 crosses **Altamont Pass**, one of the windiest spots on the coast. It is marked by an exquisitely rural sight – a windmill farm, overhead power lines and dairy cows peacefully coexisting. As the descent begins, the highway crosses a branch of the **California Aqueduct**. Almost immediately the freeway is full of trucks hauling double trailers of bottled tomato catsup, or canned peaches or pears. Welcome to the San Joaquin Valley.

Modesto and Fresno: Like much of California, Modesto is the creation of Leland Stanford's Central Pacific Railroad. The Tuolumne River runs almost unnoticed through the southern fringes of town. A turn-of-the-century steel arch along the main thoroughfare promotes the town's virtues: "Water, Wealth, Contentment, Health."

As in most of the valley, food is king – not food eating but food producing. A "Gourmet Taste Tour" includes stops at an almond exchange, a mushroom farm, a cheese processor, a Hershey chocolate plant and local wineries. Visitors with an appetite may want to try **Two Jerks with a Grill**, one of the notable restaurants in the downtown area.

Halfway between Modesto and Fresno, **Merced** is a major access point to Yosemite. The biggest attraction

Harvesting corn, Madera County.

132

Merced can call its own may be **Castle Air Force Base**, where lumbering B-52s provide a somewhat chilling background to the **Castle Air Museum's** collection of vintage fighters.

Fresno is the sleeping giant of central California. From a train station by the edge of a wheatfield, it has become a city with 11 freeway exits, rows of highrises and a metropolitan area of more than 300,000. It is the financial and cultural as well as the service and commercial center of the San Joaquin Valley. It is also as ethnically diverse as any city in the state, with large Mexican, Asian, Armenian and Basque communities. Cultural institutions include the **Metropolitan Museum of Art**, **Science and History**, the **Community Theater** and the **Fresno Philharmonic Orchestra**. Two wineries offer tours – **Cribari Winery** and **A. Nonini Winery**.

For people with children **Roeding Park**, right off State 99 in west Fresno, features a number of family amusements – a zoo with more than 1,000 animals, a Playland with rides, and Storyland, a quaint walk-through village where plaster fairytale figures tell their story. **Woodward Park** in central Fresno has a Japanese Garden and a bird sanctuary. But the most bizarre attraction in town is **Forestiere Underground Gardens**, 5021 Shaw Avenue. The gardens were once the domicile of sculptor-horticulturist Baldasare Forestiere, who single-handedly carved out the maze of 100 rooms, passageways and courtyards over 40 years.

The annual rodeo in nearby **Clovis** brings buckeroos together for two days of roping, riding and bronco-busting the last weekend in April. Buffalo roam year-round 40 miles (64 km) northwest at **Safari World** in **Coarsegold**.

The San Joaquin Valley has a life of its own. Certainly it is unlike any other part of California. Fig orchards stand between suburban houses, outlying hills reflect brilliant sunsets, the seasons are distinct, and in springtime fields and orchards blossom for miles in spectacular color.

Melon farmer displays his produce.

BIG SUR AND MONTEREY BAY

The stretch of Northern California coast from San Simeon to Santa Cruz is one region that does not exist in a state of implicit apology for not being San Francisco. The pace might be slow, but the highly differentiated and individualistic communities which occupy this shore are so busy leading their own lives, the thought of doing otherwise does not occur to them.

Driving north on State Highway 1, the traveler first encounters ruggedly beautiful Big Sur, to which no other stretch of coastline can compare. The boutiques and quaint restaurants of Carmel match anything that Union Street can offer. Quiet little Monterey, the former Spanish capital, exists in its own time warp. Santa Cruz is a liberal university community grafted onto a conservative backwater. Despite a rocky beginning, their union now shows surprising hybrid vigor.

Spectacular Big Sur: Between the two great world wars of this century, convict labor built a narrow, twisting road over the virgin California coastline from the Hearst Castle at San Simeon 93 miles (150 km) north to the Monterey Peninsula. Except for the road itself, it's not much different today than it was then – there are no billboards or streetlights, only occasional scattered mailboxes and, with the possible exception of Big Sur village itself, nothing even recognizable as a town.

In some parts, the road (State Highway 1) rises as much as 1,000 feet above sea level in a matter of a few miles. One minute, travelers are shivering in a cold gray mist, sharp with the smell of salt water and kelp. Five minutes later, they are standing atop a sunny hillside looking over a billowy white blanket of ocean fog as far as the eye can see. On really hot days in the inland valleys, air currents pull the fog up the mountainside, turning State 1 into an endless gray tunnel with fog skimming overhead like an upward flowing waterfall.

Because the blasting needed to build the road weakened the underlying rock, the highway is prone to damage. During heavy winter rains, huge chunks of roadway sometimes slide into the ocean, cutting off local residents for days or weeks at a time.

There are a number of inns, lodges, motels and campgrounds scattered along State 1. There are also places out of sight of the highway where persistent wayfarers can make camp, sip their wine and listen to the barking of sea lions high above the crashing surf.

Until the end of World War II, Big Sur was mainly populated by ranchers, loggers and miners. But following the war, literary people began turning up to live cheaply, grow marijuana in remote canyons, and commune with what long-time resident Henry Miller called "the face of the earth as the creator intended it to look". (Actually, not everyone found it that attractive. Jack Kerouac, for one, couldn't stand the solitude.)

By the end of the 1960s, Big Sur had become a cultural fad where neoagrarian hippies lived off the land (and food stamps), made non-negotiable demands on behalf of the environment and, every dry season, inadvertently set fire to sections of the hills. At the same time, affluent San Franciscans, having discovered that there's nothing like an ocean view to bring out the subtle taste of Brie and Chablis, began arriving by Porsche and BMW in an ever-increasing stream.

Cute and cozy Carmel: Two chance factors made **Carmel** what it is today – starving writers and unwanted painters fleeing the devastation of the 1906 San Francisco earthquake, and canny developers who, to reduce their real-estate taxes, covered the previously treeless site with a thick carpet of Monterey pines. The result is one of the most endearing little seaside towns on the entire West Coast. When the evening fog rolls in from the bay, the lights inside the cozy little houses, combined with the faint whiff of wood smoke, give Carmel the peaceful feeling of an 18th-century European village.

Although some 3 or 4 million people visit this southern gateway to the **Monterey Peninsula** each year, Carmel

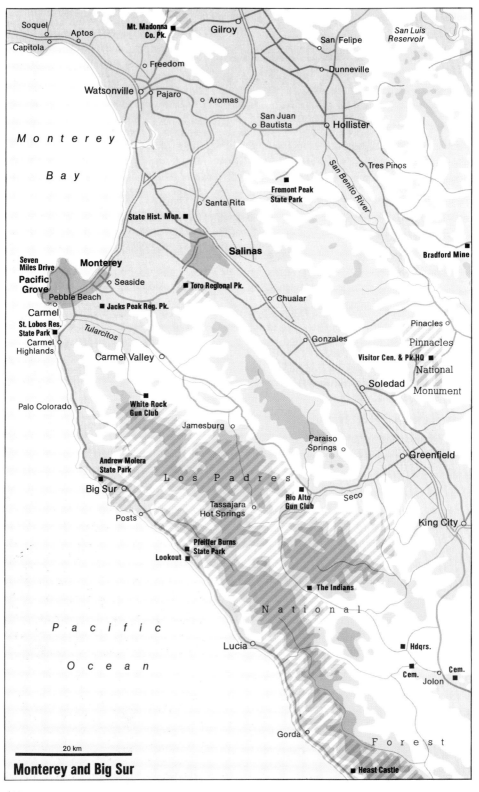

Soquel
Capitola
Aptos
Mt. Madonna Co. Pk.
Gilroy
San Felipe
San Luis Reservoir
Freedom
Dunneville
Watsonville
Pajaro
Aromas
San Juan Bautista
Hollister
M o n t e r e y
Santa Rita
Fremont Peak State Park
Tres Pinos
B a y
San Benito River
State Hist. Mon.
Salinas
Bradford Mine
Seven Miles Drive
Monterey
Seaside
Toro Regional Pk.
Pacific Grove
Pebble Beach
Jacks Peak Reg. Pk.
Chualar
Carmel
St. Lobos Res. State Park
Tularcitos
Carmel Highlands
Carmel Valley
Gonzales
Pinacles
Pinacles
Visitor Cen. & Pk.HQ
National
Soledad
Monument
White Rock Gun Club
Palo Colorado
Jamesburg
Paraiso Springs
Greenfield
Andrew Molera State Park
L o s   P a d r e s
Big Sur
Tassajara Hot Springs
Rio Alto Gun Club
Seco
Posts
King City
Pfeiffer Burns State Park
Lookout
The Indians
N a t i o n a l
P a c i f i c
Lucia
Hdqrs.
O c e a n
Cem.
Cem.
Jolon
Gorda
F o r e s t

20 km

Monterey and Big Sur

Heast Castle

138

has firmly resisted any temptation to yield to used-car lots, fast-food franchises, high-rise buildings and neon signs. The street, plazas and quaint little malls attract pedestrians to wine shops and booksellers, antique stores, art galleries and numerous boutiques. The local market offers freshly picked artichokes (from fields barely a mile away), sweet basil, French cheeses, German sausages, liver pâté, and floor-to-ceiling racks of imported and domestic wines. At night, on the side streets, a dozen couples might be dining quietly by candlelight behind dark restaurant windows. In the residential parts of town, the streets meander casually through the forest, sometimes even splitting in two to accommodate an especially praiseworthy pine.

The 17 Mile Drive: Just north of the foot of Ocean Avenue is the Carmel Gate entrance to the **17 Mile Drive**, which meanders around the Monterey Peninsula, via the **Del Monte Forest**, to Pacific Grove. Because all the roads in the Del Monte Forest are privately owned, travelers on the 17 Mile Drive must pay a $4 use fee to the Pebble Beach Company. The trip is worth it, if for no other reason than to see the big **stone mansion** (looking like something out of a flash of lightning in a dark night on the Scottish Moors) next to **The Ghost Tree** cypress.

Still, the attitude of the Pebble Beach Company toward tourists seem more than a little condescending. Along their exclusive golf courses are signs every 100 feet or so warning visitors that trespassing on the course is a misdemeanor punishable by a fine and imprisonment. At the famous **Lone Pine Cypress**, a single gnarled and windswept tree near the top of a huge wave-battered rock, the sign on the protective fence reads "No Trespassing Beyond This Point", as if merely being in the forest were a trespass in itself.

Historic Monterey: The history of the people who passed through **Monterey** is the history of California itself. First there were the native Indians, then the Spanish explorers, the Mexican ranchers, the American settlers, the Sicilian

fishermen and finally the most ubiquitous and persistent invader of all, the tourist.

Thanks to John Steinbeck, the most famous attraction in town is the former Ocean View Avenue, now known as **Cannery Row**. During World War II, Monterey was the sardine capital of the Western Hemisphere, processing some 200,000 tons of the fish a year. As Steinbeck described it then, the street was "a poem, a stink, a grating noise, a quality of light, a tone, a habit, a nostalgia, a dream". When the fishing boats came in heavy with their catch, the canneries blew their whistles and the residents of Monterey came streaming down the hill to take their places amid the rumbling, rattling, squealing machinery of the canning plants. When finally the last sardine was cleaned, cut, cooked and canned, the whistle blew again, and the workers trudged back up the hill, dripping, wet and smelly.

After the war, for reasons variously blamed on overfishing, changing currents and divine retribution, the sardines

"The Lone Cypress" on 17 Mile Drive.

suddenly disappeared from Monterey Bay and all the canneries went broke. But as Steinbeck has pointed out, it was not a total loss. In those heady early years, the beaches were so deeply covered with fish guts and flies that a sickening stench covered the whole town. Today the beaches are bright and clean, and the air is sparkling fresh. Cannery Row, located along the waterfront on the northwest side of town just beyond the **Presidio**, has become an impressive tourist attraction. Its old buildings are filled with lusty bars, gaudy restaurants, a wax museum, dozens of shops, a carousel, an arcade and peddlers selling hot pretzels and caramel corn.

In downtown Monterey today the main visitor attraction is **Fisherman's Wharf**. (The real working wharf is two blocks east.) Fisherman's Wharf is lined with restaurants, shops, an organ grinder with a monkey, fishmarkets and noisy sea lions who swim among the pilings.

To see the rest of Monterey, a 3-mile (5-km) walking tour called **The Path of History** leads past the more important historical buildings and sites. These include the **Customs House**, the oldest public building in California, now a museum; **Pacific House**, a two-story adobe with a Monterey balcony around the second floor and impressive historical exhibits from the Spanish, Mexican and early American periods; **Colton Hall**, a two-story building with a classical portico which was the site of the state's first (1849) constitutional convention; **Stevenson House**, a smaller former hotel where the romantic (and sickly) Robert Louis Stevenson lived for a few months while courting his wife; and the **Royal Presidio Chapel**, in constant use since 1794. (US President Herbert Hoover was married in a courtyard there.)

The Presidio, founded in 1770 by Gaspar de Portolá, now serves as the **US Army Language School**. Other points of interest in Monterey include the **Monterey Peninsula Museum** of regional art and the **Allen Knight Maritime Museum**, featuring relics of the era of sailing ships and whaling. In mid-

Cannery Row, Monterey.

September each year, the acclaimed **Monterey Jazz Festival** attracts many of the biggest names in contemporary music to the Monterey Fairgrounds.

Nonconformist Santa Cruz: At the northern end of Monterey Bay – 28 miles (45 km) from Monterey via State 1 – is **Santa Cruz**, a cool, green, redwood-shingled beach town hoisted for the moment on the leftward swing of its own political pendulum. In 1965, when the **University of California** opened its Santa Cruz campus on remote hills high above the city, the intent was to create an Oxford-style university where students could devote themselves to four years of intense semi-cloistered study, uninterrupted by the hue and cry of the outside world.

It was a good idea at the wrong time. What students craved in the 1960s was "relevance", not ivory-tower scholarship. And within a few years their energy and sense of mission had transformed what had previously been a quiet backwater town into an activist community.

The students may have originally come down off their hilltop campus to demonstrate, but they stayed to open dozens of excellent restaurants, cafes, pastry shops, bookstores and a multitude of shops selling everything from 10-speed bicycles to Japanese kites. In the process, they restored and rejuvenated downtown Santa Cruz, restaining the oak on the turn-of-the-century buildings, polishing the brass, installing stained glass, replacing cement block and aluminium with natural redwood and hanging ferns. Santa Cruz has sparkling clean air in the summer; its only drawback is the torrential winter rain that turns canyons into rivers.

The Santa Cruz **municipal pier** features restaurants, fish markets and fishing facilities. Next to it is a wide white sandy beach. On the other side is the **Boardwalk Amusement Park**, a throwback to an earlier era with its carousel, Ferris wheel, thrilling roller coaster and old-fashioned arcade containing shooting galleries as well as an unwelcome invasion of video games.

Pacific coastine north of Santa Cruz.

FORESTS AND FISH: THE NORTH COAST

There are few places as wild as California's North Coast. Developers may have recreated Southern California's coastline in their own image, but here, north of Marin, the elements still rule. Although most of the towns along Highway 1 tend to be small, visitors are welcome, and accommodations are plentiful. There are few ways more pleasant to pass a few days than traveling from one bed-and-breakfast to another, shopping in quaint coastal villages, enjoying the breathtaking views, and walking along unspoiled beaches.

The absence of development along the North Coast is partly due to the California Coastal Commission, formed in the Seventies when the state seemed fated to become a 400-mile ribbon of private marinas and ocean-view condominiums. The only sign of unchecked development on the North Coast is the Sea Ranch, a chic subdivision designed to blend into the environment. There are trick codes forbidding residents to paint their homes or to do anything but minimal landscaping.

Sonoma Coast: North of **Bodega Bay**, most of the Sonoma County coast is a state beach, with comfortable access, plenty of parking, thrilling views, no camping, and appropriate beach names like **Mussel Point, Salmon Creek, Hog Back, Shell Beach** and **Goat Rock.**

As one travels north on State Highway 1 from Bodega Bay, the prevailing scenery is fog, cypress trees, pines, old barns and grazing sheep and cows – plus slow-moving motor homes struggling with the road's twisting curves and quick ascents. As real estate, this grazing land is so valuable that local ranchers are termed "boutique farmers", because they don't really have to farm. They could sell the land immediately for more money than they'd make in a lifetime of farming.

"I'd rather look at my cows than count money in a bank," said one North Coast dairyman. "If my cows are happy, I'm happy." This same man once owned a chunk of Marin County pasture land that was recently sold for unknown millions of dollars to filmmaker George Lucas for his Skywalker Ranch.

Tourism is the growth industry on the North Coast, overtaking logging and fishing which are both suffering from depression. Although demand for trees and fish is on the increase, the supply is diminishing. The boats in the Bodega Bay salmon fishery, declared an official "economic disaster" in the early 1980s, now remain berthed during the salmon season because it is too expensive to cruise for a product that may not be there. Bodega salmon fishermen sell freshly caught albacore directly from their boats to recoup losses. The winner in this market may be the camping traveler. Fresh barbecued albacore is far better than the deep-fried frozen fish served with professional indifference in tourist cafes along State 1.

North of Jenner, State 1 weaves through daily fog, rolling pastures and sudden canyons that drop 1,000 feet (over 300 meters) into the blue and

Preceding pages: primary and secondary growth in Redwood National Park. *Left*, Crescent City fishing fleet. *Right*, a local fisherman, Bodega Bay.

foamy Pacific. The road passes historic **Fort Ross**, a careful reconstruction of the original fort built by Russian traders in the early 19th century. There are tours, but the best way to see the fort is to stroll through on one's own. The small Russian Orthodox chapel is worth a special stop.

One of the more compelling ways to pass an afternoon in north Sonoma County is to visit the coastal tidepools. At **Stewart's Point State Park**, a popular place for abalone divers, the pools are accessible at most tides, and there is little risk (present at some North Coast beaches) that the explorer will be swept to a tragic death at sea by what the state's warning signs call "sleeper" waves.

The Mendocino Coast: Travelers enter Mendocino County just north of Sea Ranch at **Guadala,** notable for its fine old hotel in the center of town. Fifteen miles (24 km) north, a coastal access path leads to **Point Arena Harbor**, a tiny bayside beach that comprises several dozens of weathered mobile homes, two

disintegrating and dangerous piers and the **Arena Cove Cafe** ("short orders"), which also sells bait and fishing tackle and is everything one might imagine a battered old shoreline coffee shop to be.

The Coast Guard's **Point Arena Lighthouse** occupies the point of the US mainland closest to Hawaii. Lots of ships have crashed near Point Arena. Lots of free literature is available to tell visitors which ships, and where, and what was lost as a result.

Many travelers choose to spend the night in the town of **Mendocino** in a "B&B" – a bed-and-breakfast inn. It is not hard to find one. The B&Bs are proliferating so quickly in Mendocino – 32 miles (51 km) north of Point Arena – that city officials have passed laws prohibiting any new ones from opening.

In a sense, Mendocino is a victim of its own beauty: it's just too lovely to be ignored. A century-old former logging village, it's set on a long bluff above a small bay and is full of picturesque Victorian structures. The town is now treading the narrow line between **Fisherman repairs his nets.**

"quaint" and "cute". One inn, for example, has a sod roof. Another is called the **Fools Rush In**. "Built in 1877 AD," says the entrance of **Heritage House**, a local lodge where the standard accommodations are named "Romeo" and "Juliet".

For a small town with a population under 1,000, Mendocino is hectic. Once visitors find (with difficulty) a place to park, they are confronted with restaurants bearing names like **Whale Watch**, and menus listing such delicacies as "Sempervirens Steak" – a "highly seasoned tofu loaf made with whole grains and vegetables and covered with sauteed mushrooms, onions and jack cheese". Travelers can escape from this leisure chic at two nearby state parks, **Van Damme** and **Russian Gulch**, which offer camping, hiking, beach-combing and other quiet pleasures.

To the north, the city of **Fort Bragg** is the frumpy flipside of Mendocino. It is an unpretentious, blue-collar, beer-bellied rube who greets the wayfarer not with an historical B&B, but with a road-side cafe named Jerko's Koffee Kup. Fort Bragg's love affair with the architectural present (Safeway supermarkets and Payless drugstores) can be a shock to the traveler, like a breath of air freshener.

Some of the best of Fort Bragg's unpretentiousness can be found in **Noyo Harbor**, a sunny inlet lined by docks, charter boats and seafood restaurants. Among them is **Cap'n Flint's**, a simple cafe with plastic tablecloths, paper-napkin dispensers and bottles of McIlhenny's tabasco sauce on the tables. The fish is fresh, breaded, deepfried and served in a basket with french fries. It represents the best of the North Coast – simple, relaxed and tasty.

The cloud of steam over Fort Bragg is produced by the Georgia-Pacific Corporation's lumber mill. As the largest coastal settlement between San Francisco and Eureka, Fort Bragg is an old logging town that hasn't been abandoned, nor does it seem to show the effects of the recently depressed North Coast timber industry. Trucks loaded

California brown pelican, a common sight at coastal communities.

with fir and redwood logs hurtle along State 1 toward Fort Bragg at the rate of one every two or three minutes. The shoulders of the highway north of the city are strewn with red fuzz from redwood bark blown off the trucks.

Redwood mystique: Much of the mystique of the North Coast is in the tall redwood trees, which have survived attempts to transform them into everything from lumber and ashtrays to mulch for suburban rose gardens. Most of California's remaining old-growth redwoods are now protected in parks, where tourists are invited to look up at the trees, to drive through holes burnt or cut through the larger ones, and to buy something made of their wood.

A number of things have been done to sell redwood as a souvenir. There are redwood clocks, lamp shades, hats, purses and lipstick caddies.

Notices tacked to buildings and utility poles all along the North Coast offer "Sinsemilla Tips". Says another bulletin: "Don't get caught with your plants down." The plant in question is mari-juana, which has become a multimillion dollar black market commodity. Until 1981, it was listed in the annual Mendocino County agricultural report as the county's largest cash crop; since then, county officials have chosen not to include the estimated marijuana gross. During the late summer harvest, local and federal police in helicopters, jets and jeeps dedicate themselves to raids on known dope fields. In **Garberville**, in southern Humboldt County, the weekly newspaper runs a "Bust Barometer", a map on which the week's pot raids are charted. The information is provided by the sheriff.

Avenue of the Giants: North of Garberville a 33-mile (53-km) scenic drive called the **Avenue of the Giants** follows the South Fork of the Eel River through **Humboldt Redwoods State Park**. The giants – redwood trees, otherwise known as *Sequoia sempervirens* – are tall and sometimes wide. Their size can be marketed: "Drive through a living tree" is the come-on from the Shrine Drive-Thru Tree in **Myers Flat**.

Carson House, Eureka.

Eventually the Avenue of the Giants can make the traveler wonder about, even long for, an avenue of the midgets, or possibly a boulevard of the about-average size. Those seeking to avoid the commercialism can take the difficult road west from Garberville over the **King Mountains** to **Shelter Cove**. North of this isolated outpost is **Petrolia**, site of the first oil well in California.

An honest glimpse into the spirit of the early Anglo life along the North Coast is aptly afforded by **Scotia**, a crisp neat little company town built entirely of redwood and dominated by the **Pacific Lumber Company mill**, the largest redwood mill in the world. The mill owns the town and keeps it looking remarkably tidy. There is a visitors' center built entirely of redwood in the style of a classic Greek temple. Redwood logs represent the fluted doric columns. There are no trees growing in Scotia's gardens, nor is there any distinctly modern architecture.

Grotto with a motto: From the moment you arrive, it is obvious that **Eureka** is a good place to buy sewer pipe, lumber, a slab of redwood burl, a life-sized statue of a lumberjack carved from a redwood log, or a fresh fish dinner.

Often shrouded in fog, Eureka (population 24,000) is the largest Pacific Coast enclave in North America north of San Francisco. It is a sprawling, busy, industrial place, and it is in that spirit that it prepares its fish dinners. The **Seafood Grotto**, a restaurant on US 101, is also the retail outlet of Eureka Fisheries, which processes 40 million pounds of fresh and frozen seafoods each year. "We Ketch 'em, Cook 'em, Serve 'em" is the motto of the Grotto. The portions are immense. A plate of clams is actually a stack of clams (each the size of a human hand), piled up like pancakes.

Eureka's ubiquitous and impressive Victorian architecture in **Old Town** is highlighted by the **Carson House** at the end of 2nd Street. Visitors can't go inside the house because it is now a private men's club – which makes it seem all the more Victorian. (The little town of **Ferndale**, 10 miles (16 km) southwest of Eureka, has a remarkable collection of well-maintained Victorians to excite the architectural connoisseur.) Eureka is also the location of the North Coast's only institution of higher learning, **Humboldt State University.**

At Orick, the traveler enters **Redwood National Park**, established in 1968 to consolidate 40 miles (64 km) of majestic forested coastline under federal jurisdiction. A visitor center in Orick gives directions and shuttle-bus information for excursions up **Redwood Creek**, where (8½ miles/14 km, southeast of Orick) three of the six tallest trees ever identified on this planet, including the record holder – 368 feet (112 meters) in height – are located. They are clustered in the unimaginatively named **Tall Trees Grove.**

It is difficult to recommend much of the scenery north of the **Klamath River** bridge, because you probably won't see much of it. The stands of redwood in **Del Norte Coast Redwoods State Park** and **Jedediah Smith Redwoods State Park**, both extensions of Redwood National Park, are noteworthy. But the foremost fact of life in this area is fog. In **Crescent City**, one of the principal civic ironies is that someone had the chutzpah to name a seaside restaurant "Harbor View". To be charitable, though, Crescent City – a grim, gray gathering of plain houses and vacant lots around a semi-circular harbor – has never fully recovered from a 1962 typhoon which devastated the town.

For the traveler looking for a place to have a pleasant time, the best bet is to head inland to higher and hotter ground. Fifteen minutes east of Crescent City, on US Highway 199 toward Grants Pass, Oregon, the last un-dammed river in California flows gin-clear through the 90°F (32°C) summer twilight. Although the **Smith River** is wild, its accommodations are civilized. There's a lodge on **Patrick Creek** with a restaurant and bar. There are clean campgrounds, public and private, under the peeling red madronas. Jagged boulder-lined banks, unrepaired landslides, clear pools, rattlesnakes, good fishing, a great feeling and no redwood souvenirs are to be found along the Smith River.

THE HIGH NORTH: A STORY IN ROCKS

The key to unlocking the secrets of California's High North is State Highway 299. Running 321 miles (517 km) from the Humboldt County redwoods to the Nevada border, one could easily drive in two days. But one shouldn't .

Mountainous State 299 should be savored like a fine wine, something this route doesn't offer. The restaurant guides can be left behind; no one undertakes this journey for the cuisine. Weeks could be spent here. At least five days should be allowed.

State 299 is the only paved highway that crosses the state's isolated north. On its winding, two-lane blacktop trek, it cuts across some of California's least populated wilderness – a remote domain of mountains, valleys, volcanoes, rivers, canyons, basins and, at the end, desert. Other paved roads penetrate the High North, including the north-south Inter-state 5, running roughly along the boundary between the Klamath and Cascade mountain ranges. Every journey through this region should include side trips on secondary roads. But when it comes to offering visitors the most topographically varied exposure to the region, State 299 is the road to ride.

The time to visit is between mid-April and mid-November. The northern third of California gets two-thirds of the state's precipitation. Winter snows and spring floods make State 299 dangerous; they often close the route altogether. Even under the best conditions, rock slides and heart-stopping curves make driving in this district no experience for the timid, the inebriated or the impatient.

Home of Bigfoot: Coming from the Pacific Coast, State 299 branches off US Highway 101 at Arcata, north of Eureka, and crosses the low **Coast Range** to the wilderness realm of the **Klamath** and **Trinity rivers**. These two principal rivers drain the Coast Range and **Klamath Mountains**.

The Klamaths comprise a series of smaller ranges – the **Siskiyou**, the **Trinity**, the **Trinity Alps**, the **Marble**, the **Scott Bar**, the **South Fork** and the **Salmon** mountains. They cover about 12,000 sq. miles (about 31,000 sq. km) of northern California and southern Oregon. **Mount Hilton**, 8,964 feet (2,732 meters), is the highest peak in the region; most vary between 5,000 and 7,000 feet (about 1,500–2,100 meters).

The Klamaths are famous as the home of Bigfoot, also know as Sasquatch, the giant humanoid who – according to legend – stalks these mountains. Whether or not Bigfoot really exists, it is an appropriate and cherished myth. There *is* something wild about the Klamaths: with more than 70 inches (1,780 mm) of annual rainfall in some parts, they sustain a lush forest of ferns, hemlocks, pines and spruce. Except for the highest of the Trinity Alps, glaciers are rare, so most peaks retain a raw, jagged quality. River canyons lack the graceful horseshoe shape of their glaciated Sierra Nevada counterparts.

Three national forests contain most of California's Klamaths – Klamath, Shasta and Trinity. Within these forests are more strictly protected wilderness areas. The best-known and most popular is the **Salmon-Trinity Alps Primitive Area**, laced with hundreds of miles of trails for hiking and camping. Ranger stations along State 299 at **Burnt Ranch, Big Bar** and **Weaverville**, and on State 3 at **Trinity Center**, will issue free permits, answer flora and fauna questions, and provide up-to-date information on weather and trail conditions.

About 10 miles (16 km) east of the Trinity River bridge marking the Humboldt-Trinity county line, near the community of Burnt Ranch, State 299 passes just south of **Ironside Mountain** (5,255 feet/1,602 meters). Ironside's sheer, scenic face is the eroded, exposed tip of a much larger piece of granite – the Ironside Mountain Batholith. About 165 million years old, this batholith is typical of other such intrusions in the Sierra Nevada and Klamaths. Batholiths distinguish the Klamaths from the neighboring Coast Range.

The warp and woof of Weaverville: The Klamath-Trinity drainage system includes hundreds of smaller creeks, lakes and rivers. In high mountain streams, the spring melting of Klamath snowpacks creates a fearsome torrent of a volume and velocity that can move large boulders more than a mile downstream. Recently, some Klamath residents have begun to see money in these currents. Under a recent federal law, local power companies must purchase any electricity generated by small entrepreneurs. With this in mind, some mountain residents have developed small hydroelectric plants – like the one run by Mom & Pop Power Company in Trinity's tiny **Minersville**. Only a few such plants now operate, but others are planned.

For residents of Trinity County, a "night on the town" usually means a trip to Weaverville, the county seat with a population of 3,500. It saw its glory days during the mid-19th century, when it was a supply post for Klamath region gold prospectors. Gold hunters still haunt the creeks of Trinity County, but timbering sustains the economy. As is typical in rural California, 72 percent of Trinity County is owned by the federal government, another 10 percent by Southern Pacific Railroad. Although, ironically, no railroads cross the county. Southern Pacific received huge 19th-century land grants here as elsewhere in the West.

Although lumber ranks first, marijuana ranks second in Trinity cash crops. This juxtaposition of enterprises – one traditional, one contraband – is typical of Trinity. Those who go in either of Weaverville's principal Main Street bars, **The New York Hotel** (which isn't) or **The Diggin's** will soon understand: Trinity County's population breaks into two groups – natives and those who have come here since the end of the 1960s. Generally, natives tend to be conservative, the newcomers less so.

Despite their differences, Trinitarians share an individualism and a jealous regard for the natural environment. While Trinity often votes conservative in general elections, it also displays an abiding sensitivity to ecological issues – a sort of environmental populism.

Chinese joss house in Weaverville.

This is not so much a matter of ideology as one of simple self-interest. Many residents hunt their own food and draw water directly from springs, rivers and creeks. (The bedrock of granite and serpentine is too impermeable for aquifers.) So when the county recently tried to stop the federal government from spraying Trinity's woodlands with an herbicide many feared would end up in water supplies, no politicians – Democrat or Republican – openly opposed the grass-roots effort. This closeness to one another and to the land breeds a native suspicion of outsiders.

Visiting motorists should know that Trinity County, like most of California's north, has "open range". Cattle has never been a major part of the economy here, and open range is mostly a symbolic vestige of the region's frontier heritage. Open range means that cattle wander beyond their owner's unfenced rangelands. It also means that any driver whose vehicle strikes a cow has just purchased damaged livestock. Hikers must be careful to stay away from creek bottoms on which gold prospectors have staked claims. Likewise, those who come across a patch of marijuana should leave quickly before (a) they are shot at by its grower or (b) they are arrested on suspicion of being its growers.

Weaverville is the site of the **Joss House State Historic Park**, a tribute to Chinese history in California, particularly of the Gold Rush days. The oldest Chinese temple still in use in the state is open daily; tours are available. Nearby is the eclectic **J.J. "Jake" Jackson Museum**. Weaverville is also the gateway to **Clair Engle** and **Lewiston Lakes,** part of the expansive **Whiskeytown-Shasta-Trinity National Recreation Area**. A short drive north of town, these lakes were created in the '60s with the damming of the upper Trinity River. They offer fishing, hiking, boating and camping.

The Volcanic Cascades: The Cascades run almost due north from California to Canada's British Columbia. In California, the range runs 40 to 50 miles (70–80 km) across, in Washington state more

Logging operation, Trinity National Forest.

than 80 miles (130 km). Farther north, glaciers dominate the range. Here in California, only the highest peaks bear these Ice Age relics. The dominant snow-capped Cascade peaks are young volcanoes. Some, like Washington's Mount St Helens, are still active. Unlike the Klamaths, the higher Cascade peaks present a sharply vertical profile of high conical peaks surrounded by lower mountains of the 4,500 to 5,000-foot (1,370 to 1,520-meter) range.

There are few better places to study volcanology than Lassen Volcanic National Park. It is reached via State 36 east from **Red Bluff**, State 44 east from Redding, or State 89 south from State 299 beyond **Burney**. Lassen Peak (elevation 10,457 feet/3,187 meters) marks the southern terminus of the Cascade Range, and is one of only two Cascade volcanoes to have erupted in the 20th century.

Much of 108,000-acre (43,700-hectare) Lassen Park lies within a caldera, the giant crater left by the collapse of an ancient volcano. Out of this caldera, Lassen Peak later rose to dominate this expanse of wilderness, but there are small volcanoes in the park as well. There is also **Bumpass Hell**, a steaming valley of active geothermal pools and vents. And there are lakes, rivers, meadows, pine forests and fine trails for hiking and camping.

Most of the California Cascades fall within two national forests, Lassen and Shasta. At Shasta's southern boundary lies another prime wilderness, **Plumas National Forest**. These upland woods cover the northern end of the Sierra Nevada and cradle the **Feather River**, one of California's most celebrated wild streams.

Between Redding and Burney, a distance of 53 miles (85 km), State 299 climbs into a gently undulating country of ranches and volcanic debris. The red rocks that litter the landscape and pastures to the south of the road were deposited by hot mud flows from the eruption of Mount Maidu 7 million years ago. This posthumously named volcano collapsed to form the caldera within Lassen Park.

East of **Bella Vista**, on the south banks of **Cow Creek**, are the ruins of **Afterthought Mine**, a resource of zinc and copper from the late 19th century until the end of World War II.

Just beyond the lumber and livestock marketing center of Burney (population 3,200) is the State 89 intersection. South is Lassen Park; north is Mount Shasta. About 6 miles (10 km) north is lovely 129-foot (39-meter) **Burney Falls**. Volcanic terrain is inhospitable to rivers, and this state park gives a clear indication why. Before it gets to the falls, Burney Creek disappears into a porous lava flow, but reappears just in time to drop over the spectacular moss-covered precipice.

East of Burney is **Fall River Mills**, and from here to the Nevada border State 299 runs across the basins and fault-block mountains of the Modoc Plateau. For a large part of its route, the highway follows the deep canyon of the Pitt River, the plateau's main drainage.

The Modoc Plateau is a lava plain similar to the Columbia Plateau to the north. In California, the Modoc covers 13,000 sq. miles (33,670 sq. km), taking in all of Modoc County and parts of Lassen, Shasta and Siskiyou counties.

The Modoc doesn't look like a plateau. It looks more like a scrubby basin on which someone left some block-like piney mountains that don't seem to belong. Vestiges of volcanism make up much of the **Modoc National Forest**, which covers 1.97 million acres (797,000 hectares). A pristine example of this volcanic past is **Glass Mountain**, a huge flow of obsidian lava on the forest's western edge.

The focus of any geologic tour of the Modoc Plateau is **Lava Beds National Monument**. A finer example of basalt flows cannot be found than this moonlike landscape of lava flows, columns and caves. (Yes, there are basalt flows on the moon.) In one of the caves, a Modoc Indian chief known as "Captain Jack" and the warriors of his tribe held out against the US Army during the final days of the 1872–73 Modoc Indian War. This was one of the last such conflicts in American history.

Helen Lake, Lassen Volcanic National Park.

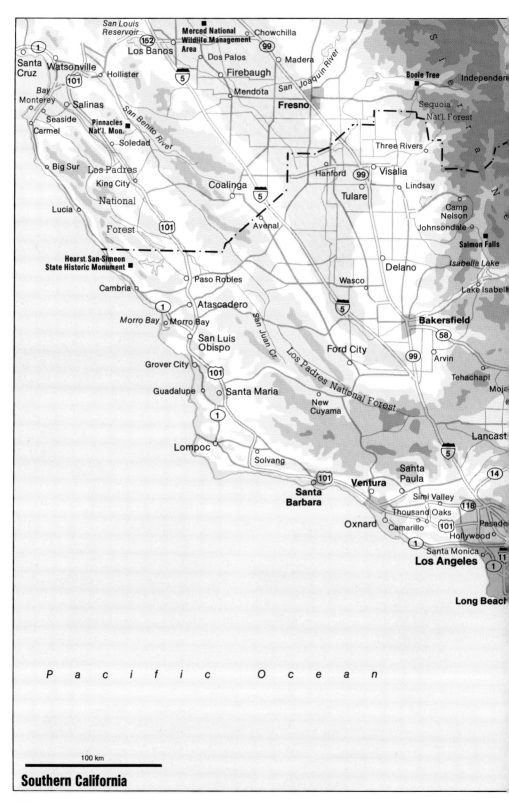

Southern California

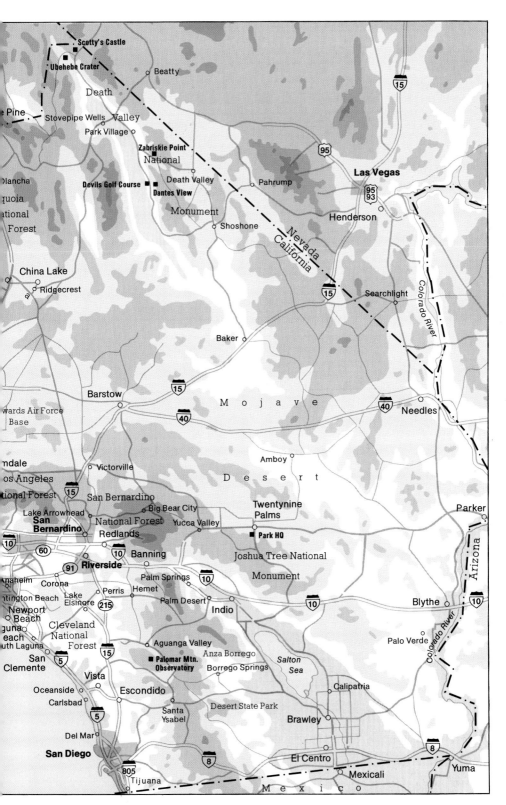

SOUTHERN CALIFORNIA

Southern California is Hollywood and Disneyland, Sea World and Knott's Berry Farm, Universal Studios and the San Diego Zoo. Glitter, glamour, Donald Duck, performing whales, roller coasters, movie stars, koalas: such images come readily to mind at the mention of these place names. Here are "LA Law" and "Dynasty", Beverly Hills and the fabulous Hearst Castle. Here are Howard Hughes' bizarre *Spruce Goose* and the opulent J. Paul Getty Museum at Malibu.

But Southern California is also San Juan Capistrano and Santa Catalina, Palm Springs, and Bakersfield, Death Valley and the Rose Bow. Rough and rugged terrain challenges backpackers to turn off the roads and vanish into looming woods, leaving civilization behind. There are desert areas sprinkled with cacti, Indian dwellings built before Europeans ever imagined a "New World", snow-capped mountains, valleys drowned in wildflowers and wildlife, parks, lakes and canyons.

Most of all, Southern California is Los Angeles, the sprawling, smoggy metropolis straddling the notorious San Andreas Fault. Wedged between the rolling Pacific surf and the arid Mojave Desert, it has maintained much of its old Spanish flavor while becoming a cosmopoliatan 20th-century entertainment capital. In downtown LA, the ambience is informal and intimate. Stroll through the narrow alleyways off Olvera Street; listen to the echoes of the past within museum walls; shop for Mexican and Japanese crafts; kick off your shoes and feel the track on which Olympic heroes sprinted to international fame.

164

LOS ANGLES: CITY OF THE ANGELS

Los Angeles is hypnotically seductive. Graceful, gravity-defying palm trees sway next to rippling aquamarine pools. Perfect bronzed bodies recline under the hushed midday sun in exotic beach areas. Sleek automobiles with sunroofs open dodge in and out of traffic at sunset.

The images live on, perpetuated by the very LA residents who created them. Los Angeles has digested its own astounding mythology and embraced its own narcissistic reflection to the point that there is no longer a dividing line between the factual LA and the fantastical one.

Non-Southern Californians often hold a very different image of Los Angeles – that of a concrete, smog-breathing monster. In fact, visitors complain about the technicolor air far more vociferously than LA residents themselves. In the past two decades, Angelenos (as the residents are known) have taken major steps to reduce the amount of smog in their air. Had they not done so, they might have had to match their clothes to the polluted hues of the sky.

There are very few other cities in the world which have been so thoroughly shaped by itinerant dream-makers. The alluring appeal of the golden city poised on the edge of the Pacific, ripe for new beginnings, has enticed thousands from every corner of America. Consequently, this unique city is just beginning to create its own traditions.

Heart like a wheel: One tradition near and dear to the Angeleno's heart guzzles gas and is air-conditioned. There is no doubt that Los Angeles is consumed by its affair with the automobile.

Most of America's major urban centers had their boundaries rigidly set before the internal combustion engine belched to life. But LA was and is geographically amorphous, constantly evolving along an undisturbed, seemingly endless, Pacific coastline. Other American cities patterned themselves after Europe's "walking cities"; LA embraced the automobile and soon spilled over its original boundaries.

Thanks to Henry Ford and the assembly-line process, the City of the Angels quickly became the City of the Automobile. Los Angeles became a kaleidoscopically uneven patchwork of suburban areas, linked casually under the vague concept of "Greater LA" To many, Los Angeles seemed to say: "Have your cake and eat it, too." Here was the centrality and glamour of a sophisticated metropolis coupled with the treasured tranquility of country living.

But what started out decades ago as a carefree, flirtatious affair with the passenger car soon careened into a full-blown relationship with a lifetime commitment. The automobile has united the city to the point where distances are measured not in miles but in estimated driving time.

The downside of Los Angeles' sense of absolute mobility and freeway freedom is that drivers spend an inordinate part of each working day behind the wheel, often combating bumper-to-

Left, rush hour on the Hollywood Freeway. **Right**, actress Debra Wakeham.

bumper bottlenecks on one of the country's busiest freeway systems.

After more than 10 years of planning, construction of Metro Rail, the city's first underground train system, was begun in 1987. The entire project is expected to cost $4.5 billion.

From the start, Metro Rail has been surrounded by controversy. Critics argue that it will serve fewer commuters than city planners projected but supporters justify the expense by arguing that LA is the only major American city without an underground system and that expanding the city's network of public transportation is their best hope of solving an increasingly unmanageable traffic problem.

The California Look: It is hardly surprising that all of these hours of freeway frustration have exploded into an obsession with health spas, gymnasiums and aerobic centers. As if to compensate for the stressful hours spent nervously inhaling exhaust fumes, residents of the city have flocked to sweat emporiums in nearly every part of the suburban basin. Whether it be pumping iron or just luxuriating in a heated jacuzzi, residents have found a new social institution for the inimitable LA lifestyle.

Of course, Los Angeles' passion for all things physical is hardly new. Thanks to the city's semi-tropical climate, residents always have been able to exhibit a maximum of skin nearly year-round. Local fashion designers have cooperated, creating the *California Look*, which revolves around the concept that assets shouldn't be hidden. They should be flaunted.

Not only are health spas the new cathedrals of the physically inclined, the workout spots have eclipsed the infamous single bars as gathering places to finalize new fast-lane contacts. Co-sexual aerobic classes and whirlpool dips have ushered a whole new, slightly sweaty vocabulary into LA's dating lexicon. In the 1970s, the cliché opener was: "So what's your sign?" In the 1980s, at least in Los Angeles, it was clearly: "So where do you work out?" What's next?

Realization of the California dream.

In the palm-festooned atmosphere that fostered an appreciation for pet rocks, terrariums and macramé, few are surprised by this fad. National trends have a way of sprouting up first in Southern California, and health spas are the newest in a long list of popular LA-born diversions to infect the rest of America.

Celluloid idols: Los Angeles' infatuation with the physical is historically rooted. Ever since D.W. Griffith pointed a camera at his stable of aspiring starlets, Hollywood's film efforts have celebrated seductive physicality. With these colossal silver-screen projections, LA presented celluloid idols with uncanny regularity. Hollywood's sexuality became a passion (many would argue an obsession) for most of Los Angeles.

LA is a company town – or more accurately, an industry town. Movie and television shows are "The Industry's" products, with the studios that make them dotting the suburban landscape like the steel furnaces of the American Northeast. The city of Los Angeles is kept in a perpetual state of show-biz dazzle, with film crews continually invading local neighborhoods like renegade battalions on frequent military maneuvers.

Few would dispute that Los Angeles is the world's film capital. No wonder, then, that great talents from around the globe have gravitated to LA and made a remarkable difference in the quality of the city's life. During the past 60 years, some of the century's greatest writers, directors and artists have fashioned one of the most electric, unpredictable, creative cities around. They have produced milestones in the film industry while contributing to the artistic evolution of the region.

Los Angeles is a mesmerizing study in diverse, mutually appreciative lifestyles. From the relaxed beach scene where local surfers spend unhurried days paddling for the ultimate ride, to the city's bustling commercial centers where the business-oriented anxiously negotiate for the ultimate deal, LA fosters a climate of limitless possibilities for nearly everyone.

Left, keeping in shape with Jane Fonda at her workout studio. **Right**, "The Look".

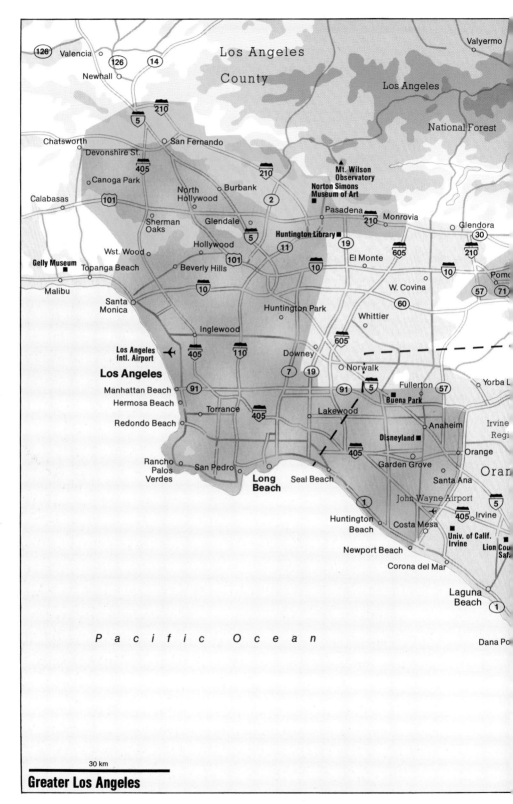

Greater Los Angeles

170

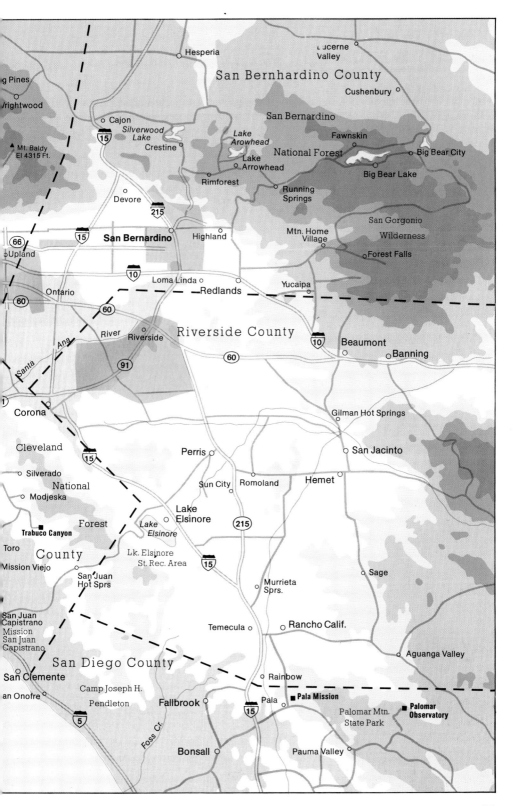

DOWNTOWN LA, THE CITY WITHIN

Downtown Los Angeles is often dismissed as the antithesis of Southern California's endless line of suburbs, the forgotten wasteland dedicated to railriding tramps and Bible-thumping fanatics. But beyond the grim facade lies a vital, wildly diverse city-within-a-city, sporting hidden cultural treasures and historic significance not always visible to the hurried traveler.

The City of the Angels has replaced Ellis Island as the most heavily burdened immigrant entry point in the United States, and the weighted cultural baggage of the newly arrived is usually dumped first at the heart of LA's downtown urban core. Street life is animated and sometimes illuminating as dozens of different languages reverberate along the busy sidewalks, crowded with throngs bent on survival. The air is thick with the competing aromas of hundreds of fledgling ethnic cafes and luncheonettes specializing in regional cookery, all vying for the attention of the casual passerby as well as the curious visitor.

Los Angeles' downtown, in fact, is currently undergoing a renaissance of sorts, emerging with a reenergized spirit of entrepreneurship and a sense of the creative. With all the possibilities of transforming itself into another stylish Soho, new art galleries and fashionable cafes are opening their doors to an enthusiastic public anxious to embrace the arts. Abandoned warehouses and industrial spaces are rapidly metamorphosing into imaginative living spaces, inhabited by the new tribe of urban pioneers – artists, scholars and musicians ready to experiment with new concepts of contemporary urban living.

Historic Olvera Street: The casual visitor may not immediately grasp the fascinating cultural history, the diverse ethnic building blocks, upon which Los Angeles was so securely founded more than 200 years ago. The city's overwhelming Spanish beginnings are no-

Preceding pages: LA glitter from Griffith Park Observatory. Below, afternoon colors on the downtown LA skyline.

where more evident than along festive, manicured **Olvera Street** in the heart of bustling downtown near Sunset Boulevard and Main Street. The cobblestone walkway celebrates the first actual settlement in Los Angeles. Some of the curious architectural feats along the animated avenue date back to the 18th century, while others are merely replicas of pre-existing structures.

Olvera Street is a combination of the picturesquely ethnic and the outrageously contrived. A casual stroll down this historical street, restored as a Mexican market-place in 1930, will rarely prove to be a dull experience. Vendors hawking everything from hand-painted *piñatas* to velvet paintings designed to glow in the dark are tirelessly enthusiastic about their wares, and several Mexican restaurants offer homemade *tortillas* and margaritas.

Of particular historical note along the avenue is the **Avila Adobe**, 14 Olvera Street, the oldest (1818) residential dwelling in Los Angeles. And just a few steps away stands one of LA's first brick houses, **La Casa Pelanconi**, 33–35 Olvera Street.

Olvera Street opens onto a quiet, shady plaza where the **Church of Nuestra Señora la Reina de Los Angeles** (Old Plaza Church) has hosted religious services since 1822. Currently undergoing restoration, the nearby **Pico House** (built by former governor Pio Pico) and the **Merced Theater** (the city's first) are expected to reopen as soon as funds become available to finish the work. This 44-acre (18-hectare) historical area, best known as **El Pueblo de Los Angeles State Historic Park**, is also the site of the city's oldest firehouse. **Firehouse No. 1**, now a museum of antique firefighting equipment, is open to the public year-round.

The Asian connection: Although Spain and Mexico have undoubtedly influenced the evolution of Los Angeles more than any other single ethnic force, pioneering Japanese and Chinese settlers have left their marks for well over a century. Los Angeles' **Chinatown**, just north of Sunset Boulevard on North

Underground shopping at the Hyatt Regency's Broadway Plaza.

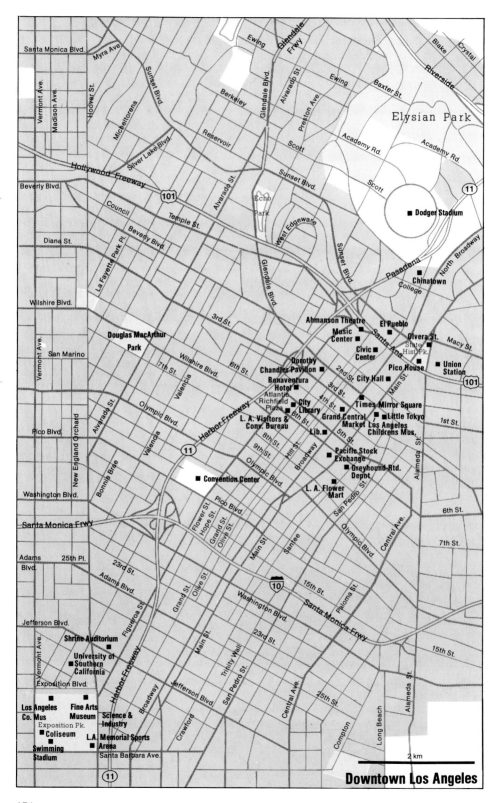

Downtown Los Angeles

Broadway, is a microscopic version of its counterpart in San Francisco. But the community's restaurants offer some of the finest Chinese cuisine on the West Coast. Small curio and other tourist-oriented shops dot the area. **The Friendly Shop**, an odd retail outlet directed by businessmen from mainland China, is of special note.

Also situated in the heart of downtown LA is **Little Tokyo**, a spotless manicured area just south of Olvera Street between 1st and 3rd streets. It is chockablock with pretty little pastry shops, crowded *sushi* piano bars, punk nightclubs, and colorful toy shops featuring the latest in Japanese robot technology.

Dignity and culture: Los Angeles' **Civic Center** provides the downtown area with a much-needed touch of quiet dignity. It centers around the classically designed 28-story **City Hall** (2nd Street near Temple and Spring streets).

Crowning the Civic Center is the much-touted **Music Center**, 135 N. Grand Avenue, home base for the Los Angeles Philharmonic Orchestra and the Civic Light Opera. Three separate theaters are nestled within the complex, offering year-round productions which run the gamut from touring Broadway musicals to the experimental.

The Society for the Preservation of the Variety Arts recently unveiled an important new contribution to the downtown theater scene, the **Variety Arts Theater**, now popular for its raucous and unpredictable comedy.

The Union Passenger Station, 800 N. Alameda Street, signaled the final chapter in the history of monumental rail terminals in the United States when it was completed in 1939. The oft-photographed station was designed by John and Donald Parkinson in an unmistakable and highly dramatic style described as "monumental Moorish".

The futuristic **Westin Bonaventure Hotel** is a courageous if solitary reminder that the 21st century is rapidly approaching. This dramatic architectural statement, made by John Portsman, incorporates 35 acres (14 hectares) of waterfalls and ponds in the lobby area alone!

The twin-tower 52-story **Atlantic Richfield Plaza**, 6th and Figueroa streets, is a huge office complex capping an underground shopping mall. The headquarters of the **Greater Los Angeles Visitor and Convention Bureau** can be found on Plaza Level B.

Exposition Park: A short distance south of these architectural behemoths on Figueroa Street is **Exposition Park**. Site of the 1932 and 1984 Olympic games, it has become a focus of the city's cultural and recreational pursuits.

In addition to two major sports arenas, the park is home to two fine museums. The **Los Angeles County Museum of Natural History** offers exhibits on the evolution of plant and animal life, including the development of human societies. It also features exhibits on the history of California from the 16th to the 20th centuries.

Just steps from the Museum of Natural History is the state-operated **California Museum of Science and Industry**. Exhibits underscore achieve-

Watts Towers.

ments in the sciences, including health, aviation, space technology, mathematics, communications, agriculture and industrial design. The "hands-on" series of inventive displays encourages the educational process and helps break the tedium of more conventional museums.

There are other fine museums at the **University of Southern California** (USC), just across Exposition Boulevard from the park. Founded in 1880, the university has more than 24,000 students on its 150-acre (61-hectare) campus. The **Fisher Gallery** has on outstanding permanent exhibit of 16th- and 17th-century Flemish and Dutch paintings, while the **Hancock Memorial Museum**, housed in an 1890 mansion, includes items from the palace of former Mexican Emperor Maximilian.

The **Museum of Contemporary Art** at 250 South Grand Avenue opened its doors to the public in 1986 and is helping to make Los Angeles one of the hottest new entries in the international circle of artists, critics, dealers and collectors. The museum's 600-piece collection was unveiled to rave reviews in a daring $23 million building of red sandstone and glass designed by Japanese architect Arata Isozaki.

In addition to the museum, Los Angeles' cultural renaissance is being fueled by the $2.8 billion J. Paul Getty Trust, which is establishing or expanding five institutions located downtown and throughout the metropolitan area.

Quiet escapes: Other museums of note in the downtown area include the **Dunbar Museum of Black Culture and History**, the **Los Angeles Children's Museum** and the **Skirball Museum**, which specializes in Judaic art and artifacts.

Boating enthusiasts can float away the afternoon at **MacArthur Park** on W. 6th Street, probably the most picturesque of the downtown area's green spots.

One of the most rustic recreational parks in Los Angeles is **Elysian Park**, dramatically overlooking the downtown Civic Center and the suburban sprawl of the San Gabriel Valley. The 575-acre (233-hectare) park is an unusual mix of wilderness and cultivated picnic areas.

Dodger Stadium, home of the Los Angeles Dodgers baseball team, traditionally among the National League's leaders, is perched high up in Elysian Park.

For a truly illuminating vision of the life-style of the Hispanic people of East Los Angeles, visitors should visit **Plaza de la Raza**, formerly known as Lincoln Park. Located just 3 miles (5 km) from the Civic Center at 3501 Valley Boulevard, its recreational facilities include a performing arts center and museum focusing on California's growing Chicano population.

Undoubtedly, Los Angeles attracts its share of creative iconoclasts. One of those eccentrics, Simon Rodia, labored in his backyard for nearly 35 years to build a monument to his personal artistic vision. Using old bits of tile and glass, the professional tile-setter sculpted the internationally celebrated **Watts Towers**. They have stood at 1765 E. 107th Street in the economically depressed area of Watts since their completion in 1954.

HOLLYWOOD:
THE WAY WE WERE

You can take Hollywood for granted like I did, or you can dismiss it with the contempt we reserve for things that we don't understand. It can be understood, too, but only dimly and in flashes.

—F. Scott Fitzgerald,
The Last Tycoon *(1939)*

Hollywood is a part of Los Angeles that visitors would no sooner bypass than they would Disneyland or the long strand of Southern California beaches. Newcomers journey to Hollywood Boulevard by rental car or tour bus or urge their friends to take them there. They expect to catch a glimpse of Robert Redford or Paul Newman, or at least, to peer into the smoked windows of a limousine and guess who's inside.

The reality is a rude awakening. Instead of limos, they find Chevys painted wild metallic-flake colors, outfitted with dangling chi-chi balls, fake fur on the dashboards and hydraulic lifts to make the cars bounce. The closest thing to movie stars are the names embedded in bronze on the district's smudged terrazzo sidewalk. Instead of stars, they find flabby-bellied bikers. In fact, they see everything but the glamour they anticipated.

To have contempt (as Fitzgerald warned) because the city cannot fulfill one's fantasies would be an unfortunate mistake. In many cases, like Frederick's of Hollywood's impressive deco facade, Hollywood's glitter is merely covered by a gaudy coat of paint. It only takes a little information and imagination to see what the town once was.

A farmland for citrus, watermelon, bell peppers and other produce, the tiny community of 700 was incorporated in 1903, and continued in pastoral harmony until the Horsely brothers leased an abandoned bar on the corner of Gower Avenue and Sunset Boulevard to shoot movies. Film studios flooded the area. The clever industry doyens saw the powerful draw of the growing film center

Hollywood hype captured on cotton.

by the early 1920s, and launched a city development program to cash in on it.

Today the census count shows that more than 50,000 Latinos (Hispanics), Asians and blacks live in Hollywood, and more than 40,000 Armenians arrived in the 1970s from the Soviet Union. Mental patients routinely ask when released from institutions to be sent to Hollywood. Vagrants and teenage runaways coverge there for the same reason. Regardless of Hollywood's tawdry physical form, in the hearts and minds of people it remains a symbol of renewed chance and opportunity.

Stardust memories: The first thing one notices while walking down Hollywood Boulevard past the T-shirt shops, pizza joints and crummy boutiques is that lots of people are staring at their feet. This isn't because (unlike New York's Times Square) it's dangerous for a person to make eye contact.

It's simply that the **Walk of Fame**, which forms a 1½-mile crisscross down the boulevard from Gower to Sycamore streets, and down Vine Street from Sunset Boulevard to Yucca Street, is hard to ignore. The 1,760-plus pink-and-charcoal speckled terrazzo stars feature the names of celebrities from the music, film, art direction and fashion industries. To be immortalized with a star, one must first be nominated and approved by a special committee, then must pay a $3,000 installation fee. Approximately one star a month is dedicated, so there are still about 50 more years of stars before the spots run out.

Another place where visitors stumble over one another is the infamous courtyard at **Mann's Chinese Theater** (6925 Hollywood Blvd). It's "the thing to do" to stick one's stiletto heels in the points left by the shoes of Marilyn Monroe and 160 other stars. Legend claims the tradition began when Norma Talmadge wandered into wet cement during the opening-night premiere of Cecil B. de Mille's *King of Kings* on May 18, 1927. Not true: owner Sid Grauman skidded into the goo himself. Knowing a good deal when he saw it, he promptly invited Talmadge, Douglas Fairbanks and Mary Pickford to do likewise.

The **Egyptian Theater**, also owned by Sid Grauman, was built to resemble the Temple of Thebes in order to capitalize on the Egyptian rage caused by the discovery of King Tutankhamen's tomb. Opened on October 18, 1922, with Fairbanks starring in *Robin Hood*, the ornate theater entryway was lined with wafting potted palms and usherettes in Cleopatra drag. Since then, the theater has fallen into unfortunate decline.

Another landmark recently saved was the 1923 **Hollywood Sign**. First erected to attract attention to a real-estate development on the side of Mount Lee, the 50-foot (16½-meter) high sign, illuminated by more than 4,000 light bulbs, originally spelled "Hollywoodland". In the early 1930s, a blonde starlet named Peg Entwhistle, despondent over the decision by RKO Studios not to renew her contract, told her uncle she was going out for a pack of cigarettes. Instead she climbed to the top of the "H" and jumped to her death. Over the years, the sign fell into a state of tattered disrepair. In 1978, the Hollywood Chamber of Commerce and several celebrities raised $243,000 and rebuilt the sign.

Frederick's of Hollywood (6608 Hollywood Blvd) is known by even the most sexually naive due to its expansive mail-order service. The zigzag modern exterior has been covered by Frederick's ridiculous purple-and-pink trademark colors. Inside, the gold-and-silver deco sales area features a smorgasbord of racy articles such as edible panties, peek-a-boo housedresses and any other trashy accessory imaginable.

Except for the four markers dedicated to the Apollo XI astronauts, the intersection of **Hollywood and Vine** is perplexingly drab. Just up the street, though, is the **Capitol Records** building (1750 Vine Avenue) designed by composer Johnny Mercer and singer Nat "King" Cole to resemble a stack of 45s topped with a symbolic phonograph needle.

The Hollywood area was home to many literati. Among those who ate and drank at **Musso and Frank's Grill** (6663–67 Hollywood Blvd) were Ernest

Cast member roars over script on set of 1920s comedy.

The House Where Marilyn Monroe Died: On the morning of August 5, 1962, actress Marilyn Monroe was found dead in the bedroom of her home at 12305 Fifth Helena Drive in Brentwood (between San Vicente and Sunset boulevards, west of Bundy Drive). Her nude body was found lying face-down on her bed, following the ingestion of 47 sleeping pills. Although numerous reports have come out that she was murdered, her death was officially ruled a suicide.

The "Mommie Dearest" House: Actress Joan Crawford bought the home at 426 N. Bristol Drive (off Sunset Blvd) in Brentwood before she married actor Douglas Fairbanks Jr in 1929. At one time, in the '40s, Crawford removed the bathtubs from the house, saying it was "unsanitary to sit in one's bathwater". In 1978, her daughter Christina wrote her *Mommie Dearest* book tracing a life of "alcoholism, abuse and terror".

Not So Funny Deaths: Comedian Freddy Prinze, who co-starred in the television show *Chico and the Man*, shot himself in 1977 at the age of 22 at an apartment located at 865–75 Comstock Street (near Wilshire and Beverly Glen boulevards) in Westwood. Prinze's idol was comedian Lenny Bruce, who died at the age of 41, at his home at 8825 Hollywood Blvd, in 1966 after injecting himself with morphine. Prinze often told friends he was the reincarnation of Bruce and many times visited the house where Bruce had died.

Hollywood's Most Bizarre Suicide: Albert Dekker, who appeared in several horror movies and was best known for his role as *Dr Cyclops*, killed himself in 1968 at his apartment at 1731 N. Normandie in Hollywood. Dekker, who also was elected to the California State Assembly, was found in his bathroom hanging by his neck at the end of a rope that was tied to a shower curtain rod. The rope was also tied around both his legs and one of his arms, and two hypodermic needles were stuck in his body. Police ruled the death a suicide, although they could find "no information why he wanted to take his own life".

Marilyn and Joe's Honeymoon Home: When actress Marilyn Monroe married baseball star Joe DiMaggio in 1954, they settled down at 508 N. Palm Drive in Beverly Hills. The house is next door to the last home of actress Jean Harlow. Monroe and DiMaggio met on a blind date at the Villa Nova restaurant, 9015 Sunset Blvd. The restaurant is now called the Rainbow Bar and Grill.

Janis Joplin's Final Night: Rock singer Janis ("Pearl") Joplin died of a heroin-morphine overdose in 1970 in a room that was part of the old Landmark Hotel, 7047 Franklin Street in Hollywood. She was 27. She had earlier set aside $2,500 for her own wake. The Grateful Dead provided music for more than 200 guests who had invitations that read: "Drinks are on Pearl."

Chateau Marmont Hotel, site of many a Hollywood intrigue.

Hemingway, Dorothy Parker and William Faulkner. They also stopped by the **Brown Derby** (1620–28 Vine Street). The Hollywood atmosphere inspired locations and characters that could be found in the pages of many novels – particularly the Hollywood detective stories. Raymond Chandler used the **Montecito** (6650 Franklin Avenue) as a model for *Chateau Bercy* and *Little Sister*. The **High Tower** (at the north end of Hightower Avenue) was used as Jules Amthor's house in *Farewell, My Lovely* and later as the home of Elliott Gould's Philip Marlowe in Robert Altman's film *The Long Goodbye*. Geiger's pornographic bookstore from *The Big Sleep* was actually the **Book Treasury** (6707 Hollywood Blvd). Marlowe's Cahuenga Building, formerly the beaux-arts Guaranty Building where gossip columnist Hedda Hopper had her office for many years, is now the Bank of America (6331 Hollywood Blvd).

The **Hollywood Bowl** (2301 Highland Avenue) is above Hollywood Boulevard, just south of the Hollywood Freeway (US Route 101). This huge outdoor amphitheater seats 17,000 in its 116-acre (47-hectare) park. Since 1923, the Bowl has hosted "Symphonies Under the Stars" from July to September. It is also popular for its spectacular peresentation of Tchaikovsky's "1812 Overture" on the Fourth of July, to the accompaniment of a brilliant fireworks display and a real cannon-blast finale.

In the heat of the night: The best-known part of the district of **West Hollywood** covers Sunset Boulevard from Crescent Heights Boulevard to Doheny Drive. It is internationally famous as the **Sunset Strip**. In its heyday, the Strip was the location of steamy nightclubs such as the Mocambo, the Trocadero and Ciro's. (The latter, now occupied by **The Comedy Store**, is the only structure of the three still standing.) During the 1960s, other clubs took names like The Daisy, The Trip and Pandora's Box, making the Strip a headquarters for the so-called "Love Generation".

The only two venues to have survived since the '60s in name and substance are **The Troubador** (9081 Santa Monica Blvd) and **Gazzari's** (9039 Sunset Blvd), and both now cater to a leather-and-stud heavy-metal crowd. Forlornly decrepit is the hollow **Whisky a Go Go** (8901 Sunset Blvd). **The Roxy** (9009 Sunset Blvd) upholds the musical tradition by booking a wide mix of rock, soul, blues, country-western and new wave bands.

Laurel Canyon was one of Los Angeles' first developed canyons. In the 1920s it became a retreat for movie stars. Later, in the '60s, it was home to rock stars Joni Mitchell, David Crosby and Jim Morrison. Near the junction of Laurel Canyon Boulevard and Lookout Mountain Road are the ruins of magician Harry Houdini's once-lavish California retreat. Across the street is the charred skeleton of a log cabin which once belonged to singing cowboy Tom Mix. It was occupied briefly by avant-garde rock composer Frank Zappa.

Near the foot of Laurel Canyon, on Sunset Boulevard, is a replica of a Norman-French castle, the **Chateau**

Peek-a-boo at Frederick's of Hollywood.

Marmont Hotel. Greta Garbo lived there, as did Howard Hughes, and more recently, Robert De Niro, Tony Randall, Bianca Jagger and rock singer Sting have stayed there. It was also, sadly, the site of comedian John Belushi's tragic encounter with drug overdose.

Divine madness: From Doheny to La Brea avenues, **Melrose Avenue** is the mother of invention. Though its fashion boutiques cater to all tastes, its current "in" styles are the punk look, '50s retro and '60s mod. The entire street is worth checking out, as are many of its pedestrians' hairdos – dreadlocks, multi-colored layers and rolled spikes that radiate straight out from the skull. Currently the stores feature a melange of avant-thrift garb, pre-packaged "new wave", and oddball knickknacks.

On the other hand, the **Fairfax District**, a 2½-block area just below Melrose, is steeped in religious tradition. On any afternoon except the Sabbath, Yugoslav, Russian and Israeli immigrants mingle with an equally large population of Orthodox Jews. The neighborhood is made up of delicatessens, ethnic grocery stores and *falafel* stands.

Wilshire Boulevard is the district's cultural center. Within one block are three of Los Angeles' most respected museums. The **La Brea Tar Pits** and **George C. Page Museum** – centered around a black, bubbling morass – often cause unknowing visitors to scratch their heads. But these benign-looking pits have been a part of LA for a long time. In 1906, paleontologists discovered that this "black gunk" contains the largest collection of Pleistocene fossils ever found in one place. Within the museum, exhibitions and dioramas chart the history and evolution of the prehistoric mammals.

The **Los Angeles County Art Museum** (5905 Wilshire Blvd) is located directly adjacent to the tar pits. In 1986, the Art Museum introduced its $35 million Robert O. Anderson wing of 20th-century art. The Art Museum's Pavilion for Japanese Art houses the world-famous Japanese collection.

"Blue Whale" Pacific Design Center towers behind Melrose District boutiques.

BEVERLY HILLS & THE WEST SIDE

The dream of stardom is the essence of the west side of Los Angeles. It's in the air, as real as smog.

Visitors can almost reach out and grasp their fantasies while driving down the streets of Beverly Hills. It seems as though everyone who lives here is a star, with a star's car and a star's mansion. There are movie stars, television stars, sports stars, news stars, hairstylist stars, real-estate stars, even used-car-salesmen stars.

In fact, the spirit of this part of Los Angeles makes aspiring stars out of everyone. People who are already stars want badly to become bigger and brighter stars. The TV star wants to be a movie star. The soap opera star wants to be a prime-time star. The tourist wants to touch any of them.

Wealth and fame: The heart of this dream of stardom is **Beverly Hills**. Located midway between downtown Los Angeles and the Pacific Ocean on less than 6 sq. miles (15 sq. km) of gently sloping land, the City of Beverly Hills is world renowned as the place which the rich and famous call home.

The average home in Beverly Hills is a palatial estate, complete with swimming pool, tennis court and lush manicured greenery. It doesn't come cheap. Real-estate prices have leaped so high in recent years that million-dollar homes are commonplace.

Shops, consequently, cater to the demands of wealth, fashion and luxury. On **Rodeo Drive**, the focus of Beverly Hills commerce, merchants showcase the extravagant, the trendy and the luxurious. A $500,000 necklace is sold next to $25 keycases. Famous faces dart in and out of elegant stores like Gucci, Van Cleef, Arpels and Bijan. Some stores even provide valet parking.

With the construction in 1912 of the pink **Beverly Hills Hotel** on Sunset Boulevard, a community focus was established on what had been 12 acres of bean field. By the fall of 1913, public

Preceding pages: Saturday night road show in Westwood. Below, a Beverly Hills residence.

186

sentiment for incorporation mandated city status for Beverly Hills. The population was then 500.

Movie producers, directors, actors, writers and technicians migrated to the enclave to be near the hypnotic silver screen. On Sunday afternoons, many of them played their favorite game – polo – then gathered at the Beverly Hills Hotel to see and be seen. The **Polo Lounge** is a legacy of that glamorous time. Warm embraces and table-hopping are a part of the everyday ritual. But it isn't true that all Polo people are close personal friends. The mood in the lounge is more akin to that of feeding time in a shark tank.

Star gazing: For the visitor who cannot resist doing some star-snooping, maps of the stars' homes are sold everywhere for a few dollars. Up-to-date maps may be more expensive. It is good to remember that these maps are intended only to give directions, and are not licenses to trespass. High fences, angry Dobermans and unsmiling security guards exist for one reason: privacy.

Nearly as many stars live in lush **Bel Air** directly adjoining Beverly Hills north of Sunset Boulevard. For instance, the homes of Burt Reynolds, Barbra Streisand, Gregory Peck and Rod Stewart, as well as the former home of Elvis Presley are on **Carolwood Drive**. Not far away are the homes of Jerry Lewis and Tom Jones. A good place for a break between rounds of not-seeing stars is the **Bel Air Hotel** on Stone Canyon Road. It offers an idyllic retreat from the maddening crowd amid gliding swans and purple bougainvillea.

Westwood Village: West of Beverly Hills is **Westwood Village**, which has the most intense concentration of first-run movie theaters in the world. Thousands of shoppers and movie-goers jam the streets on *foot*, a rarity for car-crazy Los Angeles. Just behind the AVCO theaters on Wilshire Boulevard is the **Westwood Memorial Cemetery**, final resting place for screen legends like Marilyn Monroe and Natalie Wood whose names once graced the marquees of these very theaters.

The Beverly Wilshire Hotel at the foot of Rodeo Drive.

An undeveloped ranch until the 1920s, the area began to thrive in 1929 when the **University of California at Los Angeles** (UCLA) opened for classes in Westwood. The campus consists of more than 85 buildings in a variety of architectural styles, surrounded by 411 acres (167 hectares) of serene, prime Westwood real estate. Enrollment is more than 32,000. A relaxing stroll around campus include the **Franklin D. Murphy Sculpture Gardens**, the **Frederick S. Wight Art Gallery**, and the **Mathias Botanical Gardens** – 8½ acres (3½ hectares) of woodsy canyon designed as a sheltered environment.

Seaside Santa Monica: Adjacent **Santa Monica** is the center of a Southern California beach lifestyle envied the world over. The ocean breeze is refreshing, the sun warm, and the attitude laid-back. Not everyone is here on vacation; it just seems that way.

And why not? Santa Monica offers 3 miles (5 km) of sandy beach for swimming, fishing and boating. **Santa Monica Pier's** 75-year-old carousel with 56 prancing horses was featured in the movie classic, *The Sting*. Even though the pier often undergoes repairs following severe winter storms, it remains colorful. Four major boulevards – Wilshire, Santa Monica, Olympic and Pico – lead in its direction.

Santa Monica began to be developed as a seaside resort community in 1875. For many years it was a sleepy suburb, a full day's bumpy stagecoach ride from downtown LA. The character of the town changed dramatically in 1966 when the Santa Monica Freeway opened and reduced the commuting distance to downtown to less than 30 minutes. An influx of new residents ended the quieter era.

Today, many of Santa Monica's new "immigrants" can be found on **Main Street** in the **Ocean Park** area south of the pier. This has become a unique seaside shopping and dining area.

The roller-skating capital: If, as author Tom Wolfe wrote, Southern California is the great cultural laboratory of America, then **Venice** is the home of **Sunset views at Ocean Park, Santa Monica.**

188

advanced research. The fads of this bohemian beachside community seem to sweep the nation. Roller skating is the most recent manifestation: visitors must be on their quick-stepping toes to dodge skaters on **Ocean Front Walk**.

Tobacco magnate Abbot Kinney developed Venice in 1905 as a tribute to the great Italian city of the same name. In doing so, he hoped to inspire a cultural renaissance in the United States. His city plan included 15 miles (26 km) of canals with gondolas to ferry visitors from place to place. But by 1929, the community had paved over most of the waterways. Those that remain are filthy.

Today, however, Venice has its Italians. It also has many other Europeans, along with Blacks, Asians, Central Americans, Brazilians, Australians, Hare Krishnas, Mormons, Jews, burnt-out beach bums, wealthy movie directors, and every other form of humanity doing its own thing.

In recent decades, Venice has established its fame as a free-spirited stop on the young vagabond's circuit. In the 1950s, it ranked with New York's Greenwich Village and San Francisco's North Beach as a home for the beatniks. In the '60s, rock music took over: Venice spawned Jim Morrison's influential Doors and other groups.

Now, a visitor can partake of an ocean-side lunch at the **Sidewalk Cafe** and watch the passing parade of bowling ball jugglers, mimes, magicians, folk singers, Elvis Presley impersonators, unicyclists, Muscle Beach weightlifters, pretty girls in string bikinis, roller skaters and skateboarders. It's never dull. Street vendors push T-shirts, electronic gadgets, sunglasses, posters, prints, hats, watches, postcards, paisley pullovers and leopard-skin leotards.

Majestic Malibu: At the north end of Los Angeles' west side, north even of Pacific Palisades, is the chic area of **Malibu**. This isolated beach resort has a long history as LA's "last frontier", a place of tranquility overlooking the majestic Pacific.

Certainly, Malibu's wild surf and secluded beaches are its big attraction. The private **Malibu Beach Colony,** for instance, is home to some of the motion-picture industry's biggest stars. It isn't surprising, therefore, that some of the beach "cottages" are as expensive as Beverly Hills estates.

Malibu is also the home of the highly touted **J. Paul Getty Museum**. Since 1974, one of the world's greatest private art collections has been displayed free to the public within the Getty Villa, a detailed replica of the Villa del Papyri at Herculaneum in the old Roman Empire. Mosiacs, frescoes and Romanesque landscaping attempt to recapture a Mediterranean setting.

The art collection is set in several galleries connected through an atrium courtyard. There is a superb collection of Greek and Roman antiquities, a section on European paintings from the Renaissance through the baroque period, and many items from the French decorative arts.

There's one hitch: visitors can't just drop by the Getty Museum. They must call in advance for a parking reservation. It could only happen in LA's west side.

Right, would-be sailors catch the ocean breeze at Venice Beach.

191

SOUTH BAY: BLUE SKIES, BLUE WATER

When an area is host to the world's third busiest airport; when it includes a city called the aerospace center of the world; when one of its biggest attractions is the aviation industry's albatross, it's obvious that its heart is in the clouds rather than on *terra firma*.

Such is the case of Los Angeles' South Bay area. Stretching from **Los Angeles International Airport** (LAX) to Long Beach, home of the bizarre *Spruce Goose*, the South Bay looks to the sky. But it never forgets Southern California's sworn oath of providing great beach towns and loads of sun.

Before visitors – if they jet into LA, that is – can enjoy the salt air at beach communities like Manhattan Beach or the quiet life of the Palos Verdes Peninsula, they must trudge through LAX. No mean feat, this.

It's not just jobs and travel that bring people to the South Bay. Located in

Inglewood, slightly east of the airport, is **The Forum**, LA's most prestigious sports-entertainment complex.

"Playing the Forum" has become synonymous in popular music circles with having made it to the top. David Bowie, Neil Diamond, Bob Dylan, Billy Joel, Willie Nelson, Linda Ronstadt, Bruce Springsteen and Sting have all played The Forum, just to name a few.

Catch a wave: Heading south from the airport area, one passes through the communities of **Manhattan Beach, Hermosa Beach** and **Redondo Beach** – the prototype of the California lifestyle that was popularized by the "Surf Sound" of the 1960s.

While the Beach Boys hailed originally from nearby **Hawthorne**, Manhattan Beach was the Band's spiritual home. Throughout the '60s, the South Bay beach towns presented a combination of upper-class elegance and fun in the sun. The stately **Kings Harbor** in Redondo Beach was Southern California's premier private marina until San Pedro Harbor was built.

Preceding pages: *Queen Mary* and *Spruce Goose* dome, Long Beach. **Below,** surf punks, Redondo Beach.

Heading southwest on Hawthorne Boulevard, one leaves behind the jumbled mess of Los Angeles and enters the **Palos Verdes Peninsula**, a 26.3-sq.-mile (68-sq.-km) section of land that features many of LA's most attractive homes.

Palos Verdes means "green trees" in Spanish and is the home of four separate municipalities: Palos Verdes Estates, Rolling Hills, Rolling Hills Estates and Rancho Palos Verdes. While the names may differ, the mood of all four is strikingly similar.

Entering the Palos Verdes Peninsula is like taking a trip back in time to a period in Southern California history when the streets were safe for walking, when neighborhoods were quiet and shaded by tall trees.

Because the peninsula is in the path of many ocean breezes, it has the cleanest and coolest air in LA Thus it is an area that demands outdoor activity. There are four 18-hole golf courses (one is private), several public tennis courts, more than 60 miles (97 km) of maintained horse riding trails that wind through canyons and over hillsides, and several excellent fishing and diving access points.

While Palos Verdes stands as a symbol of upper-middle-class living for many, it is the beauty of the area which leaves a lasting impression. To fully appreciate this aspect of the Peninsula, one should make a trip to the **Wayfarer's Chapel**.

The Wayfarer's Chapel (5755 Palos Verdes Drive S.) was conceived by Elizabeth Schellenberg in the late 1920s. Mrs Schellenberg was a member of the Swedenborgian Church and had a dream of building a chapel on a hillside overlooking the ocean where travelers could rest and meditate on the grandeur of the area's natural beauty. The chapel, a simple construction of glass, redwood beams and Palos Verdes stone, was designed by Lloyd Wright, son of the famous architect Frank Lloyd Wright. From inside its glass walls, one may rest protected from the elements with (in Wright's words) "a sense of outer as well as inner space".

Following the completion of the chapel in 1951, work began on building a tower, visitors' center and a colonnade. The **Wayfarer Tower**, topped by a lighted cross that is visible from far out at sea, is called "God's Candle" by sailors passing through the Catalina Channel.

As one heads south from Palos Verdes, the reality of Southern California's growth quickly intrudes. Point Fermin is the last chance to sample the beauty of the coastline. Here at the 37-acre (15-hectare) **Point Fermin Park**, one may stop for a brief visit to the extensive tidepools of the **Marine Life Refuge** or just take in the magnificent vistas that overlook the harbor and the ocean. There is a wonderful old lighthouse here, built in 1874, that unfortunately is not open to the public. But it's still a good vantage point for spotting migrating whales. Further along the drive south is the **Cabrillo Beach Marine Museum** (3700 Stephen White Drive S.) where one of the world's largest seashell collections is housed.

Yachties compete off Long Beach.

Almost as commanding as the ocean is **Los Angeles Harbor**, one of the world's largest man-made ports. The 28 miles (45 km) of waterfront facilities provide berths for thousands of pleasure boats and service over 4,000 larger container ships annually. When the original port landing was built in 1835, **San Pedro Bay** was only 2 feet deep in many places. Most ocean-going vessels, therefore, had to anchor off shore. In the 1850s, Phineas Banning used a simple dredge to deepen the port to 16 feet (5 meters). The present depth is 51 feet (15½ meters).

Once one crosses onto Terminal Island, two of Long Beach's most prominent tourist attractions are close by: the *Queen Mary* and the *Spruce Goose*.

Royalty and reclusion: Ever since the *Queen Mary* arrived at her permanent berth in Long Beach, the ship has been a question in the minds of local officials and residents. For years the 81,000-ton vessel was seen as a white elephant by city fathers, whose revenues were puny compared to maintenance costs that exceeded $2 million in a year.

Then, like the cavalry coming over the hill to rescue the settlers from hostile Indians, the Wrather Corporation, operator of the Disneyland Hotel, stepped in and leased the boat from the city. The company immediately began a $12 million facelift that finally returned the ship to her former glory. With the massive refurbishing and the opening of the *Spruce Goose* next door, the crowds began to come in droves and the *Queen Mary* was spared the ignominy of making a final voyage – this time to the scrap heap.

A tour of the *Queen Mary* – which crossed the Atlantic Ocean 1,001 times – includes stops in the hospital, beauty saloon, gymnasium, Observation Lounge and Grand Salon, where a band plays music of the 1930s, '40s and '50s nightly. Staterooms are available for overnight guests. Adjacent to the ship is the theme-orientated **Londontowne** shopping village.

The ***Spruce Goose*** is located in the Howard Hughes Flying Boat Expo right next door. The 400,000-ton craft – which is made of birch, not spruce at all – made only one flight. On November 1, 1947, its designer, millionaire recluse Howard Hughes, took the plane for a 1-mile flight at a height of 70 feet (21 meters) over the harbor waters to silence government critics who complained that it was a $25-million boon-doggle. After its brief flying career, the *Hercules* (as Hughes had named the craft) was sequestered in a temperature-controlled hanger for 36 years. Its original purpose – to be a mammoth troop-carrying plane capable of transporting 750 soldiers and two tanks – was quickly forgotten.

Only on a tour of the plane, which has drawn large weekend crowds since it opened in early 1983, does one begin to absorb the craft's bizarre statistics. It has eight propeller-driven engines, is taller than an eight-story building, and has a wingspan of more than 300 feet (91 meters). Equally as fascinating are the various slide shows and photos that offer details about the life of its eccentric inventor.

Left, Formula One driver dons helmet for start of Long Beach Grand Prix. Right, volleyball at Manhattan Beach.

SAN FERNANDO: THE VALLEY SCENE

According to the 1980 census, some 1.3 million people live in the San Fernando Valley – or as it is better known to those who live in Los Angeles, *The* Valley. If the Valley were a city unto itself, it would be the sixth largest in the United States, surpassed only by New York, Chicago, Los Angeles, Philadelphia and Houston.

The San Fernando Valley is a very good place to live. Shopping is abundant and easy, parking is convenient (something the rest of Los Angeles has trouble claiming), and broad freeways make much of The Valley readily accessible – even though traffic jams at rush hours are among the worst in Southern California. Downtown LA can be reached from most parts of The Valley in less than 30 minutes. Yet The Valley also has places where orange groves still prosper, where people ride horses down shaded lanes, and where corn stalks grow tall in the summer sun.

In a way, there is still much of what Father Juan Crespi called "a very pleasant and spacious valley" when he first climbed over **Sepulveda Pass** in 1769. He named the area "Valle de Santa Catalina de Bononia de los Encinos". The only part of the original name that survived has been given to the town of **Encino**, the Spanish word for "oak".

The Valley remained essentially rural until the 1870s, when the great ranchos were sliced up like pies by men whose names (Isaac Lankershim and I.N. Van Nuys) later were given to the grand boulevards of the area. With the coming of the railroad in 1874, the California land speculation boom swept over The Valley in what would be the first of many waves. Towns such as **Burbank, Glendale, Reseda, Chatsworth** and **Pacoima** sprang up.

The railroads paid the way, and wages, of dozens of Eastern writers to come to California and publicize the good life. One journalist Charles Nordhoff, wrote a book called *California: For Health, Pleasure and Residence*. In it, he said:

It's "like so bitchin', fer sure", to be a Valley Girl.

"The cost of living is today less in California by a third than in any eastern state." To that sort of hype, the railroad added incredible incentives to the land boomers. At first, the fare from Kansas City to Los Angeles was $125; but it quickly dropped to a mere $15, and for a very brief time to only $1. California and the San Fernando Valley were touted as the Promised Land. And it cost only 10 thin dimes to get there.

The boom was short-lived, though, and the Valley boom went bust for approximately the next three decades.

What happened next is an event which historian Morrow Mayo has called "The Rape of the Owens Valley". By 1900, the population of Los Angeles had shot over 100,000, and the city had to make a choice between stopping its growth or finding a way to get more water. Fred Eaton, an engineer and former mayor, hatched a plan to build an aqueduct that would direct the melting snows of the Sierra Nevada to the Owens River some 250 miles (400 km) north of Los Angeles. He sold the idea to William Mulholland, the city's water chief, and Mulholland put a $24.5 million price tag on the project.

"Titanic Project to Give City a River" announced *The Los Angeles Times* in July 1905. Two months later, voters passed a $1.5 million bond issue to buy Owens Valley land, including that owned by Eaton, the scheme's mastermind. Work began on the "Panama Canal of the West" in 1907 after another bond issue, for $23 million, was passed.

Although many entrepreneurs got rich in behind-the-scenes dealings, the project ultimately worked. On November 5, 1913, about 40,000 Angelenos turned out to witness the Owens River water cascading into a San Fernando Valley reservoir. "There it is," said Mulholland. "Take it."

LA's bedroom: By then, the City of Los Angeles had annexed the San Fernando Valley, adding a staggering 177 sq. miles (458 sq. km) to the 107 sq. miles (277 sq. km) which already made up this burgeoning megalopolis. At the time, there was only one policeman in the whole Valley.

In the years that followed, The Valley became a major center for the motion picture and television industries. Companies such as Universal, Warner Bros. and Columbia spread across huge plots of land. In more recent years, the National Broadcasting Company (NBC) opened a vast facility in "Beautiful Downtown Burbank" and the Columbia Broadcasting System (CBS) moved onto the old Republic films lot in **Studio City.**

Most significantly, the Valley turned into "LA's bedroom", a community where single-story, ranch-style homes outnumber multiple dwellings by a ratio of at least two to one. After World War II, the Valley became one of the touchstones of the American dream, a place where anyone could afford to buy a nice house on a small lot, raise children and put in a good lawn.

Here in suburbia, however, there are a few problems. Architecture is almost uniformly boring. And the Valley's rich parents are guilty of excessively spoiling and pampering their children. Herein lies the socioeconomic basis for the Zappas' *Valley Girl* song. There is a tension between the generations, but the children aren't so much rebellious as they are parodies of their parents: obsessed with clothing, hair, fingernails, cars, shopping, credit cards and being at the right place in the right trend at the right time. Valley girls not only have their own aesthetics, they also have their own language.

The song's lyrics include numerous examples of Val Talk – phrases like "Bag your face", "Barf me out" and "Gag me with a spoon".

Touring the studios: The **Universal Studios Tour** is unquestionably the single biggest draw in the San Fernando Valley. Though films may flop, Universal can always count on a steady flow of tourists. The 4½-hour tour is so popular, in fact, that during the summer new parties are taken every five minutes from 8 a.m. to 6 p.m., seven days a week! (The rest of the year, tour parties set out every 20 minutes daily with more limited hours.)

There are two parts to the studio tour.

The Valley's agricultural history is recalled in crate label.

SILVER MOON

GROWN IN U.S.A.

Sunkist

SAN FERNANDO HEIGHTS LEMON ASSN.
SAN FERNANDO, CALIFORNIA

It begins on a "Glamourtrain", taking visitors on a constantly expanding series of thrills: a monster shark attacks the train, Cylons from *Battlestar Galactica* bombard the train with laser weapons, Conan the Barbarian wields his sword to protect passengers from a dragon. The train even passes through the Red Sea, parted for passengers courtesy of Moses.

Latest attractions at Universal include the Star Trek Adventure and the Streets of the World, the only movie sets open to the public. The Miami Vice Action Spectacular was recently added to the tour, as well as an attraction known as Earthquake – the Big One.

A short drive away is the **NBC Studio Tour** in Burbank (3000 W. Alameda Avenue). The 90-minute tour here is much more sedate than the Universal Studios tour, and a good deal more serious. The walk through the largest color studio in America leaves visitors with a sense of how hard it is to put together a television program. After the tour, many folks join the long line for admittance to *The Tonight Show* starring Johnny Carson.

A patch of green: The largest urban park in America is **Griffith Park**, which effectively separates Burbank and Glendale from Hollywood and downtown Los Angeles. As municipal parks go, it is not exactly awash with charm. Neither is it a wonderful park for strolling. But it is rather enjoyable for drivers. How typically Los Angeles!

There are two branches of **Forest Lawn Cemetery** in The Valley, almost at opposite ends of Griffith Park. One is in Glendale, the other in **Hollywood Hills**. Brochures from the park – they avoid the term "cemetery" – quote founder Hubert Eaton as wanting to build "the greenest, most enchanting park you ever saw in your life." It's not exactly that, but it is breathtaking in its strangeness.

Both cemeteries are filled with exact replicas of famous churches, such as Wee Kirk o' the Heather and Boston's Old North Church (both in Hollywood Hills). The Hollywood park also has

Left, Singapore at the Burbank Studios. Right, souvenir of a piece of Americana.

halls dedicated to the patriotic history of America. Glendale's park features mammoth murals of the crucifixion and resurrection, a stained-glass rendition of Leonardo da Vinci's "Last Supper", and a reproduction of Michelangelo's David. Many famous Hollywood personalities are buried in these parks, among them W.C. Fields and Clark Gable.

Mansions and missions: Glendale has other fine art works in its **Brand Library and Art Center**, 1601 W. Mountain Street in Brand Park. The Moorish-style mansion, built in 1904, is open afternoons, Tuesday to Saturday.

The **Mission San Fernando Rey de España** is still alive and well at 15151 San Fernando Mission Boulevard in **Mission Hills** at the northern end of the Valley. The chapel and monastery, built in 1797, have been restored. Many Indian craft and other artifacts have been preserved, including a 16th-century altar, detailed wood carvings which relate Bible stories, antique period furniture and a wine press. In Brand Park across the street from the mission are the original reservoir from which the *padres* took their water, an old soap works and a statue of Father Junipero Serra.

The fancier houses in The Valley can be found in Studio City, **Sherman Oaks,** Encino, **Woodland Hills** and Calabasas. While Beverly Hills and Bel Air claim the largest star populations in Los Angeles, there are plenty of celebrities here, too. They include comedian Bob Hope and singers Rick Springfield, Kim Carnes and Michael Jackson (and the whole Jackson family).

The further from the hills one gets, and the closer to the desert, the hotter the temperature gets. Temperatures in The Valley side of the hills are usually about 5°F (3°C) above those of downtown Los Angeles. They can go up another 10°F (5°C) on the "flats". Likewise, the "flats" population becomes poorer, more blue-collar and more Latino.

In a way, neither the trendies who live in the hills nor the workers who eke out a living on the "flats" are really the heart and soul of The Valley. The true Valley people are... well, let a Valley person explain.

"Valley People": "I like to think of my parents as definitive Valley People," said Darryl Morden, a scriptwriter who grew up in the Valley. "When they were married in the early '50s, they bought a small house in **Van Nuys** on a quiet street. After I was born, and my sister was born, they moved to a larger house in Sherman Oaks."

Morden took another bite out of his waffle at **Du-par's**, a Studio City coffee shop popular with entertainment industry people. "They've spent a lot of time putting in gardens, a swimming pool, an electric garage-door opener. But they've been more concerned with the quality of their life than with the quality of their appliances."

Du-par's is known as the "Polo Lounge of the Valley", due to the large number of people from the nearby CBS Center who meet there to rub elbows, talks contracts and come up with sitcom ideas. Not far away, **Art's Deli** displays a framed letter from Frank Sinatra praising the eatery's corned beef. When Mimi Sheraton, restaurant critic of *The New York Times*, came to Los Angeles to study West Coast food trends, one of the handful of restaurants she visited was **La Serre** in Sherman Oaks. Ventura Boulevard, in fact, is one of Southern California's greatest restaurant strips as it runs through Universal City (**Fung Lum**, the world's largest Chinese restaurant), Sherman Oaks (**Camille's, Albion, Marrakesh** and **L'Express**, in addition to La Serre), Encino (**Hatsuhana, Bouillabaisse** and **Mon Grenier**) and Tarzana (**Café de la Paix** and **Le Sanglier**).

"I used to live on the West Side," said record company executive Jill Kaufman. "Parking was bad, three people were shot dead on my block. Life was interesting, but it wasn't good. Here I grow tomatoes and zucchini all summer, and chard and carrots all winter. It feels good to come over the hill in the evening and see the street lights going on. I don't like the heat, and I don't like the smog, but I do like living here. To me, it feels like home."

Belly dancer entertains at the annual Renaissance Faire, Agoura.

Orange County, The Fun Capital

Orange County, resting on Los Angeles County's southeastern flank, is the amusement capital of America. Here are Disneyland (the original "Magic Kingdom") and Knott's Berry Farm, two of the country's three most popular theme parks, as well as a plethora of other less colossal but equally enjoyable diversions.

Perhaps there are some folks who snicker at Disneyland, who can't believe any world can really be orderly, clean… and wholesome fun. At one of Disneyland's most popular attractions, "A Small, Small World", park visitors climb aboard a small boat which cruises past small mercantile dolls in native garb from around the globe. Sometimes even the cynics come away believing the dolls' message of brotherhood when they sing – in a falsetto, no less – "It's a smaaaalll world after all."

After visiting the Magic Kingdom for the first time, journalist Robert Ferrigno reported that he was amazed that cleanliness is one of Disneyland's greatest miracles. The biggest sanitation problems, he said, are the droppings deposited by the horses who pull the trolley cars. Using a stopwatch, he found that the average time between deposit and clean-up was 23 seconds. "Anywhere in America you could pass out on the sidewalk and not be picked up as fast as horse manure on the streets of Disneyland," he wrote.

The American dream: It is easy for the more sardonic visitors to ridicule such fastidiousness and the amusement park's cornball humor and conservative maxims: good triumphs over evil, hard work is rewarded, self-reliance is the ideal, races can mix as easily as a choir can sing. They also find it easy to poke fun at inland Orange County itself – a place which named its major airport after the late actor John Wayne, that symbol of no-nonsense manhood, gun-toting capitalism and unabashed American patriotism; a place where a television

Preceding pages: Sleeping Beauty Castle, Disneyland. **Below,** modernistic Town and Country complex at South Coast Plaza in Costa Mesa.

evangelist has built a drive-in church with a sanctuary crafted out of 10,660 panes of glass; the birthplace of a disgraced president, Yorba Linda native Richard M. Nixon; a place so fundamentally new that it seems to be without roots or culture, especially in contrast to San Francisco, New York City, and even sprawling Los Angeles.

But Orange County is anything but moribund. Without much of a past, it creates ideas for the future and provides a high quality of life for its residents. It has two state universities and numerous colleges, a burgeoning cultural scene, excellent athletic facilities, theaters, hundreds of parks, sandy beaches, lakes and mountains. The county also offers exquisite restaurants, many of whose chefs number among the county's 75,000 Indochinese refugee population.

Knott's Berry Farm: In 1920, farmer Walter Knott moved to **Buena Park**. Soon after, he began to raise boysenberries, the hybrid blackberry-raspberry creation of Anaheim nurseryman Rudolph Boysen. During the Great Depression year of 1934, Knott's wife Cordelia began selling chicken dinners – initially on her wedding china – for 65 cents a meal at the farm's roadside. She added jams, jellies and pies to the menu, and by the start of World War II customers were spending an hour or more in line outside the family's restaurant.

To occupy the guests and fulfill a dream, Knott recreated an 1848 gold town, complete with narrow-gauge railroad. **Knott's Berry Farm** grew from that point until by 1966 it was attracting 4 million visitors annually. That year, Knott, a staunch conservative, witnessed the completion of a $1 million replica of Philadelphia's Independence Hall, where America's Declaration of Independence was signed in 1776. A multi-million-dollar expansion of the park began in 1975.

Knott died in 1981, but his estate carried on the work. In 1983, a new $10 million, 6-acre section called Camp Snoopy opened for children between 3 and 11 years old. Particularly inviting to

Orange Country suburban sprawl.

youngsters are the Timberline Twister roller coaster, the Beagle Ballroom (a tarpaulin filled with thousands of hollow plastic balls in which to burrow) and Tubs of Fun (spinning wooden washtubs).

In addition to the Corkscrew, the Log Ride and the Good Time Theater, the park's newer attractions include XK1, a seven-story participatory flight ride, and Bigfoot Rapids, California's longest artificial white-water experience. Also new are Kingdom of the Dinosaurs, and the Incredible Waterworks shows, which choreograph lights, music and 1,100 jets of water.

In late October, just prior to Halloween (October 31), the park changes its name to "Knott's Scary Farm". Ghosts and goblins spring from behind every rock, tree and corner within and outside of the attractions.

Knott's Berry Farm is located at 8039 Beach Boulevard in Buena Park. Visitors should have no trouble finding it: there are directional signs scattered all over the northern part of Orange County.

Disneyland: As enjoyable as guests find Knott's Berry Farm, it is generally dwarfed in their imagination by **Disneyland**, the world's best-known theme park a few miles to the southeast. So that the one won't suffer by comparison to the other, it is often recommended that the tourist visit Knott's first.

Walt Disney, the Missouri farmboy-turned-movie-mogul, opened Disneyland on July 18, 1955. Anaheim and Orange County would never be the same again. Orange groves were razed and the tourism business boomed, producing a string of motels with gaudy signs.

Disney, whose park initially had 18 attractions, promised that as long as people continued to have an imagination, his land would not be finished. His successors have been true to Uncle Walt's promise. In 1967, the year after Disney died, "Pirates of the Caribbean" opened. It has been one of the park's most popular rides since. In 1977, the high-speed "Space Mountain" ride opened. "Big Thunder Mountain Railroad" was added in 1979. By its 25th

Wild spin at the Mad Hatter's Tea Party, Fantasyland.

anniversary in 1980, the park had 59 attractions and a capital investment of $206 million.

Another $41 million was soon pumped into **Fantasyland** which, until the revamped look was unveiled in 1983, had some of the park's most forgotten rides. "It's a Small World" has always been popular, but now Fantasyland will also line up customers at the renovated "Peter Pan's Flight" and "Mr Toad's Wild Ride".

To reach Disneyland (1313 S. Harbor Blvd) by car, the visitor can choose from a number of freeways. The Riverside (State Highway 91), Santa Ana (Interstate 5), Garden Grove (State 22) and San Diego (I-405) freeways all have Harbor Boulevard ramps – southbound from the former pair, northbound from the latter two. From the Orange Freeway (State 57), visitors should head west on Katella Avenue.

Avoiding the rush: It's a good idea for the first-time visitor to arrive at Disneyland when the park opens (at 9 or 10 a.m., depending upon season and day of the week). Although the park suggests an orientation trip around the park by train, it is wiser to rush straight down **Main Street** (the park's entry corridor) to the most popular rides ahead of the crowds, thus avoiding at least one long wait in line.

Those who prefer fast, heart-stopping rides should scurry to **Tomorrowland's** "Space Mountain" or to the "Matterhorn" bobsleds haunted by abominable snowmen. Families with one or more children, or others who prefer serenity to sheer speed, should scamper to **New Orleans Square** to take the "Pirates of the Caribbean" ride and tour the "Haunted Mansion". A logical next step is a trek to nearby **Bear Country** to watch the "Country Bear Jamboree", a country-western music revue presented by 18 lovable mechanical bears. It's a lucky day if the lines are still short at **Adventureland's** "Jungle Cruise" or "Enchanted Tiki Room", where Pacific isle entertainment is provided by mechanical birds, flowers and supernatural icons.

Bird's-eye view of Fantasyland.

Only when the lines have lengthened is it time to ride the train around the park. Only then should one return to Main Street to have a photo taken beside Mickey Mouse.

If parents want a rest, Adventureland provides the "Swiss Family Treehouse" for young climbers. For a longer respite, **Frontierland** offers "Tom Sawyer Island". The children travel to the island by raft, then explore caves, cross a bridge of floating barrels, and investigate "Fort Wilderness".

Dixieland romances: Disneyland at night is a romantic setting. Teenagers primp and promenade at such dance sites as "The Tomorrowland Terrace" and "The Space Stage". Post-teen couples seem to enjoy the more intimate setting provided by the *"Mark Twain* Steamboat", a stern-wheeler circling "Tom Sawyer Island" to the accompaniment of banjo-and-clarinet Dixieland music. On many nights, fireworks light up the sky above Fantasyland's "Sleeping Beauty Castle", and an electrical parade ambles down Main Street.

Day or night, the park offers inexpensive meals at such locales as the **Carnation Plaza Gardens**, where visitors can purchase sandwiches, hamburgers, fries, salads and soft drinks for a reasonable price.

Souvenirs are also reasonably priced. This is to Disneyland's credit; with a captive audience, high prices could easily be charged, particularly if greedy or hungry children are in tow. What is lost in profit is gained several times over in good will.

Lion Country: Disneyland and Knott's Berry Farm are the obvious destinations in Orange County, but there are many other attractions, some well publicized, others little known, even to residents.

Much of the recent publicity at Irvine's Lion Country Safari has been of a negative type. In late 1982, a 2-year-old boy was critically hurt when a Siberian tiger allegedly sauntered out of its open cage, grabbed the boy by the head, and carried him 50 feet (15 meters). And in mid-1983, a park zoologist was crushed to death by a 3-ton elephant named Misty.

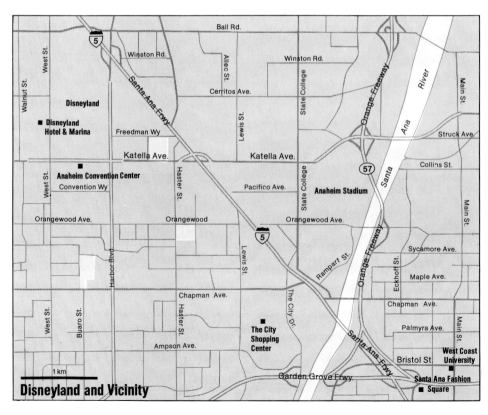

Disneyland and Vicinity

The elephant eluded capture for three hours, forcing the closure of nearby freeways.

Assuming another tiger or elephant hasn't taken to the hills, necessitating a similar road closure, visitors can reach this wild animal park via Irvine Center Drive south from I-405, or by exiting I-5 south onto the Laguna Freeway and heading south on I-405 until the Irvine Center Drive on-ramp.

Irvine is also the location of **Irvine Meadows**, an amphitheater which books big-name entertainers.

"Possibility thinking": Orange County has its own famous TV evangelist, too. The Rev. Robert Schuller preaches from the pulpit of the **Crystal Cathedral**, a **Garden Grove** congregation of the Reformed Church of America domination. Known for his "possibility thinking" theology, Schuller started a new congregation in 1955 at the Orange County Drive-In Theater because he could find no suitable hall to rent to start his Protestant church. Orating from the tar-paper roof of the theater's snack bar,

the pastor preached to a growing crowd despite the remonstrances of a minister friend for conducting worship services in a "passion pit".

Today, Schuller rules over a Garden Grove complex (Chapman Avenue at Lewis Street) with office towers, an arboretum and the multi-million-dollar Crystal Cathedral, which contains one of the world's largest pipe organs. The auto-enclosed worshipper of drive-in movie days has not been forgotten: a gigantic glass door opens during services so that penitents have a choice of sitting in pews or bucket seats.

About 10,000 worshippers attend Schuller's church. In Costa Mesa, twice that number attend services at **Calvary Chapel** (3800 S. Fairview Street) to hear the Rev. Chuck Smith, a fundamentalist preacher who began his Orange County ministry by spreading the Gospel to beach bums and drug users. His services are now so crowded that the overflow must watch on a row of television sets in an adjacent hall that is itself filled to capacity.

The Rev. Robert Schuller leads the congregation in Christmas hymns at his Crystal Cathedral, Garden Grove.

PLEASURES OF THE ORANGE COAST

The migrant and the visitor find the starkest of contrasts on the Orange Coast. For those with money or easy credit, there is a fast lane of multi-million-dollar homes on Lido and Linda isles, sports cars, yachts and yacht clubs, Mexican housekeepers, exquisite restaurants and, for those who so indulge, cocaine easily slipped into the county from Mexico, two hours by freeway to the south. And then there are the surfers and poets, living in garages, studios and battered trailers while they pursue the perfect wave or phrase. Between the two live the middle class, scraping up the money to make payments on the condo in Laguna Niguel or ante up the rent each month for an apartment in Corona del Mar or Balboa Island.

The Watergate White House: Traveling north from the county's southern border just above the controversial **San Onofre Nuclear Power Plant**, the visitor's first stop is **San Clemente**, where former President Richard M. Nixon – an Orange County native – set up his Western White House on the 25.4-acre (10.3-hectare) **La Casa Pacifica** estate. In 1980, after 11 years' residence, Nixon and his wife Pat sold their Spanish-style home on Avenida del Presidente and moved to the East Coast.

Those who want to see the house where Nixon hosted heads of state, and where he agonized over the Watergate scandal, should walk down the beach to a point where the house can be seen on the cliffs, or else glance to the right while driving southbound on the San Diego Freeway (Interstate 5).

There are six California state beaches along the Orange Coast. At **San Clemente Beach** (not far from the Nixon estate at 225 Avenida Calafia) and **Doheny Beach** (34320 Del Obispo Street), visitors may camp for a nominal fee. State fish and game wardens patrol marine-life reserves – open to the public – in Doheny Beach, Dana Point, Laguna Niguel, South Laguna Beach, Laguna Beach, Irvine Coast (south of Corona

del Mar) and Newport Beach. Snorkelers and scuba divers can look at, but not keep, underwater flora and fauna.

The swallows of San Juan Capistrano: Capistrano Beach and Dana Point are just north of San Clemente along the Pacific Coast Highway. Just inland on Del Obispo Street or I-5 is the town of **San Juan Capistrano**, home of the famous mission founded by Father Junipero Serra in 1776. The mission is located at what is now the corner of Ortega Highway and Camino Capistrano.

Father Serra's mission is a tourist magnet which attracts about 300,000 visitors annually. Work was recently finished on the Catholic congregation's replica of the **Old Stone Church**, the mission sanctuary destroyed in an 1812 earthquake. The church is built in the shape of a Latin cross with seven domes. At the center of this cross rises a giant dome housing a chandelier. It is protected against any future tremors by a steel frame and 40- to 50-foot (12- to 15-meter) pilings driven into the earth.

No one knows for sure what effect all

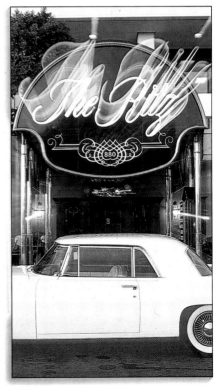

of this is having on the animal migration of swallows. The mission's gardens are particularly crowded every March 19, St Joseph's Day, when – according to a legend – the swallows return from their winter homes in Argentina to nest at the mission. Of late, pigeons have been more commonly sighted than swallows.

The decline in the swallow population has been blamed on changes in the environment. Orange groves, where insects breed, have been uprooted for development and mud flats, which provide building material for the birds, have been covered with grass. One member of a San Juan Capistrano farming family recalls having seen more than 2,000 swallows fly past his home. Now it its not uncommon to hear that March 19 is the day the tourists – but not the swallows – return to San Juan Capistrano. Still, the occasion is great fun, with *mariachi* music, a parade and other festivities. Business is especially brisk at shops which display scarfs, teacups, glass bells and other other knickknacks bearing likenesses of swallows.

Laguna and Newport: From Capistrano, the Pacific Coast Highway continues north past Three Arch Bay and South Laguna to **Laguna Beach**, known for its artists' colony, burgeoning gay population and landslides. In Laguna Beach, a person can get lazy: eat a croissant, sip cappuccino, catch some sunshine, and people-watch from a sea-facing bench along the promenade. More active types can dive through the air playing beach volleyball, wade into the water, wander through such art galleries as the **Vorpal** and the **Laguna Beach Museum of Art** (307 Cliff Drive), window-shop at the stylish boutiques, or eat dinner at a restaurant serving Mexican seafood or Hawaiian-style barbecued ribs.

Bluffs overlook the Pacific Ocean north of Laguna Beach. On one bluff, a stable rents horses for rides along the beach. There's a beautiful sandy beach in **Corona del Mar**. Nearby are caves and tidepools to attract the explorer. The town of Corona del Mar, actually a part of **Newport Beach**, has a shopping

Two visions of San Juan Capistrano Mission: left, Father Serra points the way; and right, tourists explore corridors of history.

area along the Pacific Coast Highway with gourmet restaurants, singles' saloons and clothing shops, including several selling the wealthy's high-fashion hand-me-downs.

Seaward, Newport Beach has everything a sailor could ask, no matter how big or small the wad in this wallet. On **Lido** and **Linda isles**, some homes come equipped with docks for several yachts. (The late John Wayne lived in one of them.) And there are places where the low-cost sailor can push his inflatable kayak into **Lower Newport Bay** for a brisk respite from city life.

To go to **Balboa Peninsula**, visitors can turn south from Pacific Coast Highway to Newport or Balboa boulevards, or – more romantically – take the short ferry ride from **Balboa Island**, which can be reached from the Pacific Coast Highway by taking Jamboree Road south.

Like Laguna Beach, Corona del Mar and (to the north) Seal Beach, Balboa Island and the areas around the Balboa and Newport piers are great for indulging in chocolate-chip cookies, fruit drinks and ice cream. One way to work off a few of those calories is to rent roller skates and wheel down the cement walkway connecting the two piers. Skaters should be prepared, however, for the grating of their wheels on sand blown into their path.

At the base of **Newport Pier** is the weathered outdoor plywood market of the country's only dory fleet. More than a dozen boats go out to sea at dawn each day and bring back fresh rock cod, bonito, mackerel and sea trout.

Harbor tours leave Balboa Pavilion and take their passengers out to the breakwater, past the island homes of movie stars and other rich folks.

North on Pacific Coast Highway from Newport Beach and its components is **Huntington Beach**, the surfing capital of the Orange Coast and possibly all of California. Like **Seal Beach** to the north, Huntington Beach has a pier and the usual collection of grizzled fishermen flanked by nubile teenaged girls showing off the latest in swimwear.

218

CALFORNIA'S FIRST CITY: SAN DIEGO

"San Diego," the *Wall Street Journal* once observed, "is so laid back it sometimes seems comatose."

Untrue? Not necessarily. Unfair? Definitely.

The writer should have known better. San Diegans work hard at what they do best: enjoying themselves and their coastal city. And if the posture they assume in pursuit of enjoyment seems laid back, well, a true San Diegan probably wouldn't deny it.

But comatose is hardly the word to describe the changes that have occurred in the past few years in California's second largest city. There's a pleasing new skyline and lifestyle downtown, the arts are flourishing and the population (now about 1,060,000) is climbing at a rate of about 42,000 a year. It is estimated that the population of San Diego County may reach 3.5 million by the year 2020. With northward expansion checked by Camp Pendleton Marine Base at the Orange County line, and southward growth stunted by the Mexican border, the only real room for affordable development is to the mountainous east.

So newcomers and long-time residents alike are making the most of their urban spaces. Cool sea breezes help scrub the sky clean of pollution and make for short-sleeve weather most of the year. San Diego is a nice place to visit, and an even nicer place to live. The Convention and Visitors Bureau's trademark slogan seems to invite further arrivals: "San Diego feels good all over." But a popular bumper sticker summarizes the opinion of many other San Diegans toward their crowded future: "Welcome to San Diego. Now go home."

With the diverse and pleasing mix of activities that the city offers – ranging from cosmopolitan to, well, laid back – San Diego will find it hard to keep visitors away.

Historic Presidio Hill: California began in San Diego. Here, on July 16, 1769, Father Junípero Serra conducted a solemn mass dedicating California's first mission "to the glory of God". Father Serra, who subsequently moved north from San Diego to found California's famed mission chain, then dedicated the state's first military settlement, which surrounded and protected **Mission San Diego de Alcala**. This all took place on **Presidio Hill**, earning it the seldom heard nickname, "The Plymouth Rock of the West Coast".

Today, Presidio Hill is flanked by Interstates 5 and 8 to the west and north, and even though the freeways' roar is omnipresent, a hike or drive up is worth the effort. From Taylor Street east of Old Town, a short, curving road marked **Presidio Hill Observation Point** turns off just before the I-8 on-ramp. At the top of this road is a rarely visited city park consisting of a steep slope sometimes frequented by grass skiers (who have tractor-type treads on the bottoms of their skis).

Tombstones and whales: Probably the best place to get a complete look at San Diego is from the southern tip of **Point**

Preceding pages: San Diego's burgeoning downtown. Left, San Diego Bay and Shelter Island yacht harbor. Right, Mission San Diego de Alcala.

Loma. The drive on Cabrillo Memorial Highway leads through an expensive neighborhood with some fine ocean and city views. The scenery changes abruptly at the gate to the US Navy's **Fort Rosecrans Military Reservation**, home to a variety of military facilities including eerily beautiful Fort Rosecrans National Cemetery. The neat white markers marching down to the Navy station below are mute testimony to San Diego's deep military roots. The road ends at **Cabrillo National Monument**, named for Juan Rodriguez Cabrillo, the Portuguese explorer who discovered the point and upper California itself on September 28, 1542. The visitors' center has displays explaining the city's discovery; daily programs about the monument itself are also presented.

A short stroll south is **San Diego Lighthouse**, first illuminated in 1853. Often obscured by fog, it was replaced in 1895 by the Coast Guard lighthouse at the ocean's edge. There's also an observation point for watching the California gray whales on their southern migration from the Bering Sea to the warm waters of Scammon's Lagoon and Magdalena Bay in Baja California. From late December to early March, the behemoths are plainly visible from most of San Diego's coast. Numerous charters and private boats will shuttle adventurers out.

Heading back toward the city on Cabrillo Highway, a left turn on aptly named Hill Street leads into **Ocean Beach**, one of the city's oldest beach communities. Its reputation as a haven for hippie hold-outs is not undeserved; long-haired males and flowers-in-her-hair females are abundant in the flatlands near the beach and municipal fishing pier.

Sunset Cliffs Boulevard leads north to **Sea World**, where visitors come nose-to-dorsal fin with a happy clan of killer whales, dolphins, porpoises and other marine life from around the world. The brilliant new Penguin Encounter has quickly become the park's most popular attraction, but Shamu the whale, sharks and walruses still pack 'em in for a

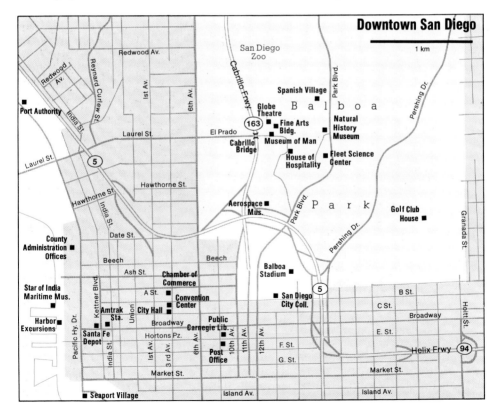

Downtown San Diego

round of daily performances that would tire a vaudevillian. There are ample interpretative exhibits to satisfy those who prefer aquarium-type settings.

"**Ducking around the bay**": North of Sea World on Ingraham Street is **Vacation Village**, a resort on carefully named Vacation Isle. The secluded village typifies just about everything the resort-goer seeks in San Diego: soft white beaches, lily-filled ponds, an immense heated swimming pool, rental sailboats and bicycles, plus fine dining. At the center of all this bliss is an observation tower that offers another excellent view of the city's coastline. For closer looks at 4,600-acre (1,860-hectare) Mission Bay without getting wet, Duck Tours' amphibious landing craft pick visitors up at land-locked hotels for guided tours. The tours have become the fashionable way to "duck around the bay".

Across Vacation Isle are **Mission Beach** and **Pacific Beach**, two of the most popular areas with out-of-towners and locals alike. Residents make a point of stating whether they're from North or South Mission. Homes in the latter are more exclusive because the neighborhood ends at Mission Bay's entrance channel, a wonderful place to watch boats or go fishing from the jetties. South Mission has **The Pennant** and **The Beachcomber**, side-by-side bars that are the ultimate San Diego beach hangouts – especially on Sunday afternoons, when it is presumed most of the tourists have headed back to the inland valleys.

Pacific beach is a tidy community nestled between the coast, Mission Bay and La Jolla. The ocean beach itself extends about 4 miles (6½ km), but is barely visible on nice summer days when swarms of glistening bodies crowd the sand. The bay has miles of less-crowded beaches, but no waves except the wake from ski boats. Activities tend to center on the beach by **Crystal Pier** and in the area along Mission Boulevard and up Garnet Avenue, where the locals shop, dine and congregate.

Standard garb for most of the year in this locality is OP shorts, Hawaiian shirt

Killer whales take a bow at Sea World.

(the gaudier the better), strapped-on sunglasses and stylish rubber sandals which are referred to simply as "zoris". A deep-toned suntan is *de rigeur* of course. An optional extra might include Walkman-type headphones for tuning things out when jogging along the beach, bike-riding or just browsing in the bookstores.

Mission Boulevard continues north toward **La Jolla**. Mystery writer Raymond Chandler, who lived there, claimed the community was "a nice place for old people and their parents". La Jolla does have its fair share of senior citizens, but their numbers are at least equalled by the *nouveau riche* who can be observed running errands on their mopeds or in their Mercedes and always in their designer shirts.

La Jolla, "The Jewel": La Jolla means "The Jewel" in Spanish, and the name's literal and geographical meanings both apply. The town's scenic coastal edge meanders from **Tourmaline Surfing Beach** on the south to **Torrey Pines State Beach** on the north. In between are a number of easily accessible ocean-view sites across from homes that grow more gorgeous as one heads north up La Jolla Boulevard. **Bird Rock** is an interesting tidepool area at the end of a street with the same name. **Windansea**, at the end of Rosemont Street, is the locals' beach immortalized by Tom Wolfe in *The Pumphouse Gang*.

La Jolla Boulevard ends at Coast Boulevard, which rims central La Jolla's string of grassy beach parks, each with its own blend of rocky bluffs, sand, palms, and local color. **La Jolla Caves**, at the east end of Coast, are a snorkeler's haven and home of a local rite of passage. While snorkelers dart in and out of the ocean caves, teenagers above wait for waves to surge in, then take running leaps between the rock formations 20 feet (6½ meters) below.

Coast Boulevard climbs back up to **Prospect Street**, where La Jollans and visitors stroll, shop and dine. There are fine jewelry stores, boutiques, art galleries, restaurants, bars and hotels, including the elegant pink **La Valencia**. La

A tender moment at the San Diego Zoo.

Jolla extends several blocks southward in this same vein, with high-class department stores, gourmet food and antiques stores. For those with time to explore, the **La Jolla Museum of Contemporary Art** always has a well-publicized exhibit or two.

Treats for body and mind: Prospect proceeds north to Torrey Pines Boulevard and **La Jolla Shores**, one of the prettiest beach areas in San Diego. A fair hike to the north is notorious **Black's Beach**, once a legal nude beach ("swimsuit-optional" is what the city called it) in an isolated area with high cliffs and a narrow shoreline. Numerous problems, including gaggles of gawkers, made the city rescind its blessing several years ago, but the all-over-tan bunch still makes its pilgrimages.

The past in the present: A visit to **Old Town** often satisfies the traveler's desire for a trip south of the border. Much of the neighborhood falls within **Old Town State Historic Park**, a fairly accurate depiction of a mission-era Mexican plaza with early American influence. The park proper is off-limits to vehicular traffic. It includes such sites as the small room where the first edition of *The San Diego Union* was printed; **Whaley House Museum**, the oldest brick structure in San Diego; and **Casa de Estudillo**, a sprawling adobe residence that housed the original commander of the Presidio.

The tourist centerpiece of Old Town is **Bazaar Del Mundo**, another adobe rescued from neglect and converted into a lush complex of high-quality shops and restaurants.

San Diegans have always been proud of **Balboa Park**, a 1,400-acre (566-hectare) recreational and cultural oasis that grows more urbane as the city blossoms. On weekends, the park is an ever-changing wonderland of picnickers, roller skaters, families, art lovers, jugglers, mimes and Hare Krishnas – some seeking attention, most shying away from it. The **El Prado** and **House of Hospitality** areas, right in the center of things, are a good place to get acquainted with the park and its gardens.

The park houses several excellent museums, including the **Aerospace Museum**, one of the most extensive of its kind in the nation; the **Natural History Museum**; **Timken Art Gallery**, featuring European old masters and 19th-century American paintings; the **San Diego Museum of Art**; the **Reuben H. Fleet Space Theater and Science Center**, home of a spectacular multimedia Omnitheater and the largest planetarium in the United States; and the **Museum of Man**, which emphasizes the Western Americas.

Most of the park's facilities are in Spanish Moorish-style buildings created for the Panama-California Exposition of 1915–16 and the California-Pacific International Exposition of 1935–36. One of the most interesting of the latter is **Spanish Village**, where dozens of artists' studios ring a colorful, fading courtyard.

The park is home of the city's most visited attraction, the internationally famous **San Diego Zoo**. Nearly 3,500 representatives of 760 species reside within this 100-acre (40-hectare) tropi-

cal garden. Most are in barless, moated enclosures in an attempt to recreate as much as possible the animals' natural homes in the wild. In addition to the usual assortment of elephants, lions, tigers, giraffes and bears, the zoo has more koalas – 30-plus at last count – than any other zoo in America. The cuddly creatures have become the institution's unofficial mascot.

A good way to get to San Diego's new downtown is through its old downtown. Drivers headed southeast on Harbor Drive can turn left at Fifth Avenue and enter **The Gaslamp Quarter**. The brick-paved sidewalks, turn-of-the-century architecture, Victorian benches and gaslight-style street lamps are here to bring new life to the city's first true commercial district. This long-neglected neighborhood has undergone the transformation that occurs in many central cities: young, upwardly mobile artists, entrepreneurs and urbanites have moved in and renovated. City incentives helped smooth the way, along with The Gaslamp's designation as a historic district. A walk along Fifth Avenue takes in the **Stingaree Building**, site of a historic brothel raided early this century in a futile effort to clean up downtown; the gilded **Louis Bank of Commerce Building**, with twin crow's nest towers that once reigned as downtown's highest points; and the **Jewelers' Exchange Building**, headquarters for the city's wholesale jewelry market.

There's still a curious mixture of porno shops, dingy bars and transient hotels left over from the neighborhood's heyday as a playground for sailors on leave. All of that will probably remain even though the city's most ambitious inner-city project, **Horton Plaza** regional shopping center, was recently built between The Gaslamp and downtown's new highrises. Completed in the spring of 1985, the plaza, named for San Diego visionary and developer Alonso Horton, features a deluxe hotel, major department stores, a theater and more in a sophisticated ensemble that is beginning to herald a new era in downtown living. Several new housing complexes have already proved popular, and their number should grow as San Diegans discover the joys of living two feet from work.

Perhaps the best symbol of the new movement downtown is the **San Diego Trolley**, whose bright red cars whisk thousands of commuters daily between the **Santa Fe Depot** and 17 other stations south to the international border. The light-rail system has proved so successful in its first two years of operation that an eastern extension is on the drawing board.

Downtown also has its own version of Off-Broadway. Several eminently professional and affordable small theaters offer a wide scope of styles and subject matter. These include the **Gaslamp Quarter Theater** in that neighborhood, the intimate **Bowery** in the basement of an old apartment hotel and **San Diego Repertory Theater** in what was once a church. Many of the actors and actresses have performed at the Old Globe and other major venues and represent an important ingredient in the reputation for professionalism that these theaters enjoy. The venues are popular among performers and theater-goers alike. San Diego is very rapidly becoming a major American city in terms of its theater presentations.

Coronado and a view across the bay: A pleasant way to wind up a San Diego visit is to travel to **Coronado**, an island-like community across the bay from downtown at the north end of the **Silver Strand Peninsula**. The ferry used to be the fastest way to get to Coronado. But it was replaced in 1964 by the **Coronado Bay Bridge**, a graceful 2.2-mile (3.5-km) archway. A return trip across this span yields a 360-degree look at the bay and city to the north, Point Loma and the coast to the west, downtown Golden Hill to the east, and Mexican border communities to the south. **North Island** at Coronado's western city limit is home of a massive naval air station, the noise of which is among the few negatives of Coronado life. The town is a handsome blend of cottages, custom homes, beach houses, condos and stately Victorians laid out in neat streets leading to the bay on one side and the Pacific on the other.

The historic Hotel Del Coronado.

225

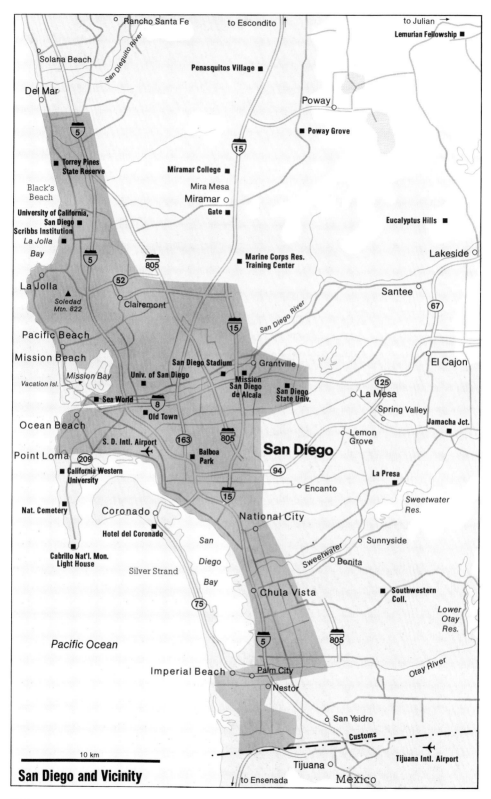

San Diego and Vicinity

10 km

to Escondito

to Julian →

Lemurian Fellowship ■

Rancho Santa Fe

Solana Beach

Del Mar

Penasquitos Village ■

Poway

Poway Grove ■

Torrey Pines State Reserve ■

Black's Beach

Miramar College ■

Mira Mesa

Miramar ○

Gate ■

Eucalyptus Hills ■

University of California, San Diego ■

Scribbs Institution ■

La Jolla Bay

Marine Corps Res. Training Center

Lakeside ○

La Jolla ▲

Soledad Mtn. 822

Clairemont

Santee

Pacific Beach

San Diego River

El Cajon

Mission Beach

Vacation Isl.

Mission Bay

Univ. of San Diego

San Diego Stadium

Grantville

Mission San Diego de Alcala

San Diego State Univ.

La Mesa ○

Spring Valley

Sea World ■

Old Town

Jamacha Jct. ■

Ocean Beach

S. D. Intl. Airport

Balboa Park ■

San Diego

Lemon Grove

Point Loma

California Western University ■

209

94

La Presa ■

Encanto ○

Sweetwater Res.

Nat. Cemetery ■

Coronado ○

National City

Hotel del Coronado ■

San Diego Bay

Sweetwater

Sunnyside ○

Cabrillo Nat'l. Mon. Light House ■

Silver Strand

Bonita ○

Chula Vista ○

Southwestern Coll. ■

Lower Otay Res.

Pacific Ocean

75

Otay River

Imperial Beach ○

Palm City ○

Nestor ○

San Ysidro ○

Customs

Tijuana Intl. Airport

Tijuana ○

Mexico

to Ensenada

226

SAN DIEGO – THE COUNTY

San Diego County is a microcosm of the Golden State – its western boundary is totally ocean, its southern border is totally Mexico, and the east and north are laced with a combination of mountains and desert.

Stretching inland some 110 miles (176 km) at its widest point, and northward 65 miles (104 km) from Mexico, San Diego County represents a diverse lifestyle, climate and landscape. And its 2 million-plus people are a cross section of California ethnic groups.

The North Coast: Stretching north of San Diego city along the coast are a string of Pacific Coast communities whose identities are much more interesting than the exit signs on Interstate 5 would indicate.

The first of these coastal towns beyond La Jolla is **Del Mar**, a beautiful spot with a sweeping hillside view of the Pacific. Site of the **Southern California Exposition** and national horse show over two weeks in June and July, and home of the **Del Mar Thoroughbred Club** racetrack, it is truly a community where "the turf meets the surf".

Actor Pat O'Brien and the late singer Bing Crosby rescued the struggling Del Mar racetrack in the early 1930s, pumping a huge amount of money into the facility and turning it into one of America's most popular racing circuit venues. The season begins in July, a week after the big fair (which draws 700,000 people annually) has ended, and runs until mid-September.

On the east side of I-5, inland some 5 miles (8 km), is the crown of North Coast communities – **Rancho Santa Fe**. Here is where the affluent of San Diego County's affluent live. Considered a country-style Beverly Hills, Rancho Santa Fe first became a popular retreat for many of Hollywood's celebrities in the late '20s when actor Douglas Fairbanks and his wife, actress Mary Pickford, built their majestic **Fairbanks Ranch**. The ranch was the site of the 1984 Olympic equestrian events. Many other stars followed the Fairbanks to Rancho Santa Fe over the years, building plush homes in the hills (which are covered by a thick growth of native trees). Such stars as Victor Mature, Robert Young and Patti Page make their homes today in Rancho Santa Fe.

Valley Center, a community to the north of Escondido on Road S6, is the gateway to massive **Palomar Mountain**. Rising 6,100 feet (1,859 meters) above sea level and stretching some 20 miles (32 km) in length, Palomar is the home of the Western world's largest reflecting telescope. The 200-inch Hale Telescope is within the **Mount Palomar Observatory**, owned and operated by the California Institute of Technology. It is world-famous for its many celestial discoveries of the past three decades. Open for limited tours and visitation daily, the observatory includes the **Greenway Museum** with photographs of important sightings.

West of Palomar, on State 76 toward Oceanside, is the community of **Pala**. This village of 500 people proudly

The world-famous Mount Palomar Observatory.

maintains its **Mission San Antonio de Pala**, an *asistancia* (extension mission) built in 1810. It is of special interest as the only California mission still serving Indians – it is on the **Pala Indian Reservation**. The Corpus Christi Festival, featuring an open-air mass, dances and games, has been held here the first Sunday of June since 1816.

East County: East on I-8 from San Diego's Mission Valley, travelers climb a long hill past **San Diego State University** and enter the city of **La Mesa**, population 52,000. Often called "the Jewel of the Hills", La Mesa is home for many of San Diego's more affluent families. From the top of **Mount Helix**, reached by car via Fuerte Drive off I-8, there is a spectacular view.

Present-day historical points of interest include the old **McKinney House**, home of the city historical society. Built in 1908, it was first the home of a Methodist minister and later served as the city's first library.

The fully-restored passenger train that serviced this region in the 1920s is featured in the **Pacific Southwest Railway Museum** at the La Mesa Depot on Nebo Drive. This "Cannonball" train still operates excursion runs on special occasions.

On State 94 is the county's border crossing at Tecate. The California side of this community is nothing more than a small shopping center and a post office, but the Mexican side is a thriving community of 5,000 and a rather popular brewery named for the town.

Those traveling into Baja California Norte from San Diego County who want to avoid the crowded Tijuana border crossing will be pleased to know there is never a crowd in Tecate. In fact, there is seldom more than one Customs agent on duty, and he closes the border each night at 11, earlier if there's no traffic.

The South Bay: The South Bay region of San Diego County is a string of communities surrounding the lower end of San Diego Bay. National City, Chula Vista, Palm City, San Ysidro, Imperial Beach and Coronado make up these suburbs of greater San Diego.

National City and Chula Vista have growing commercial districts which depend heavily on Mexican shoppers coming across the border. The first shopping center ever built in America was the **South Bay Plaza** on National Avenue in **National City**. Opened in 1953, the center was the prototype which changed the face of American merchandising and shopping habits. National City has much of its past preserved in **Granger Hall**, which capsulizes the history of the South Bay.

San Ysidro, gateway to Mexico, is a booming community where it is of great benefit to be able to speak both English and Spanish. It is the busiest international border crossing in the world: some 40 million people pass in and out of the US and Mexico here annually.

Imperial Beach, population 23,000, has beaches that lead right to the Tijuana Bullring to the south and the historic Hotel Del Coronado to the north. It is also fast becoming home to the well-heeled of Los Angeles and Orange County who are buying up as much beach and adjacent property as possible.

Left, a Mexican resident of San Diego's South Bay. **Right**, a sunset flight over Black's Beach at Torrey Pines Hang Glider Park.

Tijuana And Northern Baja

Baja California is most Americans' introduction to Mexico. To some, it's paradise. To others, it's the pits. The truth, of course, lies somewhere between the tourist brochure puffery and years of girl-and-donkey-show stories.

The people of this region are as rich and poor, as warm and gracious, as enterprising and nationalistic as their *compadres* farther south of the border. But by its very location, Northern Baja (as everyone on both sides of the border tends to call it) is a world unto itself.

US citizens don't even need a passport if they're visiting for less than 72 hours or plan to go beyond the State Highway 1 checkpoint below Ensenada. If so, they must pick up a tourist visa in San Diego from any travel agent, the Mexican Consulate General, the Mexico Government Tourism Office or the Automobile Club of Southern California. Proof of nationality must accompany the visa. Drivers should carry some daily auto insurance, obtainable at any of the dozens of drive-throughs just north of the border. US insurance is *not* valid in Mexico.

Eighteen miles (29 km) south of downtown San Diego, Interstates 5 and 805 converge at the decidedly funkier Mexican side of the **International Border Crossing**. Here, agents casually wave drivers past their barren inspection booths. Straight ahead you will find the refurbished, tourist-oriented part of downtown **Tijuana** (say "tee-wanna").

On **Avenida Revolución**, Tijuana's renovated main drag, the visitor can still hop on a burro painted like a zebra, don a *sombrero* with "Drunk Again" scrawled on the brim, and pay a street photographer to make an instant postcard of the whole embarrassing scene.

There are enough bars and 50-cent margaritas to hang a person head-over-heels for the rest of his life. There are a seemingly endless number of *mariachi* bands, discos and night clubs. It's not necessary to go looking for them; they make their presence known soon enough.

But for those who prefer loftier forms of stimulation, a superb way to learn about Mexico's heritage can be found less than a half-mile from the border. The new **Tijuana Cultural Center** on Avenida Paseo de los Heroes is a block of national pride in the heart of the city's redevelopment district. The museum in this futuristic-looking complex houses an outstanding collection of folk art, relics, handicrafts and artifact replicas. All are displayed on both sides of a 35-foot (11-meter) wide, mile-long indoor ramp.

Next door is another eye-popper, the 85-foot (26-meter) high **Omnitheater**. Within the giant dome is presented a super-wide-angle film tour of Mexico's historical and cultural sites.

Across the street is Tijuana's closest rival to the suburban shopping malls found a few miles north. **Plaza Rio Tijuana**, the largest shopping center in northwestern Mexico, will gladden visitors' hearts and possibly empty their wallets. Baja California is a free port, so most goods cost less than in San Diego.

Tijuana craftsman adds colourful touches to pottery in his shop.

But shoppers should remember that US Customs demands receipts for any daily purchases exceeding $400 per person.

Avenida Revolución and its side streets offer somewhat less cosmopolitan merchandise, although some of the finest clothing and jewelry shops are mixed among the *sarapes* and sandals. Mexican-made goods are priced in pesos, imported goods in US dollars. If no price is posted, bargaining wins the prize.

Just southwest of Tijuana is the beach and the **Bullring-by-the-Sea**, newer and sturdier but far less popular than the rickety old bullring downtown. Bullfight season is May to September, with half the season held at each ring.

There are two routes south from Tijuana. The *Cuota* toll road, at $2.40 for a round-trip to Ensenada, includes some fine ocean scenery. It is recommended over the *Libre* free road, which parallels the *Cuota* as far as **Rosarito** (13 miles/20 km from Tijuana), then dips inland.

Rosarito is a beach town whose popularity is growing rapidly. It is no Mexican Riviera, but a recent proliferation of time-share resorts has pumped new life into the town.

A visit to the **Rosarito Beach Hotel** is obligatory. Guests of the 60-year-old former gambling palace have included Lana Turner, Mickey Rooney, Prince Ali Khan and other celebrities and heads of state. The hotel features glorious indoor murals by Matias Santoyo and a large swimming pool and bar area above the clean, wide beach.

Ensenada is another 30 miles (48 km) south, but worth the drive on the toll road. At the **El Mirador** exit, there is a bluff-top view of **Bahia de Todos Santos**, home of Ensenada's deep-sea charter fleet, naval drydock and various pleasure craft including the *S.S. Azure Seas* cruise liner from Los Angeles.

A few blocks from the bay is the main tourist shopping zone along **Avenida Lopez Mateos**. Merchants on the avenue display an astounding assortment of traditional Mexican crafts, from sandals, sombreros and leather jackets to onyx chess sets, guitars and silverware. But prices are better in the "nontourist" part of town off **Avenida Ruiz** a few blocks away.

No visit to Ensenada is complete without a stop at **Hussong's**, one of the oldest continually operating bars on the West Coast. Established in 1892, the wooden-frame cantina on Avenida Ruiz just east of Avenida Mateos is usually overflowing with *gringos* yukking it up and slurping down *cervezas* (beers) at record rates.

The return to California can be a bit more tense than the entry into Mexico. At the International Border Crossing, polished US officers come out of their computerized hutches to make drivers sweat about the cigarettes in the trunk as if they were bricks of Acapulco Gold. The constant buzzing of a US Border Patrol helicopter over nearby **Deadman's Gulch**, a notorious port of entry for illegal aliens, does little to soothe one's nerves. During busy American holiday periods, such as Independence Day (July 4) and Labor Day (early September), waits of up to two hours are not uncommon.

Traditional clothing and leather goods are only some of the many products sold in Tijuana's ubiquitous bazaars.

SANTA CATALINA ISLAND

It shouldn't really be there. Nature, having already endowed Southern California with enough scenic splendor and climatic favor, needn't have added the proverbial frosting on the cake by providing an island paradise as well.

Yet, there lies **Santa Catalina Island**, 26 miles (42 km) off the coast of Los Angeles. This 8-by-21 mile (13-by-33 km) piece of real estate lacks only television's tiny Tattoo to fulfill the traveler's postcard-perfect "Fantasy Island". A peaceful, unhurried life continues here, buffered by blue skies and warm breezes. Catalina exists serene and unimpressed with civilization, content to ignore progress in favor of conserving a pace which recalls simpler times.

Although it *is* possible to swim to Catalina – contests have occasionally been held with mixed success – easier access may be gained by air or sea from San Pedro, Long Beach or Newport Beach. Air travelers may spend the short flight gazing upon migrating gray whales below, while the seafarer's two-hour pilgrimage is sweetened with an arm's length view of the porpoises which seem to escort voyagers toward Atlantis.

While air travel is quicker, sailing is the preferred way to go. The lapping waves provide the most appropriate introduction to the gentle rhythm of California's only island resort. Breeching the early morning haze off the coast, one wonders if he hasn't been caught in some space warp and transported somehow to the French Riviera, circa 1930. When entering the harbor at **Avalon**, Catalina's only town, the narrow beaches, private yachts and huge circular casino, which marks the harbor's entrance, encourage this reverie.

State of nature: The natives, anything but restless, are identifiable by their tribal costume of bathing suits, T-shirts and sandals. All sport disquietingly uniform tropical tans. In contrast, visitors are adorned with cameras, hardsoled shoes and pale pink skins.

Walking along **Crescent Avenue**, Avalon's main beachfront street, the visitor notices that no glass-and-chrome skyscrapers block the sun from the 2,000 permanent residents. Victorian hotels retain the charm employed in their construction 60 years ago, and side streets are sized for horse-and-buggies, not Oldsmobiles. Elderly residents occupy the plentiful benches which dot the streets.

Conversations are uninterrupted by blaring portable stereos. They are prohibited from the beaches by city ordinance. Stepping slowly across the street to pick up a paper or exchange gossip with a neighbor, citizens don't bother to look both ways: cars are prohibited in most of Avalon. In fact, automobiles are rare – their usage limited to islanders, 125 of whom are on a waiting list. Traffic lights, "Don't Walk" signs, freeway jams and parking jousts have all been left on the mainland.

Avalon is virtually a pedestrian's dream, a small village where nearly all points of interest are accessible by foot.

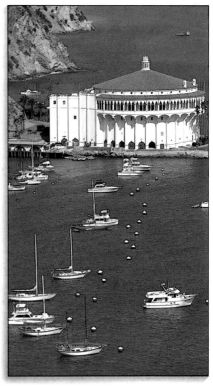

Left, a ketch from Newport Beach sails toward a weekend visit to Santa Catalina Island's Avalon Bay, **right**, dominated by its landmark Casino.

Visitors may stroll through the many souvenir and clothing shops along Crescent Avenue (or as it's more commonly called, "Front Street"). Fresh seafood is the ticket at the many patio restaurants which face the sea. There are no McDonald's or Burger Kings here; nothing is fast, particularly the food service.

Beer and Polynesian drinks are favored beverages, consumed most enthusiastically by the natives. Jaded, perhaps, by the slow pace of this island Shangri-La, drinking has become a pastime cultivated by islanders. The analogy to the mythical land of *Lost Horizon* is further supported by the permanent exodus of island-born as soon as they reach college age, abandoning Paradise in search of more worldly experiences. A real generation gap exists between Catalina's children and elderly.

Hotels, tours and the Catalina wilderness: Visitors planning to stay awhile should make hotel reservations six months in advance. Occupancy soars to 10,000 or more from Easter to Labor Day. Hous-

ing, even for residents, is scarce – so scarce that government-financed developments had to be built to accommodate island employees who could not otherwise find shelter. Construction on Catalina is severely restricted by the Santa Catalina Island Conservancy which owns 86 percent of the island. Its goal of preserving Catalina in its natural state is viewed with mixed emotions by those who live in one-room dwellings.

There are about 40 hotels around the island, the most intriguing of which is the **Zane Grey Pueblo**. Perched on a hillside, the former home of the Western novelist offers rooms named after his works and provides a spectacular and romantic evening view of Avalon Bay. (Information on all Santa Catalina hotels can be obtained by telephoning 213-510-1520.)

The day-tripper is best left to his or her own devices in exploring Catalina. Tours which visit all parts of the island and its waters are available, but so are free guides to everything worth seeing. One big attraction is a glass-bottomed

Bison graze in Catalina's undeveloped interior.

boat cruise to look at the ocean floor.

It's best on Catalina to take matters into one's own hands – or flippers, as the case may be. The clear azure waters of Avalon Bay yield rich kelp beds with aquatic life forms not often seen elsewhere. Skin divers can rent the necessary equipment (license required for scuba) and explore the northwest corner of **Crescent Bay** with its mysterious shipwrecks.

The visitor can see all the attractions of Avalon in about half a day. But the *real* Catalina lies in the island's interior, a virtual pristine wilderness. Camping and hiking in this rugged land are permitted, and an overnight at **Little Harbor**, **Two Harbors** or the mountainous **Blackjack Campsite** is recommended. The less energetic can take a half-day motor tour for $11.50.

The isolation of the Blackjack wilderness is broken only by a pay telephone, available for emergencies. What emergencies? Some campers have awakened to find a wild boar devouring their breakfast. Others have had surprise tête-à-têtes with 1,500-lbs (680-kg) buffalo foraging in the brush. Such encounters do make one pause and reflect.

One might well wonder just what buffaloes are doing on Santa Catalina Island. Fourteen of the woolly beasts were brought to Catalina for co-starring roles in *The Vanishing American*, filmed here in 1924. Encouraged by the romantic nature of the island, the creatures have since multiplied their numbers to more than 400. The sight of these gargantuan beasts celebrating the rites of spring is something not easily forgotten.

After a trip to the island's interior, Avalon seems especially charming after sundown. Its harbor is gaily lit in the manner of a Mediterranean seaport. Couples stroll hand-in-hand along the shore and watch flying fishes in the starlit sea.

Meanwhile, college students drink to each others' health at **Big Mike's Tavern**. If the deliberate and preserved peacefulness of Catalina has any effect, they may live to be a hundred.

A peaceful anchorage at Little Harbor on Catalina's windward side.

CENTRAL COAST: A QUIET CHARM

Unrushed, contemplative, friendly: these are adjectives frequently used to describe the stretch of California coastline from Ventura north to San Simeon.

Concentrated within this coastal region of about 200 miles (320 km) are the restored remnants of a significant chapter in California's historical development: the missions. Five of the state's 21 missions, founded by Franciscan *padres* from Spain, are located along the Central Coast. Their locations were neither mistake nor coincidence. The priests were creating a chain linking the state from San Diego to Sonoma, and they chose prime sites with good water sources, fertile farm and pasture lands, pleasant surroundings, an occasional harbor, and always a supply of Indians who could provide farm labor once they became Christians.

The mission heritage has not been forgotten elsewhere in California, but the Central Coast has woven that era more tightly into its modern fabric than other areas. US 101 parallels the famous **El Camino Real**, the King's Road, once a narrow Indian trail, then widened to a rutty road for the *padres*. Today it is a smooth, modern thoroughfare. Traveling up the coast along El Camino Real, the visitor becomes a modern missionary rediscovering the state.

San Buenaventura: As if to guarantee that the historical connection won't be forgotten, El Camino Real is frequently marked by mission-type bells hung along the roadway. One of the first is at the southern gateway to the town of **Ventura**. At this point, US 101 has finally reached the ocean after crossing a rather dull stretch of overdeveloped smoggy land.

Ventura is the site of the **San Buenaventura Mission**, the last mission founded under the leadership of Father Junípero Serra. The mission which once maintained extensive grazing land and fabulous gardens, now lies at the edge of an area called **Old San Buenaventura**. Its quaint shops are reminiscent of pioneering days. Close to the mission are modern buildings created in mission-style architecture, and nearby are a historical museum and an excavation project. Prehistoric Indian artifacts have been uncovered here, as well as the foundations of five early buildings.

The town is also the embarkation point for cruises to the nearby Channel Islands and has an extensive marina.

East of Ventura, there are dramatic mountain vistas along State Highway 33. The first important stop on this route is the small town of **Ojai** (say "oh-hi"), nestled among the hills.

Glossed horizon: Ojai has managed a rare, eccentric mix of people and interests. Some residents are wealthy country-club types who relish Ojai's renowned classical music festival in June and its famous spring tennis tournament. Others are "health nuts" drawn to the area for the healing powers attributed to its several hot springs; or philosophers who have established numerous esoteric institutes among the oak trees of

Preceding pages: a windswept view of Morro Rock. **Left,** the emblem of El Camino Real.

this community of 7,000. Artists are drawn to Ojai's quiet rural atmosphere and scenic beauty: east of town on Ojai Avenue is the vantage point from which Ronald Colman viewed Shangri-La in the movie classic *Lost Horizon*. Small farmers still maintain their land in the area around town.

Ojai's charmless business strip is surrounded by verdant groves of oranges and avocados, country clubs and golf courses, and a well-known health spa, **The Oaks**. Close by is **Lake Casitas**, site of the 1984 Olympic rowing and canoeing competitions.

What initially drew people to the area in the 1870s – besides the discovery of oil – was Eastern journalist Charles Nordhoff's glowing description of a town with mild temperatures, natural mineral baths and an outstanding climate for agriculture. Initially named Nordhoff after the newsman, the town acquired its current moniker in 1917. It supposedly meant "The Nest" to native Indians, although a Toledo, Ohio, glassmaker named E.D. Libby was responsible for

the name change. Libby also helped turn the town into a resort with Spanish architecture and an emphasis on the arts and sports.

Northeast of Ojai along State 33 is the **Wheeler's Gorge** camping area. It's the beginning of the stunning **Los Padres National Forest**, a mecca for backpackers and campers. West of Ojai, State 150 winds along some of the 60 miles (97 km) of Lake Casitas' shoreline, then through hilly orchards and back to US 101. This route is full of impressive vistas. But so is the invigorating stretch of US 101 north of Ventura that travelers miss when they take the Lake Casitas route.

Surprising Santa Barbara: As the highway enters **Santa Barbara**, there's a surprising splash of greenery – much of it borrowed from other countries and climes. As California chronicler Carey McWilliams noted, when people learned that anything would grow in Southern California, everything was planted here, most conspicuously eucalyptus and palm trees. McWilliams called the latter "an

Offshore oil rigs glow in the Santa Barbara Channel.

abomination, a blot on the landscape, hideous beyond description."

Most would disagree, especially when driving along Santa Barbara's 5 miles (8 km) of palm-lined beachfront. It is one of the most inviting ocean stretchers in the United States. At its eastern end are dozens of beach volleyball courts, across from Santa Barbara's strip of luxury hotels. To the west, the hotel rates go down a bit, but the beach continues its unmarred expanse, further brightened on weekends with art festivals along the boardwalk. At night, those twinkling lights offshore might resemble a distant shore, but they're actually oil derricks, a reminder of the millions of gallons of black goo that covered the pristine beaches in 1969's widely publicized environmental disaster.

But Santa Barbara has been lucky enough to avoid many of the misfortunes that plague other mid-sized cities. It started its existence fortuitously hemmed in by mountains on one side and a treacherous sea on the other. Because of its year-round sun and pleasant climate, it became famous as a rich man's resort by the 1890s. In fact, by the 1920s the neighboring town of **Montecito** reportedly had the largest concentration of wealth in the nation.

An earthquake nearly destroyed Santa Barbara in 1925, allowing it to be rebuilt in a uniform Spanish colonial style favoring white walls, red-tiled roofs, rounded archways and iron grillwork. The style was inspired by the 1915 San Diego Panama-California Exposition, and has remained the hallmark of the town. Santa Barbara has been cited as one of the best examples of how architecture can be regulated to the lasting benefit of a city.

Mission and museum: Located high above the town, with a view of the ocean, the **Santa Barbara Mission** is still one of the town's chief attractions. A self-guided tour includes a visit to the mission's cemetery and chapel, still in use today. About a block away is Santa Barbara's **Museum of Natural History**, where visitors can learn about the Chumash Indians.

The museum has preserved remnants of the Chumash culture – baskets, bowls, charms, beads (their monetary unit) and tools. One of the most spectacular Chumash relics, a modern recreation of their structurally remarkable wood-plant canoe, is not located in the museum, however. Reinforced by only a single crossbeam, the 20-foot (6-meter) *tomol* could carry 10 persons back and forth to the Channel Islands for fishing and trade. The canoe can be seen in the **Santa Barbara County Courthouse**, the most grandiose building in the city. Constructed in the late 1920s, it is a magnificent Spanish-Moorish castle, decorated inside with murals, mosaics, woodcarvings and tile. Filling in the square of the L-shaped building is an exquisite sunken garden shaded by tall trees.

The courthouse is just a block from State Street, the city's main thoroughfare. Although the north end of the street is filled with newer shopping centers, the southern part carries out the city's Spanish motif with many blocks of red-

Left, the Santa Barbara Wharf. Right, a rooftop view of residential Santa Barbara.

241

tiled roofs, rounded porticos, wooden balconies and adobe-like walls. The streets inspire leisurely strolls past a variety of shops and restaurants, as well as nearby historic adobes such as **Casa de la Guerra**, made famous in the book *Two Years Before the Mast*, and a classic-style **Museum of Art**. In August, the city celebrates "**Old Spanish Days**" with an outdoor breakfast in historic **El Paseo** arcade and with traditional costumes and dances.

Even away from the State Street area, there is no dearth of restaurants in Santa Barbara. This is a town that relishes good food as much as a good tan. Three of the best restaurants are plopped in an otherwise deserted cul-de-sac just across the road from the **Andrée Clark Bird Refuge**, a lagoon located a winding drive southeast from **East Beach**.

Those who leave Santa Barbara on US 101 travel along the coast, passing lemon groves, circling hawks and a number of state beaches. The first town is **Goleta**, home of the **University of California, Santa Barbara**. Known to many as a laid-back surf-and-party campus, it briefly spoiled its reputation in the turbulent 1960s when students burned down a branch of the Bank of America in neighboring **Isla Vista.**

Further along the coast are **El Capitan State Beach**, **Refugio State Beach**, a delightful cove surrounded by palms, and **Gaviota State Beach**, which sports a fishing pier.

The home of former US President Ronald Reagan, Ranch del Cielo, is located about 30 minutes north of Santa Barbara off US 101. Access to the ranch is via Refugio Road, an inland turnoff, opposite signs pointing to the state beach. Although Reagan is no longer President, visitors are still discouraged.

Pismo clams: From Santa Maria, US 101 continues inland. It rejoins the coast and State 1, near **Pismo Beach,** a resort known primarily for its clams and its sand dunes.

The Pismo clam, which ranges up the Big Sur coast as far as Monterey, has a heavy circular shell that grows to the size of a dinner plate and weighs as

much as 1½ lbs (nearly 700 g). The meat has a distinctive, sweet flavor. In the past, these clams were easy to obtain, dug from the sand with large forks at low tide. Now Pismo Beach has been seriously depleted of the thing that once made it the world's clam capital. "You get a clam these days," says one resident, "you make it a meal for three." Nonetheless, clams can still be found in unrestricted areas. If they're at least 4.5 inches (11.4 cm) in diameter, they're keepers.

Unlike the clams, Pismo's dunes are doing just fine despite years of use by all-terrain vehicles which drive merrily over the hilly piles of sand. **Pismo Beach State Park** has about 6 miles (10 km) of shoreline dunes, running south to the tiny beach community of **Oceano**. Only certain areas are open to dune buggies and other all-terrain vehicles. But any motorist may drive on the beach itself! The rest of the park includes areas for surfing, surf fishing, pier fishing and muskrat-watching.

San Luis Obispo: The next major town is **San Luis Obispo**, situated in a forested area below the **Santa Lucia Mountains**. It is less ritzy than Santa Barbara, with an inexpensive but intriguing variety of restaurants, Victorian homes and a youthful shopping area.

It's no surprise that San Luis Obispo's history began with a mission. **San Luis Obispo de Tolosa**, founded by Father Serra in 1772, was originally built out of logs and tule. The thatched roof was repeatedly torched by Indians, leading the missionaries to come up with a major innovation: fireproof roof *tiles*, a theme quickly adopted by the rest of the missions in the chain.

Morro Rock and Morro Bay: Travelers in a hurry to get to the San Francisco Bay area head north from San Luis Obispo inland on US 101. Those with more time, however, prefer State Highway 1, which clings to a magnificent coastline all the way to the Monterey Peninsula. Though this route is sometimes closed just below Big Sur due to landslides, there are few (if any) finer drives in California.

Morro Rock guards the harbor.

About 15 miles (24 km) north of San Luis Obispo on State 1, a massive rock formation juts from the ocean. This monolith, actually the last in line of nine prehistoric volcanic peaks in the area, is **Morro Rock**. The bay surrounding it, and the town that grew on its hinterland, are both called **Morro Bay.**

The 576-foot (176-meter) rock was once even larger than it is today. Earlier in the 20th century, the great monolith was used as a quarry. But in 1969 it was given national monument status. Once an island at high tide, like France's Mont-Saint-Michel, Morro Rock since the 1930s has been reachable by car at any hour. There's a small beach beside the rock.

The town of Morro Bay centers around the waterfront. At the **San Francisco Wharf** or along the **Embarcadero**, seafood lovers can eat fish to their stomachs' delight. The marine delicacies are hauled in by the town's own fishing fleet. The "Clam Taxi" ferries passengers to the bay's **Sand Spit**, a finger of sandy dunes emerging from the south part of the bay; here one can sunbathe, surf-fish or dig for the elusive Pismo clam.

Hearst's Incredible Castle: Nothing really prepares visitors for what awaits them at the top of a hill high above the little village of **San Simeon**. It was here that newspaper tycoon William Randolph Hearst built his vacation mansion. He called it La Cuesta Encantada, "The Enchanted Hill"; but everyone else refers to it as **Hearst Castle**, and it's the No. 2 visitor attraction in California, behind only Disneyland.

Hearst's father, George, who had struck it very, very rich in gold, silver and copper, had originally bought 40,000 acres (16,188 hectares) of the Piedras Blancas Ranch in the 19th century. Running from San Simeon Bay through the Santa Lucia Mountains, the ranch cost 70 cents an acre. The senior Hearst later expanded his land holdings to 275,000 acres (111,291 hectares) and 50 miles (80 km) of oceanfront. He used the ranch as a family campsite, calling it "Camp Hill".

But his son, who inherited the ranch after his parents died, had more grandiose ideas. William Randolph, who added to the family fortune by building a media empire that included dozens of newspapers, magazines and two film studios, decided to build a house on Camp Hill as a museum for his extensive art collection. He hired Julia Morgan, a favorite family architect and the first female graduate of the École des Beaux Arts in Paris, and together they worked for 28 years to bring his dreams to fruition.

And what dreams they were, especially since money was absolutely no object. Often Hearst would start a room design with an *objet* he owned – say, a 400-year-old, 83-foot (25-meter) long carved wooden ceiling from Italy – then have the room built to fit it. Using the remains of European castles and cathedrals, he and Morgan blended carvings, furnishings and art work from different eras and countries into a single room, yet somehow unified them into a convincing, and often breathtaking, whole.

The grounds were an equally amazing conglomeration of plants and animals brought together from all over the world. At one time, Hearst maintained the largest private zoo and animal reserve in the world.

Hearst still hadn't finished building his monument when he died in 1951, but the result in no way seems incomplete. The hill includes three guest houses – each looking like a Mediterranean villa fit for royalty – and a main house that's a town-towered mansion with 38 bedrooms. It also includes an 83-foot (25 m) assembly hall (built around that Italian ceiling), a Gothic dining room, an indoor mosaic pool called "The Roman Bath" and a movie theater with giant Greek-inspired caryatids along the walls. Outside, Hearst built a marble-lined "Neptune Pool" – probably the highlight of the entire place – that holds 345,000 gallons (1.3 million liters) of water and looks out onto the ocean below. There are four separate tours of the castle and you must make reservations in advance.

The Neptune Pool is one of Hearst Castle's spectacular attractions.

247

DEATH VALLEY
AND THE MOJAVE

The Mojave Desert is packed with many treasures – more varied, and even more accessible – than most travelers realize.

"I cried the first time I drove through the Mojave," said one of the naturalists assigned to Death Valley National Monument. "God knows, it wasn't the beauty of the place. But there was something awesome about it. I still remember wondering, 'Can anything be this big?'"

The Mojave (named after a southwestern Indian tribe, pronounced "mo-*hahv*-ee") lies between US Highway 395 and Interstate 40, snuggled against the Nevada state border. It has come to mean different things to different people. Since the back-to-the-land movement of the 1960s, the Mojave Desert has become a battleground of conflicting interests between backpackers, miners, ranchers, scientists, environmentalists and off-road vehicle groups.

Most of the time, the Federal Bureau of Land Management must referee the fights.

What generates such an interest in the huge, hot Mojave? Most Californians who travel here do so to escape the confines of urban life. They also come to experience for themselves the truth about one of the most desolate, challenging landscapes in the Americas.

Centuries ago, explorer Juan Bautista de Anza experienced the Mojave's natural furnace and in his diary referred to the region as *Tierra del Muertos*, literally, "Land of the Dead". Those words came back to haunt the first settlers who had the misfortune to wander into Death Valley in 1849 on their way to the Gold Rush.

These days Mojave Desert travel, regardless of the season, is infinitely easier and safer, with well-supervised roads and good accommodations. (Death Valley has two inns and a luxury hotel.) The climate between November and April is ideal for outdoor travel, while May through October burn with heat like the North African Sahara.

A fascinating two or three-day trip can be made from Los Angeles through the Mojave to Death Valley and back. Perhaps the best route is to set out from the San Fernando Valley on State Highway 14 through Lancaster and return via I-15 and Barstow.

Mojave: Miners and mules: At the junction of State Highways 14 and 58 is the small desert town of **Mojave**. From borax to the B-1 bomber, it has seen more history than most settlements many times its size.

Located just a short distance from **Edwards Air Force Base**, Mojave is part of the Antelope Valley aerospace boom. As such, it is earmarked to become one of the high-technology desert centers of the 21st century. Its current role is very much that of a bedroom community for the aerospace workers, as well as those employed in agriculture and railroads. The winter season is busiest in Mojave; that's when weekend skiers, heading to and from Sierra slopes, pack the motels and roadside cafes.

North of Mojave some 25 miles (40

Preceding pages: the jagged Devil's Golf Course at Death Valley. **Left**, US 395 stretches across the Mojave north of Barstow.

km) along State 14 is the **Red Rock Canyon State Recreation Area**. This unusual camping and picnic spot is one of the important geological treasures of Southern California, but it's just enough off the beaten path to be one of the area's best-kept secrets. Nicknamed "Grand Canyon of the West", it's actually more akin to Utah's Bryce Canyon. Great, brightly colored columns of sandstone rise off the desert floor on either side of the highway.

Formed after the last Ice Age, these sculpted towers in the foothills of the eastern Sierras were once the home of a desert Indian tribe now known only as "the old ones". Much later, about the middle of last century, traffic picked up considerably when desert prospectors began discovering gold nuggets on the surface of dry stream beds. A miniboom followed, and before long some $16 million in ore had been removed, including one 5-lbs (2.27-kg) nugget.

On weekends, state rangers give guided nature walks. Picnic tables and some 50 primitive campsites are pro-vided for tenters and recreational-vehicle enthusiasts. There are no concessions at the park, however, so visitors must bring their own food and water.

Randsburg, a 19th-century ghost town that isn't a ghost, is about 20 miles (32 km) due east of Red Rock Canyon on US 395. Named for one of the big gold boomtowns of South Africa, Randsburg is living proof that lightning can strike the same place twice... er, three times.

From 1895 to 1947, this hilltop enclave – and two others just over the hill, **Johannesburg** and **Atolia** – struck it rich first with gold, then with silver, and finally with tungsten. Gold fever struck in the 19th century's final decade with the discovery of the Yellow Aster mine, which yielded $20 million in paydirt before it was exhausted.

After the mine's owners celebrated their good fortune on San Francisco's Market Street with a marching band, stories of Yellow Aster's success raced up and down the California coast. Turn-of-the-century Randsburg was as wild

Red Rock Canyon State Recreation Area.

and woolly as any Western boomtown, with saloons and dance halls, scoundrels and rogues. Local legend says one of the town gunmen took second place to local vigilantes and was buried cradling a bottle of whisky in each arm.

Today Randsburg is a small but thriving mining community. Among the ramshackle remains of the original wood-and-corrugated iron buildings on the main street is the **Desert Museum.** Open weekends, it contains a small but fascinating collection of mining and geological artifacts. Also open are the town saloon, dance hall and barber shop, which have been quaintly converted to shops offering rocks, bottles and mining curios. The **Randsburg General Store** is open every day, selling everything from dungarees to dynamite! Thirsty wayfarers can sip a chocolate soda at the same swivel-chaired soda fountain that was hauled into town by mules a century ago.

Paleontologists have given the world such famous fossil finds as Java Man and Peking Man. There are those who suspect that, one day, a China Lake Man may be discovered beneath the rock and sagebrush of these Mojave flatlands.

Recent discoveries of Stone Age tools indicate human habitation in North America is older than anyone previously suspected. Scientists originally believed the first paleo-Indians didn't cross the Bering land bridge into the New World until the end of the last glacial period, 11,000 to 14,000 years ago. Now, as a result of discoveries at **China Lake**, some scientists are tempted to say that humans migrated from Asia at least 40,000 years ago, and perhaps as long as 100,000 years ago.

China Lake is a dry lake near **Ridgecrest** off US 395. It is best known as the focus of the important **China Lake Naval Weapons Center**. Near the main gate of the naval station is the small **Maturango Museum**, open weekend afternoons. The museum occasionally conducts public field trips to study aboriginal rock inscriptions found at China Lake, perhaps the best collection of them in California.

Descent from the barren summit of Mount Whitney.

Not far from China Lake, near the banks of the equally dry **Searles Lake**, are the **Trona Pinnacles**. This great pincushion of ancient limestone columns in the middle of the Mojave Desert is as rare as it is bizarre. The spooky stone spires are "national natural landmarks", probably the outstanding example of tufa formations in North America and a marvelous moonscape to explore for hikers and rock climbers of all ages.

Access to the Trona Pinnacles is via State 178 north from Johannesburg. They are found in a 2-sq.-mile (5-sq.-km) area on the west side of Searles Lake, a bleak and awesome bit of real estate, seemingly untouched by human hands. Camping is permitted at the Pinnacles. Motorists can get local directions in the community of Trona.

Ninety-four miles (151 km) north of Johannesburg on US 395 is **Lone Pine**, a picturesque village that has often been used as a location for Hollywood westerns. From here, **Mount Whitney** – at 14,494 feet (4,418 meters) the highest peak in the continental United States –

is accessible, if one wants to stretch the meaning of that word. It's a two- to three-day, 11-mile (18-km) challenge from the end of Whitney Portal Road to reach the summit.

After the climb, a good place for a break is **Keeler**, a ghost town about 10 miles (16 km) from Lone Pine.

The Lowest Spot on Earth: State highway 190, is the main artery through **Death Valley National Monument**.

Ever since Death Valley was established as a national monument by decree of President Franklin D. Roosevelt in 1933, it has attracted more and more visitors, and increasingly international ones. Winter or summer – it doesn't seem to matter much – sightseers, hikers and amateur naturalists come to scramble up the sand dunes near **Stovepipe Wells**, marvel at the view from **Zabriskie Point**, gasp at ancient **Ubehebe Crater**, study old mines and ghosts towns, look perplexedly at abandoned charcoal kilns, and snap whole photo albums of themselves at humble **Badwater**, 282 feet (86 meters)

below sea level, the lowest spot on earth.

Death Valley's temperatures are exceeded only in the Libyan Sahara. This depression – 120 miles (193 km) long and 4–16 miles (6½–26 km) wide – is the result of a geological phenomenon. Eons ago, the deep gap between the **Panamint** and **Funeral mountains** was formed by a folding of the earth's crust. Gradually erosion wore rock debris away from the mountains and filled the valley floor. The ice ages left it flattened and swathed in a vast cool sea, which evaporated to leave alternating layers of mud and salt. Cut off from cooling breezes by the surrounding mountains, this basin has been left to parch with an average annual rainfall of less than 2 inches (50 mm).

Autumn through spring, the climate is made to order for exploring Death Valley. Daytime temperatures range in the 60s and 70s Fahrenheit (about 15–25°C), chillier at night. Skies are usually bright and rain-free.

Summers are another story. The *average* daily high in July for the past half-century has been 116°C (47°C). It commonly soars past 120°F (49°C), and once hit a national high of 134°F (57°C). In short, May to October is one continuous heat wave.

Despite the harshness of Death Valley's environment, about 900 different species of plants grow in the national monument, some throwing down roots 10 times the height of a man. In many ways, Death Valley's human population of 200 or so seems just as indomitable, enduring terrific heat and isolation. (The nearest supermarkets are in Las Vegas, Nevada, 140 miles (225 km) away, and local television reception is mediocre.)

Furnace Creek: Years ago, it was traditional for all concessions to close down in the summer. "What tourist would want to endure such heat?" asked the proprietors. Quite a few, apparently – nowadays, **Furnace Creek Ranch** and the Stovepipe Wells motel complex stay open throughout the year, and neither is ever empty.

Furnace Creek is a good focal point for a visit to Death Valley. Located not far from Badwater, it features a national monument **Visitor Center** open daily throughout the year, and until 9 p.m. from November to April. The Furnace Creek Ranch has an 18-hole golf course which is indisputably the lowest on earth. It doesn't necessarily follow that golfers' scores are that low.

There's one other golf course in Death Valley: the **Devil's Golf Course**. But no one could hire a caddy to wander through this bizarre expanse of rugged salt crystals pushing up from hundreds of feet underground.

Overlooking Badwater to the east is **Dante's View** (elevation 5,475 feet/1,669 meters). The scene from here is quite spectacular, with high mountains looming in the background. **Telescope Peak**, the highest point in the Panamint Range (11,049 feet/3,368 meters), towers directly above Badwater.

Among Death Valley's other natural beauty spots are Zabriskie Point, southeast of Furnace Creek in the **Black Mountains**, with another awesome view; **Artists Drive** and the **Golden Canyon**, vivid displays of color among old outcroppings; and Ubehebe Crater,

Left, land sailors line up for winds on a dry-lake bed east of Victorville. **Right**, contours in the sand near Stovepipe Wells.

an extinct volcano at the north end of the national monument.

At the **Harmony Borax Works** near Furnace Creek, an old cleanser-processing plant has been restored to show visitors the 19th-century manufacturing method.

In the near proximity of Ubehebe Crater is a man-made phenomenon – a graceful yet flamboyant oddity and living epitaph to one American millionaire's penchant for spending money.

This is **Scotty's Castle**, a 25-room, $2 million Spanish palace that stands poised like a prospector's dying mirage. Run by the National Park Service, it is Death Valley's biggest visitor attraction.

Chicago millionaire Albert Johnson made his fortune in mining before he was 35. In the early 20th century, he was charmed into investing thousands of dollars in a fruitless search for gold by an affable roustabout named Walter Scott, better known in these parts as "Death Valley Scott". After years of waiting for Scott to strike his fortune, Johnson's patience ran out – but not before he had grown so fond of Death Valley that he decided to build a summer retreat there.

Work on the castle began in 1926 at the foot of a natural spring-fed canyon at an elevation of 3,000 feet (about 900 meters). Construction materials from as far as Europe were transported in by ship, truck and train. Some 2,000 workmen completed the castle in 1931.

A facsimile of a Spanish-Mediterranean villa, Scotty's Castle contains beautiful continental furnishings and *objets d'art*. The Chicago financier and his wife lived on and off at the castle for many years until his death in 1948. "Death Valley Scotty", the good-natured rogue, also lived there, of course. He died in 1954, and his grave lies along a trail just behind the castle. Today, the castle is open daily for public inspection. There are hourly tours.

Early men and gunfighters: State 190 exits Death Valley National Monument not far from the Nevada border, and joins State 127 at the tiny community of **Amargosa**. It's a scenic 83-mile (134-km) drive south (via **Tecopa Hot Springs**) to **Baker** and I-15. From Baker, another 50 road miles (80 km) take the traveler to **Calico**.

Some of the earliest traces of human habitation on the North American continent were discovered on this wind-blown desert. Paleontologists are still carrying on the work of the late Dr Louis Leakey, leader of a team of scientists who believed they found a prehistoric "tool factory" estimated to be some 200,000 years old. The so-called **Calico Early Man Site** is open for public viewing, with guided tours Wednesday through Sunday. Arrangements can be made with the Federal Bureau of Land Management office in nearby Barstow.

The town of Calico was established by silver miners in the 1880s. A clever restoration of that boomtown is the **Calico Ghost Town**. Half history and half Hollywood, Calico is an amusement park where visitors can explore mining tunnels, ride the ore train, and browse through the dry-goods shops.

Just west of Calico is **Barstow**, a bustling desert town, part-suburb and part-military community. Situated at the junction of Interstates 15 and 40, it has a 5-mile stretch of motels, gas stations and grocery stores that make it a good base for desert adventures.

Surviving in the desert: The Mojave Desert is just a few hours drive from Los Angeles. It is so close and so accessible that travelers often are amazingly casual about what to expect in this alien environment. Smart travelers take plenty of precautions.

The Mojave covers an enormous amount of land – roughly that of the states of Massachusetts, Connecticut and Rhode Island combined. It's easy to get lost and, with conventional vehicles, even to get stranded off the main roads.

Visitors who have never experienced summer desert heat, and who haven't a clue how to pace themselves, should be warned: It is quite literally life-threatening to be under the desert sun too long.

"You lose the thirst impulse," said Shirley Harding, museum curator at the Death Valley National Monument. "People have died out here with a full canteen of water beside them."

Living history at Calico Ghost Town.

PALM SPRINGS AND THE DESERT

Where the high Mojave Desert greets the lower Colorado Desert, the landscapes speak.

They make stark statements in shades of brown and beige, arid platitudes punctuated by snow-capped mountain peaks. What might be perceived as nature's harshness really offers an enveloping sense of warmth and tranquility to those who learn to know the many moods of California's southern desert.

This desert area is one of great contrasts – hot and cold, lush and sparse, populous and barren. Urbanization hasn't extended its tentacles here yet. There are cities, but no metropolises. There are people, but no crowds. And there are three separate wilderness designations (totaling more than 500,000 acres) where the impudent roadrunner, the majestic desert bighorn sheep and the wedge-snouted, fringe-toed lizard are the main residents. Humans are only visitors.

Southeastern California's upper reaches (those between Interstates 10 and 40) are indeed parched and mainly unpopulated. Further south, however, the region comes to life. It stretches beyond the shimmering Salton Sea to the Colorado River and the state of Arizona. In the west, the resort-oriented Coachella Valley surrounding Palm Springs is a favored destination of "newlyweds and nearly deads" – or so one cynic has said.

Palm Springs: While it is true that the abundance of sunshine and recreational opportunities make the **Palm Springs** region appealing to honeymooners, retirees and the wealthy, there is an ever-increasing middle class. They, too, are captivated by the accessibility of myriad activities and terrains. On a hot summer day, with temperatures topping 100°F (38°C) in the shade, a 15- to 20-minute ride on the **Palm Springs Aerial Tramway** will carry sojourners 8,516 feet (2,596 meters) up **Mount San Jacinto**, where snow can still be found in July amid a peaceful alpine atmos-

phere. In the winter, cross-country skiers enjoy the mountaintop terrain, and there are annual dog-sled races.

Many people know Palm Springs (population 32,000) by two of its more luxurious features – lush golf courses and celebrities' homes. Bob Hope's house, built on a ridge overlooking the swimming-pool-dotted **Coachella Valley**, was likened by one writer to a Trans World Airlines' terminal. It is not quite that large, but it is as large as a fair-sized department store and easily visible from the desert floor.

Hope – along with such other celebrities as Frank Sinatra, Kirk Douglas, Red Skelton, Dinah Shore and the late Jack Benny – has brought fame to Palm Springs, along with fortune. But long before the Hollywood luminaries and Midwestern business tycoons lived here, the area was inhabited by the Agua Caliente Indians, a band of the Cahuilla. Their name, which means "hot water" in Spanish, came from the ancient mineral springs on which the resort city rests.

Preceding pages: Joshua Tree National Monument. Left, sun worshippers at Anza-Borrego's Palm Canyon. Right, Bob Hope sinks another putt at Palm Springs.

Every other square mile of Palm Springs, in fact, is part of the **Agua Caliente Indian Reservation**, a checker-board arrangement devised by the United States government when it sought to give a right-of-way to the Southern Pacific Railroad. The result is a hodge-podge of development, a continual squabble over who has the right to zone Indian land. About 100 separate members of the Agua Caliente each own land worth more than $2 million.

By the mid-1860s, many non-Indians knew about the desert's mineral springs. Railroad surveyors discovered them in 1853, stagecoachers in the 1860s. Tourism was not far behind. In 1886, Dr Welwood Murray, a canny Scotsman who today has a downtown library named after him (not to mention the canyon), built the **Palm Springs Spa Hotel**, its first lodging house.

Two years earlier, John Guthrie McCallum had become the first permanent white settler. He laid out the first irrigation system, planted figs, citrus, alfalfa and vineyards. Later residents called McCallum "Judge", an honorary title but one befitting his position as an attorney and the community's founder. Palm Springs flourished. In the 1920s, it became a popular hideaway for movie stars and executives. After all, "The Springs" were only 105 miles (169 km) east of Los Angeles.

On New Year's Eve 1928, **El Mirador Hotel**, built by oilman P.T. Stevens, opened in an isolated location in the northern part of the city. Skeptics snickered, but Stevens knew what he was doing, and the 200-room grand hotel hosted the toast of filmdom along with such serious-minded folk as Albert Einstein. In 1931, the *Amos 'n' Andy* radio program, a favorite of President Franklin D. Roosevelt, was broadcast from the hotel's Byzantine-Moorish tower. El Mirador was taken over by the federal government as an Army hospital during World War II, had many glory days in the '50s and '60s, then was closed in 1973 when bought by its neighbor, Desert Hospital.

El Mirador played a part in the gen-

Spectators pack the stands at the annual mid-February international tennis classic at La Quinta.

esis of the famed **Palm Springs Racquet Club**. Since the hotel had only one tennis court at the time, actors Charlie Farrell and Ralph Bellamy often had to wait to play. Having their own court seemed a solution, so they bought 200 windswept acres a few blocks north of the hotel for $30 an acre. The club opened on Christmas Day 1933 with two courts and a small dressing room. A swimming pool and snack bar followed. So did movie stars such as Humphrey Bogart, Marlene Dietrich, Douglas Fairbanks, Henry Fonda, Clark Gable, Greta Garbo, Carole Lombard and Mary Pickford.

Palm Springs fostered the image of a "Playground of the Stars and Presidents". Though tennis brought the original acclaim, it soon became known as the "Golf Capital of the World". Today there are more than 50 golf courses in the Coachella Valley from Palm Springs east to Indio.

The culture vultures: In Palm Springs, it is easy to buy one's way into the social structure. A large contribution to char-

ity or a fancy party guarantees a photo in the local society pages. No doubt, most visitors think of Palm Springs as a collection of hotels (the word "motel" is *verboten*), restaurants, nightclubs, swimming pools and bejeweled women walking poodles.

Perhaps because of this stereotype, "culture" is a word taken seriously by many in Palm Springs. Residents are somewhat sensitive to criticism. They are vastly proud of the **Desert Museum**, an $8.5-million arts center at the base of the San Jacinto Mountains near the Desert Fashion Plaza.

The Denney Western Art Wing houses an ever-expanding collection of American sculptures, paintings, graphics and photography. The McCallum Natural Science Wing (named after the "Judge") has four extensive galleries devoted to desert landscape, climate, plant and animal life. Also in the bi-level structure are the Annenberg Art Wing and the 450-seat Annenberg Theater. (Funds were donated by Walter Annenberg, publisher and former am-

Relaxing in a jacuzzi at La Quinta Hotel.

bassador to the United Kingdom, and his wife, Lee.) The Walt Disney Gallery, the Helena Rubenstein Children's Art Studio and the (Frank) Sinatra Sculpture Court round out the museum.

Annenberg and Sinatra live a few miles down State Highway 111 in **Rancho Mirage**, a bedroom community of country clubs, golf courses and tennis courts. Former US President Gerald Ford and Leonard Firestone, industrialist and former ambassador to Belgium, also reside there, side by side on a fairway at Thunderbird Country Club. The Annenberg estate is a few blocks away at the corner of Frank Sinatra and Bob Hope drives. (Having a street named after a person has become the desert's ultimate status symbol.)

South of Indio and north of the Salton Sea is **Lake Cahuilla**. Created from the adjacent waters of the **All America Canal**, the lake is stocked with rainbow trout, striped bass and catfish. For non-anglers, there are hiking and equestrian trails, shady picnic spots, special campsites and a children's play area on the sandy beach – away from fishermen.

What can be said of the **Salton Sea**? To be honest, it was all a big mistake. When engineers attempted in 1905 to divert Colorado River water to the Imperial Valley, the river changed course and reflooded the ancient Salton Basin, 235 feet (72 meters) below sea level. This formed a sea of 360 sq. miles (968 sq. km) with royal blue water filling the area where the Coachella and Imperial valleys merge.

Sportsmen love it. The sea's saltiness creates a buoyancy popular with water skiers and swimmers. It also provides a habitat for salt-water game-fish. Adjoining marshlands are a refuge for migrating birds and a haven for bird-watchers. The **Salton Sea State Recreation Area** is an 18,000-acre (about 7,300-hectare) park with both developed and primitive campsites. There is a large boat basin at **Varner Harbor**. And geology buffs have a field day with ancient shorelines and layers of marine fossils visible along the base of the Santa Rosa Mountains.

Overlooking the Badlands, Anza-Borrego Desert State Park.

The Salton Sea, 38 miles (61 km) long and 9 to 15 miles (14–24 km) wide, is flanked by State 111 on the east and State 86 on the west. Local residents like to avoid the latter road, a two-lane thoroughfare they have dubbed "the killer highway" because of the unusually high number of fatal traffic accidents it records.

The northeastern tip of **Anza-Borrego Desert State Park** is only a couple of miles from the Salton Sea. The largest state park in California, it contains some 600,000 acres (243,000 hectares) of Colorado Desert, and extends nearly to the Mexican border. The park is chock full of canyons and *arroyos* (dry gullies) easily reached by car. It also has its share of badlands, inhospitable except to the jackrabbits, coyotes, kangaroo rats and chuckwalla lizards who call them home. Camping is permitted.

More than 150 species of birds have been sighted in Anza-Borrego park. The vegetation is equally varied, ranging from junipers and pines at the 5,000-foot (1,500-meters) level to palm trees at sea level. A 3-mile hike from **Campfire Center** to **Palm Grove** reveals plants used by the Cahuilla Indians for medicines, dyes and food.

The Colorado River: About 58 miles (93 km) due east of El Centro is **Yuma**, Arizona, a desert town built on the banks of the Colorado River where it enters Mexican territory. The Colorado forms the entire eastern border of Southern California from Mexico to Nevada. Several dams built across it have created reservoirs while providing hydroelectric power for the metropolises of Los Angeles and San Diego.

Lake Havasu, 46 miles (74 km) long, and no more than 3 miles (5 km) wide, is the reservoir behind the dam. Those who don't want to drink the water enjoy playing in it. Along Arizona State Highway 95 between Parker and Lake Havasu City are recreational-vehicle parks, marinas and campgrounds with room for tens of thousands of visitors. Everyone from water sportsmen and outboard boaters to yachtsmen, water skiers and sail-boarders, love the lake. There's fishing for bass, bluegills, trout and crappies. Small game populates the rugged south-eastern (Arizona) shore of the lake that constitutes **Lake Havasu State Park**. Birds are everywhere, as the entire body of water is contained within the **Lake Havasu National Wildlife Refuge.**

Lake Havasu City, nonexistent as recently as the late '60s, has exploded into a resort center of 15,000 residents. Developed by the late millionaire Robert P. McCulloch Sr., its most famous landmark is the original **London Bridge**. McCulloch had it shipped piece by piece to Long Beach, then trucked to the lakefront community he created.

The bridge now arches over a 1-mile channel, dredged to divert water from the lake, under the bridge and back into the lake. Beneath the bridge (but not under water) is an acre of land deeded to the City of London and featuring English shops, restaurants and other reminders of the British Isles. McCulloch died on 1977, but his promotional monument lives on, a bridge over mostly untroubled water.

Right, an *echinocereus* cactus bloom.

Everyone who lives in San Francisco feels sorry for anyone who doesn't. Other cities may have great museums, great theaters, great industries, but San Francisco has great food. While the citizens of other cities scurry through life frowning over profits, worrying about losses, and generally taking the business of living very, very seriously, San Franciscans devote themselves to the things that really matter. In fact, the life of the city is so dedicated to the pursuit of good eating that preparing food has become its major art form.

It has always been this way. When San Francisco was nothing but a shanty town filled with houses made of paper and men with dreams of gold, a historian wrote, "No people in the world live faster or more sumptuously than the people of San Francisco." That was in 1853, long before California's rich land had been tamed and tilled, long before anyone had even thought of planting crops.

In those days, vegetables and fruits were brought from the Sandwich Islands, apples and pears from Chile, and basic necessities like cheese, butter and eggs were shipped around the horn from the Atlantic coast. Cured foods came from as far away as China, and ice was towed down the Pacific coast from Alaska. At a time when most Americans were grateful for a burned piece of beef, San Francisco was already priding itself on its international cuisine. During the first flush of the gold rush, those who struck it rich spent their money on food.

Pioneer gourmands: The **Poulet D'Or**, the city's first French restaurant, opened in 1849, was soon renamed The Poodle Dog by miners who couldn't wrap their tongues around the French vowels. By 1855 reporters noted that San Franciscans had a choice of "American dining rooms, English lunch houses, French *cabarets*, Spanish *fondas*, German *wirtschafts*, Italian *osterie* and Chinese chowchows". San Franciscans chose them

all, reveling in the diversity of their restaurants. By the turn of the century, the city became known as the "American Paris". When the earthquake leveled San Francisco in 1906, more sober Americans muttered darkly that the city was only getting its just deserts, and prophesized that this would teach the snooty city to be more temperate in its appetites.

How wrong they were! San Francisco restaurateurs set up trestle-tables and served meals amidst the rubble. Dinner over, they cheerfully set about the business of rebuilding. It takes more than an earthquake to dull the appetites of San Francisco, probably the only American city which has had a mayor known primarily for the quality of his cooking. (Mayor Tilden was so jealous of his culinary secrets that it was not until after his death that his recipes were published in 1907.)

Mayor Tilden is long gone, but a taste of the past lingers on in some old San Francisco restaurants. There's **Jack's** on Sacramento Street, tables nudging one another in the masculine clutter of its downstairs dining room, blithely unchanged after all these years. The menu remains much the same; and as one eats the sweet, tiny Olympia oysters (which filled the local waters until a greedy populace ate them almost into extinction), the fat mutton chops accompanied by hash brown potatoes and followed by thin jelly-filled French pancakes, it is easy to imagine the sound of horse-drawn carriages just outside the door.

When Mayor Tilden was in the mood for a piece of fish, he went to **Sam's** or **Tadich's** with their old wooden booths and spartan interiors. Generations of San Franciscans have known that the city's finest fresh fish comes to these old establishments, and lines have stretched out their doors at every mealtime for the past 100 years. San Franciscans do their best to hide this information from the non-native. Only tourists eat at Fisherman's Wharf. The locals head inland when they want grilled native petrale sole, or crab Louis, or the locally invented "hangtown fry" (an omelette of oysters topped with bacon, which reputedly came by its name when it was requested by a thief just

Preceding pages: lobster and vegetables, the ingredients of a Big Sur seafood feast. **Left**, the Crown Room buffet at the graceful old Claremont Hotel in Oakland.

before he met his untimely end on the rope).

If Mayor Tilden wanted some excitement, he went to Chinatown. He couldn't have eaten at the **Far East Cafe**, because this last-remaining old-style Chinatown restaurant did not open until 1915, but the places he frequented were undoubtedly hung with the same exotic Chinese chandeliers and decorated with the same ornately carved wood. The Far East is the only Chinese restaurant where guests can still take a booth, pull the curtains and eat *chow mein* in complete privacy. When they need a waiter, there's a bell to ring. Even today, it is easy to imagine that just beyond the curtains lies a Chinatown of opium dens and *tong* wars.

"We might as well eat": If the earthquake failed to turn San Francisco into a sober, serious city, Prohibition came along to give it another try. With one bar for every 100 inhabitants, San Francisco may have been the most bibulous city in the States, and the advent of Prohibition was certainly a severe blow to the citizens. Many of the bars also served lavish free lunches that offered every kind of food to be found in the city. (So much free caviar was served at these bars that the native sturgeon population was entirely decimated.) But even Prohibition could not put a damper on the spirits of San Francisco. When alcohol was outlawed, local people shrugged their shoulders and said, "We might as well eat."

The city threw itself into an orgy of eating that continues to this day. Prohibition ended; times changed; and while other Americans, seduced by convenience, celebrated the glory of fast food, frozen food and fad food, San Franciscans stubbornly stuck with fine food. San Franciscans proudly claim that the Coca Cola Company does not consider this a good city for them, and when the local paper noted that San Francisco has more restaurants per capita than any other city in America, natives shook their heads and said the paper had missed the point: that San Francisco has more *good* restaurants than any other American city.

San Francisco once boasted the only restaurant in America serving pizza. Lupo's has since changed its name to **Tomasso's** but very little else has changed since they opened in 1936. The restaurant still uses the same oak-burning oven that gives the hearty Italian food its deliciously smoky quality. San

Francisco had the country's first Cantonese restaurants, and then, much later, its first northern Chinese restaurant, the **Mandarin**, now in Ghirardelli Square. It had the first Japanese restaurant in the west, **Yamato**, considered extraordinarily exotic when it began serving *sashimi* (raw fish) in 1931. The city had German restaurants, Indian restaurants, and restaurants representing almost every country – but now it has something else. San Francisco has invented a style of cooking uniquely its own.

San Franciscans, raised on this cross-cultural stew, began to feel that all these foods belonged to them. They ate so much *sushi* and *pasta* and *dim sum* and *pâté* that they

began to regard them as part of their native cuisine. For a long time, diners could go into the kitchens of Italian restaurants and find Chinese chefs at work, or discover that their favorite classic French cuisine was prepared by a Japanese chef. But all that suddenly changed. Local chefs rebelled against the idea that French food belonged in French restaurants, Chinese food in Chinese. Assuming the lead role of a new juggling act, they began experimenting, trading tastes from culture to culture, mixing ingredients, and using unorthodox techniques. A brand new cooking style was born which has been labeled "California cuisine".

The Revolution in Berkeley: This was happening all over the city, but nowhere with more passion than across the bridge in Berkeley. Once known as a hotbed of student rebellion, Berkeley is now the "gourmet ghetto". One short stretch of Shattuck Avenue makes the reason blatantly clear. At 1517 is **Chez Panisse**, a restaurant opened in 1971 by a young chef who had no formal training other than a lifetime of good eating. The restaurant started simply as a typical little French bistro but when the cooks tired of trying to imitate the food of France, the revolution began. They began to use local products only, making freshness the highest virtue.

the menu suddenly sported dishes like *ravioli* made of new potatoes and garlic, or a simply grilled lobster. Local oysters were being farmed, for the first time in years, and they became a part of the menu. Thus successful, the restaurant had a second-floor cafe with an old-fashioned oven added to it, and pizza was elevated to *haute cuisine*. The menu became even more international than ever before.

The local response was electric. Across Shattuck Avenue from Chez Panisse, the **Berkeley Co-Op** supermarket sells a heady mixture of such international foods as *tortillas*, eggroll wrappers, *phyllo* dough and *matzoh* balls. The store does more business

The restaurant encouraged local farmers to grow special vegetables for them, and had them raise animals to careful specifications. They encouraged foragers to bring them wild mushrooms, and small-time fishermen to sell their catch. Armed with these wonderful ingredients, they began experimenting and inventing. The result was food unlike anything ever tasted before in America. The strictly French food became less strict, and

Adopted tastes and indigenous styles are both part of the San Francisco eating experience. Left, a Japanese chef prepares *sushi*; and above, a label for famed sourdough bread.

than any other supermarket west of the Mississippi River. Next door the nation's first *charcuterie*, **Pig by the Tail**, tempts passersby with great clouds of herb-scented, olive oil-laden steam. Down the street the **Cheeseboard** offers warm bread and an astonishing assortment of cheeses, while the fish store next door sells crab, fish and *sushi*. Around the corner, the **Produce Market** has oranges and coconuts and mushrooms of all shapes tumbling through its aisles.

Just across the street are an Italian bakery, **Il Fornaio**; a bakery devoted exclusively to chocolate, **Cocolat**; a kosher deli and a store selling freshly roasted coffee so enticing that there is always a long line. And this is just the beginning. In the other direction are a *charcuterie* devoted to chicken, **Poulet**; a barbecue stand; another bakery; an Italian grocery store; and a couple of Chinese restaurants mixed in for good measure. Anyone still not convinced that this is an insatiable city, should consider that this is but one of four major gourmet areas in a city of only 100,000.

The availability of these foods makes Berkeley's restaurants special. Some of Chez Panisse's chefs have set up on their own, creating eclectic combinations of ingredients. At the **Santa Fe Bar and Grill** cooking is unconstrained by normal rules, borrowing

or Indonesian peanut. At **Café Americain,** the choices include grilled fish, mussels steamed with ginger, pizza, pasta or a plain old hamburger. All this, and a good wine list!

But San Francisco's most unique restaurant is undoubtedly **Green's**, run by members of a Zen sect who serve strictly vegetarian fare. The restaurant grows its own vegetables, served so fresh they still have the taste of the earth. The Chez Panisse-trained chef takes her inspiration from many places, offering grilled marinated *tofu*, *linguini* with wild mushrooms, salads made with *feta* and olives and topped with flowers.

The city's potpourri of food fare does not end in the restaurants. On any street, people

flavors from every culture. Offerings include fried black-bean cakes with *salsa* and sour cream, *fettucine* with smoked duck, grilled snapper with spicy peanut sauce, and grilled lamp chops with roasted garlic and lime sauce. At the **Fourth Street Grill**, diners can savor classics like salad mingled with Creole gumbo, *linguini* with fresh oysters, or tuna with mango-pineapple sauce.

Experimental tastes: The same experimental spirit prevails on the other side of the Bay. At **Hayes Street Grill**, fresh fish, grilled over mesquite, is served slightly undercooked and accompanied by sauces ranging from a French *beurre blanc* to Italian *pesto*, Mexican *salsa*

can be seen munching and feasting as they stroll. Many people sit in the parks, eating loaves of sourdough bread stuffed with salami and cheese, happily aware that both the bread and the meat are unique products of the city. (When researchers tried to produce sourdough bread outside of San Francisco, it was a complete flop. Some say this has to do with the weather, but the more romantic say that sourdough simply loses heart when taken out of San Francisco.)

The Italian neighborhood of North Beach is not as young as it was, and it is mostly the older people who remain, firmly set in their ways. **Gloria Sausage Company** still makes sausage like it did when it first set up business 60 years ago, and the dark interior of the store has a friendly, old-fashioned feeling. At the **Cuneo**, **Liguria** and **Italian-American** bakeries, the ladies hand over *grissini, focaccia* and *buccelato* with a few gracious words of Italian.

The flavors in Chinatown are stronger and more aggressive, not unlike the shops themselves which are pushed out onto the sidewalks, making it even more difficult to walk through the already crowded streets. Grant Avenue is filled with tourist shops and restaurants, but a block towards Stockton there is an entire street dedicated to the art of eating. Whole ducks and pigs hang in shop

windows, invitingly glazed. Women stand in the fish stores poking at the gills, examining the eyes, prodding the crabs to see if they're alive. Inside are tanks of live catfish and cages filled with frogs and turtles. Weekends see trucks pull up, piled high with cages of squawking ducks, quail and chickens.

Salsa and sashimi: Out in the Mission the mood is more lighthearted, the aromas spicier, and the music decidedly Latin. On 24th Street,

Two popular Bay Area restaurants: left, kitchen staff prepare a vegetarian meal at Green's (Fort Mason); and above, a chef makes bread at Chez Panisse (Berkeley).

the *taquerias* flash invitations to warm *tortillas* filled with grilled meats and chili-laden *salsas*, as the low-riders' big cars cruise the streets with their bellies close to the ground. The small bright *panaderias* offer sweet cakes, as well as brightly colored cookies and breads shaped into strange bewitching animals.

In Japantown the scents are brisker and saltier. Although this scene is in the heart of the city, so much fish is sold that the streets have the briny scent of the sea. In the stores are huge, deep-red chunks of tuna sitting next to the blue-white flesh of albacore, and the pale tan of buttery yellowtail brought all the way from Asia. Spread out all around are the various roe – the dull mustard-colored sea urchin, bright orange salmon roe and the flashy red eggs of flying fish which are as fine as sand.

But if there is one street in San Francisco that is a true amalgam of all the influences that are felt in this city, it has to be Clement Street. The food shops and restaurants here are so densely packed, they have elbowed almost every other kind of business off the street. There are almost 100 restaurants in a 1-mile area, with as many cheese shops, bakeries and grocery stores sprinkled in among them. At the top of the street, at Arguello, is a health-food emporium, followed immediately by a fine French restaurant, an Irish pub and a pizza stand. By the time the street slows to a halt, most major world cuisines have been represented. It would take weeks to eat in all the restaurants, but those who do would sample Russian *pelmeni*, Chinese *bao*, Indonesian *satay*, American barbecue, Japanese *teriyaki*, Vietnamese crab rolls, Viennese pastries, Philippine *lumpia*, Lebanese *shish kebab*, Spanish *paella*, Thai fish cakes, Italian *gnocci*, and would end up in **Bill's**, one of the last restaurants on Clement, where hamburgers and old-fashioned milk shakes are served.

Although the food in all these places could not be more different, the restaurants share a certain quality: they are patronized by people who joyously taste, eat and argue about food as if there were no more important things to do on earth. The truth is that in a city which revels in the joy of eating, and where people take time for all the scents and smells and savory delights of life, there isn't.

"THE INDUSTRY": MOVIES AND TELEVISION

Hollywood, dream city to much of the rest of the world, is in reality a rather tawdry collection of middle-class homes and nondescript business avenues that serve as the hub of Southern California's vast motion picture and television industries.

The city trades vigorously on its storied past – when the stars actually lived in the canyons and hills north of fabled Sunset Boulevard and caroused in such glamorous watering holes as the Trocadero, Ciro's, Macambo and the Garden of Allah, none of

symbolic value translates into millions of tourist dollars, even more at the box office. And symbolically – forget the local economic and geographic facts – Hollywood is still the biggest dream city on earth.

It's impossible to conceive of Southern California without its celebrity merchants. Before motion pictures, before Jewish glove merchants came west to make movies and become studio czars, Los Angeles was known for its orange groves. And before the orange groves, the city's sense of identity was most

which still exist. People were then in the picture business as those of other cities were into grain or bonds.

In Hollywood's myth-making days, circa 1915–50, the business of glamor belonged to a network of huge studios. Most of these studios are still churning our glamour but no longer from Hollywood. They are down the road in a sprawling amorphous area known as Greater Los Angeles. Today, in fact, only one major studio (Paramount) and one television network (CBS) have their offices in Hollywood proper.

The dream city: Nevertheless, the facade of Hollywood is of incalculable importance. Its

closely allied with its 19th-century Spanish culture. It was the introduction of motion pictures in the 1920s and the star system – which produced Chaplin, Pickford, Fairbanks, Valentino, Keaton – that permanently married the motion-picture industry to Southern California.

But the halcyon days of the Silver Screen ended a generation ago. The television industry, with corporate headquarters in New York, has been for more than a quarter of a century the dominant entertainment industry in Los Angeles. TV and theatrical films, encompassing independent stations and countless independent production houses, today influence lifestyles more than any other industry. In Los Angeles it is known simply as "The Industry".

Seven major studios dominate the film industry: Metro Goldwyn Mayer/United Artists in Culver City, 20th Century-Fox in Century City, Paramount in Hollywood, and four studios in the San Fernando Valley – Columbia Pictures, Warner Bros. and Walt Disney Productions in Burbank, and Universal Pictures in nearby Universal City.

Also in the otherwise dreary city of Burbank sits NBC. Almost totally hidden from view is ABC in the northeastern part of Los Angeles. CBS (Television City, as it is known) is in the center of Los Angeles.

fiercely competitive production companies that vie to sell programs to the networks or to fashion movies for distribution by the major studios.

Even though the overwhelming number of people in Los Angeles have nothing to do with these companies and make their living like people do all over the world, "The Industry" is the dominant economic and social force in Los Angeles. Besides the sheer impact in dollars, the film and television industries also affect the LA populace by the huge reservoir of unusual people they draw.

Easterners love to sneer about the nuts and crackpots in Los Angeles – perhaps best typified in American literature by Nathanael

These are the giants, employing thousands of workers, surrounded, in turn, by other lesser studios such as Warner Hollywood (where Sam Goldwyn used to have his Goldwyn Studios), Hollywood General, Gower-Sunset Studios (where Columbia was based during Harry Cohn's reign), and Francis Ford Coppola's bankrupt Zoetrope Studios. Sandwiched among these fiefdoms are many

Preceding pages: actors cast as Asian tribesmen stand guard on set of Columbia Pictures' *Bring 'em Back Alive*. **Left**, film crew prepares to shoot sequence. **Above**, 1920s comedy team monkeys around on set.

West's corrosive Hollywood novel, *The Day of the Locust*.

The city has always been a magnet for creative people. Whether talented people like William Faulkner and F. Scott Fitzgerald came for the money or were drawn by the muse, the effect over the years of so many popular artists on the community-at-large has given Hollywood a bizarre and fanciful image. The fact that the majority of writers, actors, musicians and assorted promoter types never find a stable income – that they are, in fact, out of work most of the year – is the underbelly of Hollywood that "outsiders" seldom hear about.

The labor unions: Creative types are no doubt a separate breed from most Angelenos. This is exemplified, strangely enough, by labor unions. Unions do not have a strong history in Los Angeles, but one of the most tightly unionized industries in Southern California is the entertainment industry. The Screen Actors' Guild (SAG) – which once elected a president named Ronald Reagan – and the American Federation of Television and Radio Artists (AFTRA) total more than 100,000 members nationwide, with the majority in Los Angeles. No one acts before a camera if he or she is not in the union. And normally an offer of employment from a producer is a prerequisite to join either SAG or AFTRA.

In the 1930s and '40s, that history was bloody, corrupt and tumultuous. The studio chiefs, such as Harry Warner at Warner Bros. and Louie B. Mayer at MGM, fought labor organizers with police and hired goons outside the studio gates. There was mafia influence at the studios. Chicago hood Willie Bioff, installed as the leader of the IATSE in Hollywood, took payoffs from studio presidents to keep down union demands. Strikes in 1945 and 1947 turned Tinseltown into a latter-day version of union-management battles at steel and iron mills in Pittsburgh.

At the same time, in the decade spanning from the mid-40s to the mid-50s, Hollywood

Directors have their Directors' Guild of America, and screen and television writers have their Writers' Guild of America. Non-union talent finds it *extremely* difficult to land work. Behind-the-camera workers such as grips, gaffers, film editors, carpenters, plasterers, publicists, costumers, art directors, sound men and cinematographers are represented by the powerful International Alliance of Theatrical Stage Employers (IATSE). Studio drivers are in the Teamsters. In short, the history of motion pictures, at least from the early days of the talkies, has been inextricably tied to the history of the labor movement in Hollywood.

endured its gloomiest era, that of the communist witch-hunts. Ten Hollywood writers, including Dalton Trumbo, went to jail. The House Un-American Activities Committee, feeding on hysteria about Reds, enjoyed a field day. Careers in Hollywood collapsed overnight. Many picture people cooperated with the witch-hunters and went to Washington, DC, to name names and thus save their careers. Many wouldn't cooperate and were exiled from the business. Half the town was suspected of being communist. It was Hollywood's Dark Age.

To make matters worse, it was the dawn of the age of television, and motion-picture houses across the country were shutting down as the studios realized too late that they had misjudged TV, and that millions of movie-goers were staying home glued to the tube.

Meanwhile, the TV networks, like the first East Coast picture studios before them, saw that Hollywood and not New York would be the production center of the future. The drain of talent from New York to Hollywood has continued ever since.

With the advent of television, the old studio contract system began to crack. Soon, stars, writers and directors became free agents, able to make the best deal to work for anybody. In perhaps the most symbolic exit of a major figure, Mayer at MGM lost a power play with stockholders in the early '50s and was gone. Suddenly a new breed – in MGM's case, Dore Schary – was calling the shots.

The rich and famous: Some of Hollywood's rich and famous moved to the "suburbs", specifically Beverly Hills. But most of the stars in the '30s stayed in Hollywood, with several – such as Sidney Greenstreet, Peter Lorre, opera singer Lawrence Tibbet, and Clark Gable and Carol Lombard (who were in pre-marital seclusion) – residing in Laurel Canyon just a stone's throw above the Sunset Strip and the legendary Schwab's drugstore where Lana Turner, according to the myth makers, was discovered in her tight sweater sipping a malt.

But all that was to change. The big money in town was moving west, toward the Pacific Ocean and the setting sun. Geographically, the entertainment people, as if tilted toward the seashore in the '40s and '50s, began invading Beverly Hills, Bel Air, Malibu and Pacific Palisades. Beverly Hills today has the highest per capita income in the country, after Greenwich, Connecticut, New York's wealthiest suburb. A lot of that money is made in deals inked after umpteen martinis at the Polo Lounge of the Beverly Hills Hotel.

This is the fantasy land where people who make movies, record albums and television shows live like royalty.

What's the effect of all this on Southern California? One good example is the little

lady who sits in her canvas chair under an umbrella every day on Sunset Boulevard in Holmby Hills. She sells maps to the stars' homes. So do others on Sunset all the way into Hollywood. They are part of the trail to the California dream.

But in a ravenous town like this, permanence is an illusion, change is swift, and security is tenuous. The average tenure of a studio executive is 18 months at the majors. The average annual income of a member of the Screen Actors' Guild is around $4,000. Most members of the Writers' Guild fare little better. The IATSE craftsmen are lucky to be employed half the year. Millions are spent at the networks on development of

projects that never get shot; and if they do get made into "pilots", most never get aired.

Among Hollywood's oldest traditions are its two trade papers, *Daily Variety*, founded in 1933, and *The Hollywood Reporter*, founded in 1931. Today, with an influence out of all proportion to their circulation, the "trades" are read by more than 20,000 people in the entertainment industry every weekday morning. Egos wax and wane at the mention of their names in the papers – or at their omission.

In a high-profile community like Hollywood, it's never business as usual. It's always a myth with a banner headline.

Left, actresses Joan Collins and Linda Evans of TV's *Dynasty* at an Emmy Awards ceremony in Pasadena. **Right**, LA television crew arrives to film a horse race at Del Mar.

TRAVEL TIPS

GETTING THERE

BY AIR

In addition to the international airports listed below, there are smaller, regional airports in several locations throughout the state including Palm Springs, Ontario, Hollywood-Burbank, Ventura County, Santa Barbara, San Luis Obispo, Fresno, Reno, Sacramento, San Jose and Orange County. Shuttle flights are available at all of the larger air terminals.

San Francisco International: SFO is 14 miles south of downtown San Francisco near the town of San Mateo. Transportation to and from the airport is provided by Airport Coaches 24 hours a day. Sam Trans, San Mateo's bus system, makes several stops between downtown San Francisco and the airport and also has services to nearby towns.

Oakland International: Oakland International is located on the east side of the Bay. It is often less crowded than SFO and parking is more convenient. Local bus service to and from Oakland is offered by AC Transit (#57 line) from 5 a.m. to midnight daily. A shuttle van links the airport with the Bay Area Rapid Transit System (BART).

Los Angeles International: Los Angeles International (LAX) is Southern California's largest airport, and it handles the major international, domestic and regional air traffic. The terminal buildings at LAX are arranged in an oval. Arrivals are on the lower level; departures are on the upper level.

Information booths just outside the terminal building direct you to a wide range of buses and limousine services. A free bus (C) runs to the parking lot which is also a terminal for buses of the Southern California Rapid Transit District (RTD). Call (213) 626-4455 for bus information.

San Diego International: Travelers who want to start their tour in San Diego can fly there directly from most major American cities. Currently there are no foreign carriers with service to San Diego airport. Public buses, taxis and limousines into the city and surrounding areas are readily available.

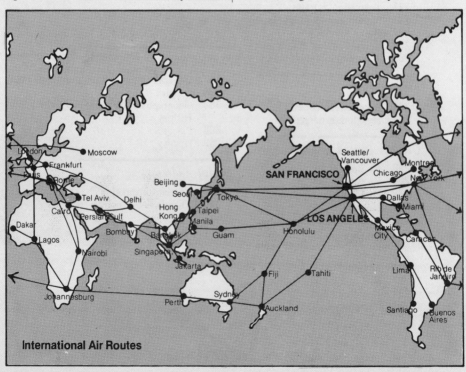

International Air Routes

AIRLINES

Air Cal	(800) 424-7225
(American Airlines)	
American Airlines	(800) 433-7300
Continental Air	(800) 525-0280
Delta Airlines	(800) 221-1212
Eastern Airlines	(800) 327-8376
Northwest	(800) 225-2525
Pan Am	(800) 221-1111
Sky West Airlines	(800) 453-9417
Southwest	(800) 531-5601
TWA	(800) 221-2000
United Airlines	(800) 241-6522
US Air	(800) 428-4322

TRAVEL ESSENTIALS

VISAS & PASSPORTS

Most foreign travelers to the US must have a passport, visa and, depending on where they are coming from, a health record. In addition, they must make prior arrangements to leave the country. Those exempt from these rules are:
• Canadian citizens
• British subjects from Bermuda or Canada entering from the western hemisphere
• certain government officials.

Any person who enters the US can visit Mexico or Canada for a period of less than 30 days and still be re-admitted into the US without a new visa. Visas can be obtained from any US embassy. If a visitor loses his or her visa while in this country, a new one may be obtained from the embassy of the visitor's respective country. Extensions are granted by the US Immigration and Naturalization Service, 425 I St, Washington, DC 20536, tel: (202) 514 2000.

WHAT TO WEAR

Northern California: With the exception of the finer restaurants, jackets, ties and formal dresses are unnecessary. San Francisco is famous for its breezy hilltops, so be sure to bring along a sweater or light jacket, even if it is warm and sunny elsewhere.

Southern California: Dress in Southern California is decidedly casual. Relatively few restaurants require jackets and ties for men. Unless you are visiting the mountain areas, the moderate climate makes heavy clothing unnecessary. Wool sweaters or lightweight overcoats are sufficient for winter evenings, and a light jacket is adequate for summer evenings.

CUSTOMS

Whether or not they have anything to declare, all people entering the country must go through US Customs. It can be a time-consuming process, but to speed things up, be prepared to open your luggage for inspection and keep the following number of restrictions in mind:
• There is no limit to the amount of money you can bring with you. If the amount exceeds $10,000, however, you must fill out a report.
• Anything you have for your own personal use may be brought in duty- and tax-free.
• Adults are allowed to bring in 1 quart (1 liter) of alcohol for personal use.
• You can bring in gifts valued at less than $400 duty- and tax-free. Anything over $400 is subject to duty charges and taxes.
• Dogs, cats and other animals may be brought into the country with certain restrictions. For details contact the US consulate nearest you or write the Department of Agriculture.
• Automobiles may be driven into the state if they are for the personal use of the visitor, family and guests only.

US Customs
1301 Constitution Ave NW, Washington, DC, tel: (202) 566-8195

GETTING ACQUAINTED

TIME ZONES

California is in the Pacific Time Zone, which is 2 hours behind Chicago and 3 hours behind New York. On the last Sunday in April, the clock is moved ahead 1 hour for Daylight Savings Time, and on the last Sunday in October the clock is moved back 1 hour to return to Standard Time.

CLIMATE

Northern California: San Francisco's climate is typical of the Northern California Coast. Daytime temperatures average in the mid-50s Fahrenheit (10–15 degrees Celsius) and drop as much as 10 degrees at night. Average temperatures are significantly higher in the South Bay and inland valleys. In fact, in the Sacramento and San Joaquin valleys, summer temperatures often reach the 90s. Summers tend to be warm and dry. Winters are generally rainy, and temperatures rarely go below freezing along the coast.

Southern California is one of the few places in the world where you can ski in the morning and surf in the afternoon. It is not uncommon for the temperature to vary 30 to 40 degrees Fahrenheit (17 to 20 degrees Celsius) as you travel from mountains to deserts to the beach. The change of seasons is not as dramatic as it is elsewhere. The winters are mild, with a rainy season that lasts from January through March. In the summer months the humidity is usually low, so discomfort is rare. The famous LA smog is at its worst in August and September.

BUSINESS HOURS

Most businesses are open from 9 a.m. to 5 p.m. Some department stores open at 10 a.m., and many stores stay open until 9 p.m.

Los Angeles and San Francisco are famous for their 24-hour restaurants. A few supermarkets are also open around the clock. Bank hours usually run from 9 a.m. to 3 p.m., although some stay open later, especially on Friday. Although some branch offices keep Saturday morning hours, most banks are closed on weekends.

Keep in mind that during the holidays listed below, post offices, banks, government offices and many private businesses are closed.

HOLIDAYS

New Year's Day
January 1
Martin Luther King, Jr's Birthday
January 15
Presidents' Day
Third Monday in February
Easter Sunday
Memorial Day
Last Monday in May
Independence Day
July 4
Labor Day
First Monday in September
Veterans' Day
November 11
Thanksgiving Day
Fourth Thursday in November
Christmas
December 25

TIPPING

Like other parts of the country, service personnel in California rely on tips for a large part of their income. In most cases, 15 to 20 percent is the going rate for tipping waiters, taxi drivers, bartenders and barbers. In the larger cities, taxi drivers tend to expect 20 percent.

The accepted rate for baggage handlers at airports and hotels is 35 to 50 cents per bag. For overnight stays, it is not necessary to tip the chambermaid. For longer stays, the rule of thumb is to leave a minimum tip of one or two dollars per day. A doorman expects to be tipped for helping unload your car or for other services; 50 cents to one dollar should cover it, depending on the nature of the service.

The final and the only tasteful rule in

tipping is that the tip should be fair and commensurate with the service provided.

FESTIVALS & EVENTS

For listings of festivals, parades, and other celebrations while you are in Los Angeles, check the Calendar section of the *Los Angeles Times* or *Los Angeles Magazine*. In San Francisco check out the *San Francisco Chronicle* or the *Bay Guardian*. Listed below are some of the more popular events:

JANUARY

Bing Crosby Golf Tournament, Pebble Beach, Monterey Peninsula.
Sacramento Symphony Pops Series, tel: (916) 756-0191.
San Diego Open Golf Tournament, tel: (619) 281-4653.
Tiburon Children's Film Festival, tel: (415) 435-1234.
Tournament of Roses Parade & Rose Bowl Football Game, Pasadena, tel: (818) 449-ROSE.

FEBRUARY

Annual Open Poetry Reading, Oakland.
Chinese New Year, Los Angeles, San Francisco.
Golden Gate Kennel Dog Club Show, Cow Palace, Daly City, tel: (415) 469-5000.
Laguna Beach Winter Festival, Laguna Beach.
Los Angeles Open Golf Tournament.
Mardi Gras, Los Angeles, tel: (213) 628-7833.
Migration Festival (Monarch Butterflies), Natural Bridges State Park, tel: (408) 688-3241.
Oakland Black Writers, tel: (415) 268-8375.
Virginia Slims Tennis Series, Oakland.

MARCH

Bay Area Music Awards, San Francisco.
Dixieland Festival, Monterey, tel: (408) 443-5260.
Living History Days, Sutter's Fort, Sacramento, tel: (916) 445-4422.
Return of the Swallows, celebrated at San Juan Capistrano, tel: (714) 493-1424.
San Francisco International Film Festival.

St Patrick's Day Parade, Los Angeles, San Francisco and San Diego.
Whale watching, tel: (805) 963-3564 for information about tours.

APRIL

Cherry Blossom Festival, San Francisco.
Daffodil Art & Craft Festival, Monterey, tel: (408) 625-0931.
Easter Sunrise service at dawn in the Hollywood Bowl, tel: (213) 419-1500.
Fisherman's Fantasy, Bodega Bay. 25,000 visit annually for the Mardi Gras parade of decorated fishing boats, bath-tub races, kite-flying championships.
The Freeway Series, Los Angeles, tel: (714) 634-2000. A three-game series between the Dodgers and the Angels.
Santa Barbara County Vintners Festival in the Santa Ynez Valley; tel: (805) 688-0881.

MAY

Bay to Breakers Marathon, San Francisco.
Calaveras County Frog-jumping Contest, Angel's Camp. 40,000 people and 3,000 frogs continue the tradition made famous by Mark Twain.
Cinco de Mayo, Los Angeles, San Francisco.
Festival of the Sea, San Francisco, tel: (415) 556-3002.
Fiesta de la Primavera, Old Town, San Diego.
National Horse Show, Del Mar.

JUNE

Haight Street Fair, San Francisco.
Lesbian and Gay Freedom Day Parade, San Francisco.
Lompoc Valley Flower Festival and parade, tel: (805) 735-8511.
National Shakespeare Festival, San Diego.
San Francisco Birthday Celebrations. Music and dance in the bandshell at Golden Gate Park. The city also stages many street fairs this month on Upper Grant Ave, in North Beach, along Union Street and in the Noe Valley.
Southern California Exposition, San Diego, tel: (619) 236-1212. A miniature world's fair.
Whale Fiesta, Cabrillo Beach, San Pedro, tel: 548-7562.

JULY

Cable Car Bell-Ringing Contest, San Francisco, tel: (415) 392-4880.
California Rodeo, Salinas, tel: (408) 757-2951.
County Fairs, state-wide.
Fourth of July Celebrations and Fireworks, state-wide.
Fourth of July Fireworks display from dawn at the Santa Monica pier, tel: (213) 624-7300.
Gilroy Garlic Festival, tel: (408) 842-1025.
Jazz Is Forever, San Diego, tel: (619) 266-1941.
Sahara Summer Blackjack Classic, Reno-Tahoe, tel: (800) 522-1500. Games in Vegas, open to all for big prize money.

AUGUST

International Surf Festival, tel: (213) 545-4502. The best wave riders in the Southland put on the most dramatic and entertaining show of the summer at Hermosa, Manhattan and Redondo beaches.
John Steinbech Festival, Salinas, tel: (408) 758-7311.
Pacific States Crafts Fair, San Francisco.
Renaissance Pleasure Fair, Novato, tel: (415) 881-2473.
San Francisco Fair and International Exposition.
San Francisco Flower Show, tel: (415) 558-3623.
South Central Los Angeles Folk Festival, at Exposition Park near the Museum of Natural History. This 2-day festival celebrates the black cultural heritage of South Central Los Angeles; tel: (213) 485-3941.
Women's Pro Volleyball Tour, at Will Rogers State Beach, Pacific Palisades, tel: (213) 457-2440.

SEPTEMBER

Fresno Fair, tel: (209) 255-3081. For 2 weeks.
Los Angeles County Fair, Pomona, tel: (714) 623-3111.
Nevada State Fair, Reno, tel: (702) 827-4914.
Oktoberfest, Big Bear Lake, tel: (714) 866-4607.
Pumpkin Festival, Half Moon Bay, tel: (415) 726-5202.

Russian River Jazz Festival, Guerneville, tel: (707) 869-9000.
Scottish Gathering and Games, Santa Rosa, tel: (707) 528-3247.
Transamerica Men's Open Tennis Championship, San Francisco.

OCTOBER

California Avocado Festival in Carpinteria, tel: (805) 684-0038.
Columbus Day Parade and Celebration, San Francisco.
Los Angeles Street Scene. A week-long block party.
Octoberfest Bavarian Festival, San Francisco.
The International Festival of Masks at the Hancock Park. Held each year on the last Sunday of October to celebrate Los Angeles' ethnic diversity; tel: (213) 934-8527.

NOVEMBER

Dickens Christmas Fair, San Francisco.
Diwali, the Festival of Lights, Life and Love, Fremont, tel: (415) 659-0655.
Doo Da Parade, Pasadena, tel: (818) 796-2591.
Hollywood Christmas Parade, tel: (213) 469-2337.
International Folk Art Market, Culver City, tel: (213) 937-5544.
Karate Championships, San Francisco, tel: (415) 974-6900.

DECEMBER

Annual Christmas on the Prado, San Diego, tel: (619) 239-0512.
Christmas Parades, in various communities; tel: (213) 393-9825.
Lighted Boat Parades, Marina del Rey and San Diego.
The Nutcracker, San Francisco Ballet and Oakland Ballet, tel: (415) 431-1210.
Victorian Christmas, San Luis Obispo, tel: (805) 514-8000.

COMMUNICATIONS

TELEVISION & RADIO

Television and radio are an invaluable source of up-to-the-minute information about weather, road conditions and current events. It is now almost standard for decent hotels and motels to include televisions in the price of a room, although you may have to pay extra for cable service. Television and radio listings are often published in local newspapers. Sunday papers usually have a special weekly guide.

NEWSPAPERS & MAGAZINES

San Francisco has two major daily newspapers, the *San Francisco Chronicle* in the morning and the *San Francisco Examiner* in the afternoon. The two papers combine into one large edition on Sunday. This weekend paper includes special sections, such as the "Pink Pages", which highlight the area's sports, entertainment and cultural events. Other papers in Northern California include the *Sacramento Bee*, the *San Jose Mercury-News* and the *San Francisco Bay Guardian*.

The *Los Angeles Times* is one of the most widely read papers in the country. There are several editions, and there is probably no better entertainment section in the country than in the *Times'* Sunday "Calendar" section. Other large daily papers are *The Daily News*, *The San Diego Union*, *The San Diego Tribune* and the *Orange County Register*.

Los Angeles Magazine, *Palm Springs Life*, *San Diego* and *Orange Coast* are monthly regional magazines that are always filled with lively feature articles on Southern California culture, as well as listings of restaurants and current events. *California Magazine* is a feature-oriented magazine covering the entire state.

POSTAL SERVICES

Post offices open between 7 a.m. and 9 a.m. and usually close at 5 p.m., Monday through Friday. Many of them are also open for a few hours on Saturday morning. All post offices are closed on Sunday. If you don't know where you will be staying in any particular town, you can receive mail by having it addressed to General Delivery, at the main post office in that town. You have to pick up General Delivery mail in person and show proper identification.

TELEPHONE

Coin-operated telephones are literally everywhere – in hotels, restaurants, shopping centers, gas stations and often in lighted booths on street corners. To operate, deposit 25 cents and dial a local number. To place a long distance call, dial 1-(area code)-local number.

The fastest way to get assistance for a telephone-communications problem is to dial "0" for operator on any phone. If the operator cannot be of assistance, he or she will probably connect you with the proper party. Another indispensable number is for information assistance. For local information dial 411. For long distance information dial 1-(area code)-555-1212. For toll-free information dial 1-800-555-1212.

Make use of toll free numbers whenever possible. For personal calls, take advantage of lower long-distance rates after 5 p.m. on weekdays and during the weekends.

TELEGRAM & TELEX

Western Union (tel: 800/257-2241) and International Telephone and Telegraph (ITT) will take telegram and telex messages by phone. Check the local phone directory, or call information for local offices.

EMERGENCIES

GETTING AROUND

SECURITY & CRIME

Like big cities all over the world, California cities have dangerous neighborhoods. Common sense is your most effective weapon. Don't walk alone at night. Keep an eye on your belongings. Never leave your car unlocked. And never leave small children by themselves.

If driving, never pick up anyone you don't know, especially if you are alone. If you have trouble on the road, stay in the car and lock the doors, but leave the hood up in order to alert passing police cars.

Hotels usually warn you that they do not guarantee the safety of belongings left in the rooms. If you have any valuables, you may want to lock them in the hotel safe.

HEALTH & EMERGENCIES

In the event you need medical assistance, consult the local yellow pages for the physician or pharmacist nearest you. In large cities, there is usually a physician referral service whose number is listed. If you need immediate attention, go directly to a hospital emergency room. Most emergency rooms are open 24 hours a day.

There is nothing cheap about being sick in the United States. It's essential to obtain adequate medical insurance before your trip and to carry an identification card or policy number at all times. If expense is a concern, turn first to county hospitals, which offer good service and do not charge patients who are indigent.

In the case of an emergency dial **911** for the police, fire department or ambulance service.

BY RAIL

Amtrak's California Zephyr is the main rail line into Northern California, stopping at Sacramento, Colfax, Davis, Martinez and Richmond before reaching Oakland's 16th Street Station, where a free bus service is provided to San Francisco. Southern Pacific Railroad also runs passengers between San Francisco and San Jose with several stops along the peninsula. Commonly called Caltrain (tel: 415/495-4546), this rail service operates from the terminal located at Fourth and Townsend streets in San Francisco.

Bay Area Rapid Transit (BART) (tel: 415/788-BART) is one of the most efficient and modern rail lines in the US Often compared to the super-subways of Europe and Russia, BART serves 34 stations in three counties, from San Francisco to Daly City and throughout the East Bay, Monday to Saturday from 6 a.m. to midnight and Sunday from 9 a.m. to midnight.

Amtrak offers several major rail lines in Southern California. The Sunset Limited from New Orleans stops at Indio, Ontario and Pomona before reaching Los Angeles. The Desert Wind, from Chicago to Los Angeles, stops at Barstow, Victorville, San Bernardino and Fullerton. The San Diegan runs between Los Angeles and San Diego with stops at Santa Anna, San Juan Capistrano, Oceanside and Belmar.

The state is tied together by the Coast Starlight which travels north from Los Angeles all the way to Seattle, stopping at Thousand Oaks, Oxnard, Ventura, Santa Barbara, San Luis Obispo, Salinas, San Jose, Oakland, Reading, Chico and Sacramento before heading across the Oregon border. Amtrak offers some local service also. Contact Amtrak (tel: 800/872-7245) directly for details.

BY BUS

The national bus line, Greyhound (tel: 800/528-0447), as well as a number of smaller charter companies provides an impressive network of ground travel throughout California as it offers daily service to major towns and cities. Beyond that, routes and schedules tend to change; it is a good idea to check in advance at local stations.

San Francisco, Oakland, Los Angeles, San Diego and most large towns also have municipal bus systems. For information on these services in San Francisco, contact MUNI at (415) 673-6364. In the East Bay call AC Transit at (415) 839-2882. In Los Angeles, call the Southern California Rapid Transit District at (213) 626-4455 for route information. And in San Diego, call the San Diego Transit Company at (619) 233-3004.

BY CAR

Driving is by far the most flexible and convenient means of travel in California, although newcomers are often confused by the many freeways. Roads are well-maintained throughout the state, and gasoline is relatively inexpensive. Before you set out, however, there are some important things to keep in mind.

MOTORING ADVISORIES

Your greatest asset as a driver is probably a good road map. In fact, it's absolutely essential to make sense of the tangle of highways surrounding most large cities. Maps can be obtained directly from the state tourism office, or purchased at most book stores, convenience stores and drugstores. Although roads are good in even the most remote areas, it is advisable to listen to local radio stations and to check with highway officials for the latest information on weather and road conditions.

Highways 1, 5, 15, 99, 101 and 395 are the principal north-south arteries in Southern California. State Highway 1, also known as the Pacific Coast Highway, runs the full length of the state and is famous for its hairpin curves and spectacular views of the California coast. The principal east-west highways are Interstate 8, 10 and 40, all of which head directly out of the state.

Keep in mind that the national speed limit on all interstate highways is now 65 miles per hour, and 55 miles per hour on most other

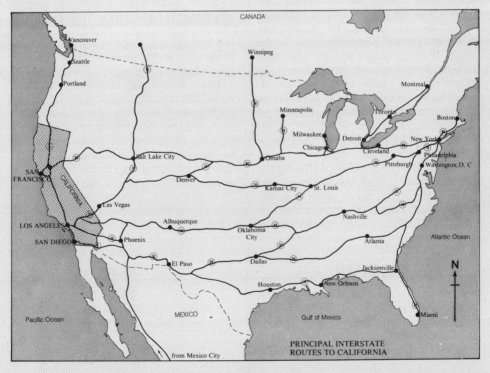

PRINCIPAL INTERSTATE
ROUTES TO CALIFORNIA

local highways. California law requires that every passenger wears a seat belt, that small children and babies be secured in youth or infant seats, and that drivers carry a valid license.

And finally, if you plan on driving any distance, it's a good idea to join the **American Automobile Association** based at 811 Gatehouse Road, Falls Church, VA 22047, tel: (703) 222-6334, or a similar organization. In addition to emergency road service, the AAA offers maps, guidebooks, insurance, bail bond protection and a $200 arrest certificate.

Travelers should check local listings for the AAA office closest to them. There are reciprocal arrangements with many international AAA organizations, such as those in Germany, Great Britain, Australia, etc... Main Los Angeles, tel: (213) 741-3111.

DESERT & MOUNTAIN TRAVEL

A word of caution for desert travelers: the single most important precaution you can make is to tell someone your destination, route and expected time of arrival. Check tires carefully before long stretches of desert driving. Heat builds pressure, so have them at slightly below normal air pressure. The desert's arid climate makes carrying extra water – both for passengers and vehicles – one of the essentials. Carry at least one gallon per person. Keep an eye on the gas gauge. It's a good idea to have a bit more than you think you need. Remember, if you should have car trouble or become lost, do not strike out on foot. A car, visible from the air and presumably on a road, is easier to spot than a person, and it affords shelter from the weather. Wait to be found rather than pursue your rescuers.

Mountain drivers are advised to be equally vigilant about weather conditions. Winter storms in the Sierras occasionally close major roads, and at times chains are required on tires. Phone ahead for road conditions before you depart.

CAR RENTAL

National car rental companies are located at all airports and large towns. These large rental agencies provide the widest selection of cars and the most extensive services. They are also usually the most expensive. Smaller,

regional rental agencies tend to cost less, but their selection and services are limited. But still, they may be perfectly suitable for local driving.

In most cases you must be at least 21 years old to rent a car (sometimes 25), and you must have a valid driver's license and at least one major credit card. Foreign travelers may need to produce an international driver's license or a license from their home country. Always take out insurance, both collision and liability. Insurance may not always be included in the base price of the rental. It usually costs somewhere between $40 and $150 per week, depending on the type of coverage. It's also a good idea to inquire about an unlimited mileage package, especially on a long trip. If not, you may be charged 5 to 25 cents per mile in addition to your rental fee.

Alamo	(800) 327-9633
Avis	(800) 331-1212
Budget	(800) 527-0700
Dollar	(800) 800-4000
Enterprise	(800) 325-8007
Hertz	(800) 654-3131
National	(800) 227-7368
Thrifty	(800) 331-4200

HITCHHIKING

Hitchhiking is the most dangerous and unpredictable way to travel. Because traffic is sparse in some regions, it can also be quite difficult. Hitchhiking is illegal on all highways and interstates and on many secondary roads as well. However, if you do decide to hitch, it's best to do it from an exit ramp (if legal) or a highway rest stop rather than on the road itself. For long distances, it's advisable to make a sign clearly stating your destination. To find the safest situations, check ride services and college campus bulletin boards for ride shares.

WHERE TO STAY

HOTELS

California offers the complete spectrum of accommodations – from elegant European-style hotels to inexpensive motels rented by the week. In Los Angeles, the most expensive hotels are situated downtown and in Beverly Hills, and have the best access to shopping and public transportation. In San Francisco, they are generally located in the Nob Hill area and the Financial District. These grand hotels are particularly well-suited to the international traveler, and many are attractive landmarks in their own right. The concierge at most finer hotels will arrange theater tickets, tours, telexes, limos with bilingual drivers and airline reservations. Rates run anywhere from $125 to $250 per night, double occupancy.

There are also a large number of smaller hotels and hotel chains for you to choose from. These establishments usually offer all of the essential comforts without the high prices of the grand hotels. If you're traveling by car and want an inexpensive alternative, motels are the best solution. Quality tends to vary considerably, but you can usually expect clean and simple accommodations. This is especially true for most of the national chains.

MOTELS

If you are traveling by car and don't intend to spend much time in your lodgings other than sleeping, motels are the best solution. Whether set along busy Sunset Boulevard in Los Angeles or along the river bank in a remote Northern Californian town, most motels provide parking lot space within paces of your room.

Degree and quality of accommodations vary, but most motels are bare bones. A restaurant or coffee shop, swimming pool and sauna are often found on the premises.

Room facilities would include a telephone, TV and radio but do not hesitate to ask the motel manager if you may inspect a room before agreeing to take it.

Other than their accessibility by auto, the other attraction of motels is their price. Motels in California range from $50 to $100 per night, double occupancy. They are less expensive in the outlying areas, usually from $35 to $75.

NATIONAL HOTELS & MOTELS

Best Western	(800) 528-1234
Hilton	(800) 445-8667
Holiday Inn	(800) 465-4329
Hyatt	(800) 228-9000
Marriot	(800) 228-9290
Quality Inn	(800) 228-5151
Ramada	(800) 272-6232
Sheraton	(800) 325-3535

BED-AND-BREAKFAST INNS

Country inns have become extremely popular in the last decade throughout the United States, especially in New England and Northern California. Most cluster in such scenic areas as the Wine Country, Gold Country, North Coast, and Monterey Peninsula. Being situated in such beautiful rural settings, they do a thriving business with city dwellers in search of a romantic weekend retreat.

Converted from mansions and farmhouses with 5 to 15 rooms, these inns offer the traveler a highly individual experience; no two inns are alike, and in most inns no two rooms are alike. Many residents have opened their homes to strangers. For those accustomed to the strict uniformity of large hotels and motel chains, the inns provide a warm, hospitable and quaint alternative.

Many inns have shared bathrooms and only a few have televisions or telephones in the rooms. Most include breakfasts with the room rental; hence, the name, bed-and-breakfast inns.

Prices vary from inn to inn and could be anywhere between $20 to $80 per night. Call or write in advance – the inns are particularly popular on weekends and in the summer. In fact, so favorable has this country inn concept become that small intimate bed-and-breakfast inns are even popping up all over urban San Francisco to compete with the large hotels.

Los Angeles Magazine devotes much of its space to recommending ways for Angelenos to get away from it all and as their recommendations are usually impeccable we have no hesitation in quoting from a recent feature "The Ritziest Little Inns in California". Bear in mind, however, that the group on the following list are pricey – rooms from $85–$200 plus per night – but all offer something special for the high tariff. The recommended are: the 18-room ("all with spectacular ocean views") **Whale Watch Inn**, Gualala (tel: 707/884-3667); the 9-room (some with "vibrating water beds") **Casa Tropicana**, San Clemente (tel: 714/492-1234); the **Victorian Gingerbread Mansion** at Ferndale (tel: 707/786-4000); the cliff-top **Blue Lantern Inn**, Dana Point (tel: 714/661-1304); the antique-filled **Mill Rose Inn**, Half Moon Bay (tel: 415/726-9794); Victorian farm house, **Wine and Roses Country Inn**, Lodi (tel: 209/334-6988); a Sonoma ranchhouse **Timberhill Ranch**, Timber Cove (where no phones or TV are allowed) (tel: 707/847-3258); and **La Jolla's Bed-and-Breakfast Inn**, once the home of composer John Philip Sousa (tel: 619/456-2066).

HOSTELS

Some travelers may also want to take advantage of California's chain of hostels. Hostels are clean, comfortable and very inexpensive (as low as $5 per night), and although suitable for people of all ages, they are definitely for the "young at heart". Beds are provided in dormitory-like rooms. Hostelers carry their own gear (knife, fork, spoon, sheets or sleeping bag, towel, washcloth) and are expected, following breakfast each day, to take 15 minutes to help at such communal tasks as vacuuming, sweeping, chopping firewood and stoking the fireplace. Hostels are closed from 9.30 a.m. to 4.30 p.m., so most guests fill their days with nearby outdoor activities. Reservations are highly recommended.

Northern California has a chain of more than 20 hostels up and down the Pacific coast, from Jedediah Smith Redwood State Park at the Oregon border down to John Little State Beach. All the hostels are along the shoreline; many are located inside old lighthouses. For lists of hostels, try these numbers:

Central California Council. P.O. Box 28148, San Jose, CA 95159, tel: (408) 298-0670.

Golden Gate Council. 425 Divisadero St #307, San Francisco, CA 94117, tel: (415) 863-1444.

LA Council. 335 W. 7th St, San Pedro, CA 90731, tel: (213) 813-8846.

San Diego Council. 1031 India St, San Diego, CA 92101, tel: (619) 226-1221.

CAMPGROUNDS

Finally, public and private campgrounds are located in or near most of the state and national parks in California. Most public campgrounds offer primitive facilities – a place to park, rest rooms within walking distance and outdoor cooking. Fees range from $1–$5 per site. Private campgrounds are usually a little more expensive and offer additional facilities such as RV hook-ups, coin laundries, swimming pools and restaurants. Most campgrounds are busy from mid-June to early September and are allotted on a first-come-first-serve basis. Again, if possible, make reservations.

The following list provides more information on camping grounds:

California State Parks & Recreation Dept. 128 Paseo de la Plaza, Los Angeles, CA, tel: (213) 620-3342.

Dept of Parks and Recreation. P.O. Box 942896, Sacramento, CA 94296. Send $2 for guide to state parks. For state park information, call (916) 445-6477.

US Forest Service. Dept of Agriculture, Washington, DC 20250.

US Forest Service. Southwest Region, 517 Gold Ave SW, Albuquerque, NM 87102.

US Park Service. Dept of Interior, Washington, DC 20240.

US Park Service. Southwest Region, P.O. Box 728, Santa Fe, NM 87501, tel: (505) 988-6375.

USDA Forest Service. 630 Sansome St, San Francisco, CA 94111, tel: (415) 556-0122.

Western Region Information Office National Park Service. Fort Mason, Bldg 201, San Francisco, CA 94123, tel: (415) 556-2766.

FOOD DIGEST

WHERE TO EAT

California is a food-lover's paradise, and it has the statistics to prove it. There are more restaurants in San Francisco per capita, for example, than in any other US city, and it's been estimated that Southern Californians dine out an average of two or three times a week. The Golden State has also been the birthplace of several culinary trends over the years, including Szechuan, sushi, nouvelle, and of course, California cuisine.

Although the most prevalent ethnic food you're likely to encounter here is Mexican, there is an endless variety of other ethnic foods as well as classic American cuisine. The following list is a mere sampling of some notable restaurants across the state.

SAN FRANCISCO

Balboa Cafe. The City's finest California cooking; warm salads, perfect pasta, handsome hamburgers and fresh fish. 3199 Fillmore, tel: (415) 922-4595.

Caffe Sport. Chaotic and crowded at all hours. Campy decor and superb shellfish. Moderate. 574 Green St, tel: (415) 981-1251.

Donatello. Luxurious and expensive. Excellent pasta, fine carpaccio, good service; the perfect place for a business meeting. Post and Mason, tel: 441-7182.

Ernie's. Formal decor (crystal chandeliers and velvet walls) and innovative French cooking; both the *nouvelle* and the *ancienne* cuisine. Coats and ties required for men. Very expensive. 847 Montgomery, tel: 397-5969.

Fournou's Ovens. Order from the oven – a succulent roast rack of lamb, fine fowl or other meats. Award-winning wine list. At the Stanford Court Hotel, 905 California, tel: 989-1910.

Gaylord. Elegant Indian cuisine. Lovely view of the Bay, especially at lunchtime. Ghirardelli Square, tel: 771-8822.

Green's. Managed by the Zen Center. Gourmet vegetarian. Dinners have to be reserved months in advance. Expensive. Fort Mason, Building A, tel: (415) 771-6222.

Julius Castle. Magnificent view. Expensive. 1541 Montgomery St, tel: (415) 362-3042.

La Rondalla. Inexpensive Mexican food; until 3.30 a.m. 901 Valencia St, tel: (415) 647-7474.

Little Joe's. Large portions, hurly-burly atmosphere and mouth-watering pasta. Moderate. 523 Broadway, tel: (415) 433-4343.

MacArthur Park. Something to please everyone: hopeful singles at the long bar in front, grilled fresh fish, tender ribs, decent hamburgers. Closed for lunch on weekends. 607 Front, tel: 398-5700.

Mai's. Vietnamese, from the Saigon-style shrimp-and-pork-noodle soup to the Hanoi-style anise-and-lemon-flavor soup. 316 Clement (tel: 221-3046) and 1838 Union (tel: 921-2861).

Mamas. Just plain good food. It's jammed on weekends, so try it during the week. Two locations: on the north side of Washington Square and 1701 Stockton St, tel: 362-6421.

Masa's. One of the finest French restaurants in town. Very expensive. 648 Bush St, tel: (415) 989-7154.

Osome. Excellent sushi bar plus usual range of cooked Japanese food. Closed Tuesday and for lunch on weekends. 1923 Fillmore, tel: 346-2311.

Prego. The perfect place for elegant pizza pie, cooked in a wood-burning brick oven. 2000 Union, tel: 563-3305.

Tadich Grill. Fresh fish and hefty drinks in an atmosphere of male conviviality. Long waiting lines. Closed Sunday. 240 California, tel: 391-2373.

Trader Vic's. This is the place where the elite meet to greet and eat. Avoid the Chinese dishes and concentrate on the *pu-pu* appetizers and remarkable rum drinks. Men must wear coat and tie. Closed for lunch on weekends. 20 Cosmo Place, tel: 776-2232.

Yank Sing. Classiest *dim sum* place in the city serving food unique to Hong Kong and San Francisco. *Dim Sum* are Chinese tea pastries, and are eaten only for brunch or lunch. A very San Francisco experience. 427 Battery, near Clay, tel: 781-1111.

Zuni. Simply cooked California cuisine made from fresh local ingredients. Moderate. 1658 Market St, tel: (415) 552-2522.

EAST BAY

Bay Wolf. A lovely little restaurant that serves fine Mediterranean food. Sundeck. 3853 Piedmont, Oakland, tel: 655-6004.

Chez Panisse. One of the most famous restaurants in the country. Expensive. 1517 Shattuck Ave, Berkeley, tel: (415) 548-5525.

Hunan. One of the few restaurants in Oakland's Chinatown serving excellent spicy food. Menus are impressive and amazingly inexpensive, don't forget to ask for the day's specials. You can't go wrong in any Chinese restaurant in this area. 366 Eighth St, tel: 444-9255.

Le Marguis. The finest French food in Contra Costa county. Dinner only; closed Sunday and Monday. 3524-B Mount Diablo Blvd, Lafayette, tel: 284-4422.

Narsai's. Mondays and Tuesdays are special dinners, honoring a celebrated chef or a particular country. On other nights, the food is elegant Mediterranean. Excellent service and wine list. Very expensive. Dinner only. 385 Colusa Ave, Kensington, tel: 527-7900.

Oakland Grill. Airy and attractive. Burgers are big; good breakfasts. Inexpensive. Third and Franklin, Oakland, tel: (415) 835-1176.

Santa Fe Bar and Grill. Restored train station and blues piano provide great atmosphere for California cuisine. Moderate. 1310 University Ave, Berkeley, tel: (415) 841-4740.

Siam. Exceptional Thai cuisine, spicy and irresistible. Moderate. 1181 University Ave, Berkeley, tel: (415) 548-3278.

PENINSULA/SAN JOSE

Caffe Santa Maddalena. This Italian-style tratoria is great: self-service cafeteria. Good for breakfast or espresso and desserts. Inexpensive. 233 University Ave, Palo Alto, tel: 322-1846.

Chantilly. From the cobblestone entry to the curtains framing the windows, this small French restaurant evokes the spirit of New Orleans. Closed Sunday and for lunch on Saturday. 530 Ramona St, Palo Alto, tel: 321-4080.

El Charro. Mexican fare – excellent margaritas and *chilies colorado* – plus some Argentinian steak specialities. Inexpensive. 2169 S. Winchester Blvd, Campbell, tel: (408) 378-1277.

Emile's Swiss Affair. Dinner only, closed Monday. 545 S. Second St, San Jose, tel: (408) 289-1960.

Fung Lum. A sumptuous and elegant environment for sampling delectable Cantonese cuisine. Moderate. 1815 S. Bascom Ave, Campbell, tel: (408) 377-6955.

Hi-Life. Good barbecued food at reasonable prices. Dinner only. 301 W. Saint John St, San Jose, tel: (408) 295-5414.

La Foret. On the site of the first adobe hotel in California (built in 1848), this charming old house is graced with tuxedo-clad waiters, traditional continental entrées, fresh mussels and clams, and tempting desserts. Dinner and Sunday brunch. Closed Monday. 21747 Bertram Road, San Jose, tel: (408) 997-3458.

La Hacienda Inn. Get a full Italian dinner here at moderate prices. 18840 Saratoga-Los Gatos Road, Los Gatos, tel: (408) 354-6669.

Liason. Friendlier and more informal than most French restaurants, the menu also features inventive Italian entrées. Closed for lunch on weekends. 4101 El Camino Way, Palo Alto, tel: 494-8848.

Original Joe's. Home of the famous "Joe's Special" – a tasty sandwich of spinach, ground beef, mushrooms, onions and scrambled eggs. 301 S. First St, San Jose, tel: (408) 292-7030.

Paolo's Continental Restaurant. Offers patrons gracious service and superb homemade pastas. Moderate. 520 E. Santa Clara St, San Jose, tel: (408) 294-2558.

Si Amigos. A tiny, narrow place that dishes up warmth and friendliness along with excellent *chilies rellenos, tacos, nachos*, and assemble-it-yourself meals. Inexpensive. Closed Sunday and Monday. 1384 Lincoln Ave, San Jose, tel: (408) 279-9083.

St Michael's Alley. The chalkboard menu at this pub/cafe changes daily. Excellent baked goods. Local folk musicians. Inexpensive. 800 Emerson St, Palo Alto, tel: (415) 329-1727.

Vahl's. In the American roadhouse tradition, this '50s-like eatery dishes up good food (not great) and plenty of it. Closed Monday and Tuesday. Taylor and El Dorado streets, Alviso, tel: (408) 262-0731.

WINE COUNTRY

Auberge du Soleil. Creative French cuisine and a view of the vineyards. Expensive. 180 Rutherford Hill Road, Rutherford, tel: (707) 963-1211.

Calistoga Inn. Casual, friendly service, large portions and excellent food. Dinner only; closed Monday. 1250 Lincoln Ave, Calistoga, tel: (707) 942-4101.

The Diner. Plain, old American breakfasts, lunches and dinners. The malts are made with real ice cream. Inexpensive. Closed Monday, and for dinner Tuesday and Wednesday. 6476 Washington St, Yountville, tel: (707) 944-2626.

John Ash & Co. California cuisine with a French and Chinese accent. Moderate. 2324 Montgomery Drive, Santa Rosa, tel: (707) 527-7687.

Miramonte. Very innovative nouvelle cuisine that looks as good as it tastes. Very expensive. 1327 Railroad Ave, Saint Helena, tel: (707) 963-3970.

SACRAMENTO

Alhambra Fuel & Transportation. Good for a late night supper, or a nice dinner and drinks. 1310 Alhambra.

Americo's. Perfect pasta and beautifully executed sauces. 2000 Capitol.

Hong Kong. Good Chinese food from a variety of regions in a converted Western barbecue place that still has the wagon-wheel light fixtures. Fifth and Broadway streets.

The Mandarin. Good Szechuan and Hunan Chinese food. Spicy. 1800 Broadway.

Torch Club. A bar with a cross-section of the community. 1612 L St.

Wakano Ura. An upstairs place in the Japanese district that can be a little noisy with Japanese revelers, although the fun becomes infectious. 2217 10th St.

Zelda's. Wonderful deep-dish pizza. 1415 21st St.

LAKE TAHOE

La Table Francaise. A bastion of French cuisine on the outskirts of Reno. Expensive. 3065 W. Fourth St, Reno, tel: (702) 323-3200.

La Vieille Maison. Every dish is flavored with garlic! All meals begin with a heaping bowl of *aioli*. Dinner only; closed Monday and Tuesday. State Highway 267 at River Road, Truckee, tel: (916) 587-2421.

Le Petit Pier. Classic French cuisine with many exotic touches. Expensive. 7252 North Lake Blvd, Tahoe Vista, tel: (916) 546-4464.

Old Post Office Coffee Shop. Crowded, friendly and inexpensive. 5245 North Lake Blvd, Carnelian Bay, tel: (916) 546-3205.

MONTEREY/BIG SUR

Casanova. Emphasis is on seafood served with light sauces, but there are also veal, lamb and beef selections. Breakfast, lunch, dinner and Sunday brunch in a French cottage setting. Fifth Street near San Carlos, Carmel, tel: (408) 625-0501.

Glen Oaks. Rustic exterior belies elegant dining room filled with fresh flowers and fine music. Large, eclectic menu. Closed for breakfast Wednesday and for dinner Monday. State Highway 1, Big Sur, tel: (408) 667-2623.

La Maisonnette. Good French food, homemade bread, very moderately priced. 218 17th St, Pacific Grove, tel: (408) 372-4481.

Maison Bergerac. This Victorian home with just 12 tables requires reservations well in advance. Fastidiously prepared *prix fixe* dinner is $30. Closed Monday. 649 Lighthouse Ave, Pacific Grove, tel: (408) 373-6996.

Mansion House. Try the homemade cheesecake topped with papaya. Closed for lunch Saturday. 418 Main St, Watsonville, tel: (408) 724-2495.

Nepenthe. Spectacular view of waves crashing 800 feet below, homemade soups and enormous chef's salads. Tourists and locals mingle comfortably. State Highway 1, Big Sur, tel: (408) 667-2345.

Ventana. A luxurious and charming resort set back in the woods. Save room for the accomplished desserts. State Highway 1, Big Sur, tel: (408) 667-2331.

The Whaling Station Inn. Seafood predominates – grilled or sautéed. Dinners only. 763 Wave St, Monterey, tel: (408) 373-3778.

NORTH COAST

Albion River Inn. Serves hearty fare. Moderate. State Highway 1, Albion, tel: (707) 937-4044.

Cafe Beaujolais. A really cozy atmosphere, fresh ingredients every night with all dishes beautifully prepared. Moderate. 961 Ukiah St, Mendocino, tel: (707) 937-5614.

Ledord House. A rustic little house overlooking the sea. Locally grown food is used when available, and always cooked to order. Dinner only. 7051 State Highway 1, Little River, tel: (707) 937-0282.

Little River Cafe. Each evening sees a different three-course dinner, with a choice of seafood, poultry or meat. The fixed price is $16.50. Dinner only; closed Monday and Tuesday. State Highway 1, Little River, tel: (707) 937-0404.

New Boonville Hotel. California cooking to the core – fresh, simple, sensitively prepared. All the food has been grown or raised right at the hotel. State Highway 128, Boonville, tel: (707) 895-3478.

Olema Inn. A restful, restored century-old inn at the gateway to the Point Reyes National Seashore. Closed Wednesday. Sir Francis Drake Blvd, Olema, tel: 663-8441.

St Orres. A beautiful restaurant emphasizing French cooking in a Russian-styled hotel. Also serves Sunday brunch. State Highway 1, in Gualala, below Mendocino, tel. (707) 884-3303.

Sea Gull Inn. Fresh fish, a buttery chicken kiev, assorted veal dishes and a nightly vegetarian special are offered. 10481 Lansing St, Mendocino, tel. (707) 937-5204.

Station House Cafe. Fresh well-cooked food in a warm, bustling atmosphere. Perfect stop after a day's hiking on Point Reyes Peninsula. Third and A streets, Point Reyes, tel: 663-1515.

Wellspring. The entire place is handmade and lovely with stained glass, high ceilings and bare wood. The vegetarian fare is creative and very good. Closed Wednesday. 955 Ukiah St, Mendocino, tel: (707) 937-4567.

EUREKA

Cafe Marina. Serves very fresh scampi, scallops and sole. If fish is not your fare, there are scrumptious sandwiches and Italian dishes. Breakfast, lunch and dinner. Woodley Island at the Eureka Marina, tel: (707) 443-2233.

Lazio's Seafood Restaurant. At Lazio's, also a seafood wholesaler, the fish couldn't be fresher. The Windjammer Lounge is as popular with the locals as the restaurant is with the tourists. 4 "C" St, tel: (707) 442-2337.

Samoa Cookhouse. Breakfast ($4) includes orange juice, scrambled eggs, pancakes, sausages, hash browns and coffee. Hefty lunches ($3.65) and dinners ($7.65) start with soup and salad, end with hot apple pie, and include plenty of homemade bread. Off US Highway 101 across Samoa Bridge, tel: (707) 442-1659.

HIGH SIERRA/YOSEMITE

Ahwahnee. The Grande Dame of hotels nestled in Yosemite Valley serves grand meals in its cathedral-like dining room. Yosemite National Park, tel: (209) 252-4848.

Erna's Elderberry House. A delightful surprise just south of Yosemite. Stunning interior design mingles with superb classic European cuisine. Erna herself greeted us and told of plans to open an adjoining inn. Highway 41, Oakhurst, CA 93644, tel: (209) 683-6800.

LOS ANGELES

Barney's Beanery. A newspaper-sized menu, pool tables for decor. Barney's is casual, funky and fun. 8447 Santa Monica Blvd, tel: (213) 654-2287.

Canter's. 24-hour Jewish deli. Inexpensive. 419 N. Faifax Ave, tel: (213) 651-2030.

Chasen's. Continental. Very expensive, but definitely worth the experience. 9039 Beverly Blvd, tel: (213) 271-2168.

Citrus. Pretty and pricey, specializing in unique California cuisine. 6703 Melrose Ave, tel: (213) 939-5354.

Dar Maghreb. The best Moroccan food to be found west of Casablanca, and one of the finest restaurants in LA. 7651 Sunset Blvd, tel: (213) 876-7651.

Gilbert's Restaurant. Crowded dive with some of the city's best Mexican food. Inexpensive. 2526 Pico Blvd, Santa Monica, tel: (213) 452-9841.

Gorky's Cafe. Funski cafeteria-style food, home-brewed beer, live music and open 24 hours. Atmospheric mix somewhere between university coffee house and communist collective. 536 E. 8th St, tel: (213) 627-4060; 1716 Cahuenga, tel: (213) 463-4060.

L'Ermitage. Elegant surroundings and creative French/Continental cuisine. Expensive. 730 N. La Cienega Blvd, tel: (213) 652-5840.

The Pantry. Always open. Basically just a coffee shop, but the steak and eggs are fabulous. Don't be surprised if you have to wait for a table – even at 3 a.m. Inexpensive. 877 S. Figueroa.

Spago. Owner and chef Wolfgang Puck is the Picasso of gastronomy. No effort is spared to procure and prepare the very best. Better than Disneyland if you've got a few bucks to burn. Expensive. 8795 Sunset Blvd, West Hollywood, tel: (213) 652-4025.

Yamishiro. The view is said to be the best in LA, because it's of LA. Surrounded by Japanese gardens, a lovely place for dinner or drinks. 1999 N. Sycamore Ave, tel: (213) 466-5125.

ORANGE COUNTY & SOUTH BEACH CITIES

Acapulco Mexican Restaurant. Award-winning Mexican food right across from Disneyland. 1410 S. Harbor Blvd, Anaheim, tel: (714) 956-7380.

Anthony's World Famous Pier 2. Terrific seafood, eclectic salad bar and over 300 California wines. Recently moved to new digs. Moderate. 640 S. Harbor Blvd, tel: (714) 774-0322.

The Cellar Restaurant. Superb French cuisine and expansive wine cellar 4 miles from Disneyland. Expensive. 305 N. Harbor Blvd, Fullerton, tel: (714) 525-5682.

Five Crowns. Award-winning food served in a beautiful two-storey building modeled after Ye Olde Bell, England's oldest inn. Moderate. 3801 East Coast Highway, Corona del Mar, tel: (714) 760-0331.

SANTA BARBARA

Acapulco. Artfully prepared and spiced Mexican food for almost three decades. 114 State St, tel: (805) 963-3469.

Bay Café. For seafood among the best. 131 Anacapa St, tel: (805) 963-2215.

Paradise Café. Always interesting – for the young chattering crowd as much as for the food. 702 Anacapa St, tel: (805) 962-4416.

PALM SPRINGS

Banducci's Bit of Italy. Steak, lobster and homemade canelloni made to perfection. Moderate. 1260 S. Palm Canyon Drive, tel: (619) 325-2537.

Elmer's Pancake and Steak House. The most crowded place in town on weekend mornings. 25 varieties of pancakes and waffles for breakfast, fine steaks and seafood for dinner. Inexpensive. 1030 E. Palm Canyon Drive, tel: (619) 327-8419.

Kobe Steak House. Hibachi-style steak and chicken in a replica of a 300-year-old Japanese country inn. Highway 111 at Frank Sinatra Drive, tel: (619) 324-1717.

Las Casuelas Terraza. Mexican-style cuisine with a pleasant outdoor patio and reasonable prices. 222 S. Palm Canyon Drive, tel: (619) 325-2794.

SAN JOAQUIN VALLEY

Harland's. Creative *nouvelle cuisine*: chicken in a raspberry *vinaigrette* sauce or veal with morels in a lovely lemon sauce. Closed Monday. 2915 N. Moroa, Fresno, tel: (209) 225-7100.

The Ripe Tomato. Quail and venison are standard menu items; typical specials include duck with apricot-garlic sauce, veal with oysters and mushrooms in vermouth sauce, and lamb with pesto sauce. 5064 N. Palm, Fresno, tel: (209) 225-1850.

Vintage Press. Fresh food with a European flair. The fish, veal, vegetables and desserts are personally prepared. Closed Monday, 216 N. Willis, Visalia, tel: (209) 733-3033.

SAN DIEGO

Anthony's Star of the Sea Room. Fabulous seafood served with dramatic flair. Located on the water. Jackets required, reservations necessary. Expensive. Harbor Drive at Ash, tel: (619) 232-7408.

Casa de Pico. Located in the Bazaar del Mundo in Old Town. Fine Mexican food and great margaritas. Inexpensive. 2754 Calhoun St, tel: (619) 296-3267.

Old Trieste. One of the best Italian restaurants in town. Expensive. 2335 Morena Blvd, tel: (619) 276-1841.

Reuben E. Lee. Dine aboard a genuine Mississippi steamboat with a great view of the surrounding harbor. Moderate to expensive. 880 E. Harbor Island Drive, tel: (619) 291-1974.

Shanghai. Mongolian barbecue, Mandarin cuisine and a nice view of the boat-filled bay. 1930 Qivira Way, Marina Village Mission, Bay Park, tel: (619) 226-6200.

THiNGS TO DO

TOURIST ATTRACTIONS

Alcatraz. A 2-hour excursion to this infamous island could be the most worthwhile visit you'll ever make to an American institution. The Red and White fleet ferries you to The Rock and back, transporting you to a time of notoriety and a concept of punishment still practiced in America. For $7.50 (less for kids and seniors), you can see where the Birdman of Alcatraz, Al Capone, and Machine Gun Kelly lived out their sentences. The ferry leaves every 30 minutes between 9 a.m. and 2.45 p.m. from Fisherman's Wharf, Pier 41 in San Francisco, daily. Park rangers lead a walking tour, covering much of the island and most of the prison. It's a hard walk (physically and emotionally). Wear comfortable shoes and dress for winter (it gets quite cold in the middle of the Bay). Reservations advised (tel: 546-2627).

Balloon Rides over the region are a popular local attraction and are offered by several companies including Pacific Horizons in San Diego (tel: 619/756-1790); Skysurfer (tel: 619/481-6800) in Del Mar; Dream Flights (tel: 619/321-5154) in Palm Desert; Piuma Aircraft in Malibu (tel: 818/888-0576); and Gold Prospecting Expeditions in Jarrestown (tel: 209/984-4653).

Bungee jumping. Being thrown from a tethered hot air ballon while tied to a long rubber cord is not everybody's idea of fun but it's a popular fad in Studio City (tel: 818/760-3957) where $99 pays for one jump from 100–300 feet above the ground. No extra charge for rebounds.

Bodie State Historic Park. A ghost mining town in a 500-acre park, 13 miles east of Highway 395, 7 miles south of Bridgeport. Information: (619) 647-6445. Museum open daily in summer, all roads closed in winter. Vehicle entry fee: $3.

Calico Ghost Town, east of Barlow north of Interstate 15, tel: (619) 254-2122, produced $86 million of silver about a century ago but its saloons and homes were deserted for years until restored by the city of San Bernadino as a regional park in 1966. It now survives on tourists who ride the (tiny) Calico and Odessa Railway, inspect a deserted mine and attend a performance at the town playhouse. Information about the area from the California Desert Information Center (tel: 619/256-8617) at Barstow.

Catalina Island. An island that is 22 by 8 miles wide and 26 miles from Los Angeles, Catalina offers swimming, hiking, horseback riding, diving, fishing, golfing, and camping as well as small-town friendliness in its solitary town, Avalon. Details from the Chamber of Commerce, P.O. Box 217, Avalon., tel: 510-1520.
Round-trip ferry from San Pedro: adults, $27.50; children, aged 2–11 $20.50; tel: (800) 257-2227. **By helicopter** it costs $100 round-trip, 15 minutes each way; tel: (800) 228-2566.

Disneyland. Disneyland features dining, shopping, entertainment and more than 55 adventures and attractions in seven magical themed lands. New rides are added yearly, with the newest attraction being a log ride called Splash Mountain. Open daily year-round. Hours: June–September, 8 a.m.–1 a.m; October–May, 9 a.m.–7 p.m. Admission: adults, $25.50; children, $20.50; senior citizen discount. 1313 S. Harbor Blvd, P.O. Box 3232, Anaheim, tel: (714) 999-4000.

Elysium Fields. Non-members may spend a day at this family-style nude ranch in Topanga canyon, by telephoning in advance to make a reservation. The cost is $15 single, $20 double, with a small extra fee for overnight stays (in your own sleeping bag or camper van). Cooking facilities, pool, sauna, tennis. 814 Robinson Road, Topanga Canyon, tel: 455-2005.

Another year-round nudist camp is the McConville mountain resort sprawled over 330 acres near the Cleveland National Forest. P.O.B. 131 Elsinore, CA 92330, tel: (714) 678-2333.

Grass Valley. Site of the 784-acre Empire Mine where hard-rock gold mining began in the US. Now a state park with museum, exhibits, hiking trails and picnic areas. Open year-round. Information from (800) 752-6222.

Hearst San Simeon State Historical Monument or Hearst Castle as it's usually called is about midway between Los Angeles and San Francisco but is well worth the 4-hour drive from either place. Because the infamous media tycoon (who died in 1951) pillaged all of Europe for his treasures the castle has so much to see that four different tours overlap each day between 8 a.m. and 5 p.m. (until 3.30 p.m. in winter; closed December 25, January 1). Reservations advisable in advance (tel: 619/452-1950 or 800/444-7275 outside California).

Knott's Berry Farm. Major theme park with a Western flavor, including a Ghost Town, a wild river ride, and miniature trains for the kids. Less automated than Disneyland, and some say more fun. Open: Monday–Friday 10 a.m.–6 p.m; Saturday 10 a.m.–10 p.m; Sunday 10 a.m.–7 p.m. Admission: adults, $21.95; children, $9.95. 8039 Beach Blvd, Buena Park, tel: (714) 220-5200.

Lake Shasta Caverns. Crystal-studded stalactites and stalagmites can be viewed from interior walkways. Open daily except Christmas and Thanksgiving. Hourly tours in summer, thrice-daily in winter. Information: (916) 238-2341.

Mount Tamalpais. Spectacular views of the entire Bay Area can be enjoyed after driving up a winding road to the summit, where there's a 6,000-acre (2,430-hectare) state park. In spring and summer, plays and musical programs are presented in the amphitheater. Six miles (10 km) west of Mill Valley, tel: 388-2070.

Mount Whitney, which towers an awesome 14,500 feet above sea level in the Sequoia National Park, is about 200 miles north of LA via Palmdale on State Highway 14 and US 395. It can be seen from the highway but the best, unobstructed views are along the Whitney Portal Road, westwards from Lone Pine. Beginning at Victorville, US 395 offers numerous landmarks and/or diversions along its route: **Death Valley** to the east; **Edwards Air Force** base (landing site for the space shuttle); the once-fertile **Owens Valley** from which LA's water supply was stolen in 1913; the desolate camp at **Manzanar** where Japanese-Americans were interned in World War II; and the Indian museum at **Independence**. Further north the road leads to relaxing Keough Hot Springs, the resorts of the Mammoth skiing area and eventually Lake Tahoe. Information about Death Valley – a place best avoided during the summer – is available from the Furnace Creek Visitor Center, tel: (619) 786-2331.

Muir Woods. This 550-acre (223-hectare) national monument, a magnificent redwood forest, offers 6 miles of trails. The main trail is an easy stroll and has trailside markers and exhibits. Seven unpaved trails offer greater challenge. The *Sequoia Sempervirens*, the tallest trees in the world, are in abundance here. Some coast redwoods are 220 feet (67 meters) tall with diameters in excess of 10 feet! No picnicking, no camping, no pets. Seventeen miles (27 km) northwest of San Francisco. Take State 1 to Stinson Beach; at Muir Beach, follow signs to the Woods. Open daily 8 a.m. to sunset. Admission free; tel: 388-2595.

National Parks. There are 20 National Park System areas in California. Although they come under a variety of guises (in Northern California, four are called "National Parks", while three are "National Monuments", two are "National Recreation Areas", and one is a "National Seashore"), they are all filled with helpful rangers and park personnel, and more scenic vistas than you can point a camera at. Last year, about 30 million people visited California's National Parks; you'll fare better to visit these areas during the week and in the off-season. For information about accommodations, campgrounds, fishing, horseback riding, backpacking and ranger programs, contact the National Park Service, 450 Golden Gate Ave, San Francisco 94102, tel: 556-4122.

Queen Mary **Shipwalk**. Explore the largest, most luxurious ocean liner afloat today on self-guided or guided tours. Spend the day witnessing lifeboat drills, nautical knot tying, semaphore flag signaling. Dining and shopping available at numerous tourist shops and restaurants. Admission price also includes the *Spruce Goose*, Howard Hughes's behemoth aircraft (*see below*). Opening hours: 10 a.m.–6 p.m. daily; extended hours (9 a.m.–9 p.m.) June 22 to Labor Day. Admission: adults, $14.95; children, $8.95; senior citizen and travel agent discounts. Visitors can take a 90-minute guided "Captain's Tour" for an additional $5. Pier J, P.O. Box 8, Long Beach, tel: 435-3511, (800) 421-3732, in California (800) 352-7883.

Redwood National Park. More than 106,000 pristine acres centered on Crescent City. Information: (707) 464-6101; campsite reservations: (800) 444-PARK. One mile south of Orick on Highway 101 is the Redwood Information Center offering slide show and tours, tel: (707) 488-3461. From Wilits (tel: 800/504-3763) 2- or 3-day train trips can be made through redwood country to Eureka.

Roaring Camp Railroad. Ride through redwood forests on this old-fashioned, steam-powered passenger train. Disembark to hike or picnic at Bear Mountain, then return to Roaring Camp for a chuck wagon barbecue (reservations required) or a walk through Henry Cowell Redwoods State Park. Four miles west of State 17 in Felton, on Graham Hill Road in the Santa Cruz mountains. Train leaves daily at 12.15 p.m; over the summer and on weekends, there are additional departures. Admission: adult, $10. Tel: (408) 335-4400.

San Diego Zoo in Balboa Park houses almost 800 different species and is sometimes said to be the best zoo in the world. Open daily: adults, $10.75; children under 15, $4. Tel: (619) 234-3153.

San Diego Wild Animal Park is an 1,800-acre preserve where wild animals roam freely. Open 9 a.m.–4 p.m. daily. Entrance fee (adults, $14.50; children, $7.50) includes animals shows and monorail tour. Off Interstate 15 east of Escondido, tel: (619) 747-8702.

Santa Cruz Beach Boardwalk. California's first and finest seashore amusement area (established in 1868) offers 24 rides, games, arcades, gift shops, entertainment and a mile-long beach. A magnificent casino, built here in 1907, has been renovated to house two restaurants. The antique merry-go-around dates from 1911. The Giant Dipper is one of the best roller roaster rides in the world. Open daily 11 a.m.–10 p.m. Boardwalk is free; fees range from $1–$2 each ride, or an all-day unlimited ticket for $16. 400 Beach St, Santa Cruz, tel: (408) 426-7433.

Sea World of California stars Baby Shamu in the "killer whale show". Open 9 a.m.–11 p.m. daily. Admission: adults, $21; children under 12, $15.50. 1720 S. Shores Road, Mission Bay, tel: (619) 226-3901.

Seventeen-Mile Drive. This scenic drive from Pacific Grove to Carmel is for all coastal visitors! Points of interest along the way include Seal Rock, Cypress Point and four of the most beautiful golf courses in the country, including Pebble Beach. Bicycling is a great way to enjoy the drive; toll for cars is $15.

Sierra Mono Indian Museum houses artifacts such as baskets, beads, tools, arrowheads and wildlife collection. Open Monday–Saturday, 9 a.m.–4 p.m. Admission: $1.50. At the intersection of 225 and 228 near North Fork, tel: (209) 877-2115.

Six Flags Magic Mountain. A 260-acre family theme park, 25 minutes north of Hollywood. Featuring over 100 thrill-seeker rides, shows and the world's largest dual-track wooden roller coaster, the Colossus. Open: daily Memorial Day through Labor Day, plus weekends and some holidays year round. Visit requires several hours. Admission: adults, $20; children, $10; senior citizen discount. 26101 Magic Mountain Pkwy, P.O. Box 5500, Valencia, tel: (818) 367-2271.

Skunk Railroad. Nicknamed for the noxious fumes originally emitted by the ancient steam train, the California Western Railroad travels from Fort Bragg (80 feet/24 meters – about sea level) to Willits (1,365 feet/416 meters). The fabulous 40-mile (64-km) trip passes through groves of towering redwood trees, crossing and recrossing the Noyo River. Round trip takes almost 8 hours. Fare $6–$15; tel: (707) 964-6371.

Sonoma County Farm Trails. Write to P.O.B. 6032, Santa Rosa, CA 95406, for free map showing trails to 100 farms in the region.

Spruce Goose. Explore Howard Hughes' all-wood 200-ton airplane inside the world's largest clear span aluminum dome. Videos, displays and exhibits tell the story. Restaurants, entertainment, shopping. Open year round from 10 a.m.–6 p.m; extended hours: June 22 to Labor Day, 9 a.m.–9 p.m. Admission: adults, $14.95; children, $8.95; senior citizen and travel agent discounts. Tours: ticket price includes *Queen Mary* Shipwalk. Pier J, Long Beach, tel: 435-3511, (800) 421-3732, in California (800) 352-7883.

State Capitol. Built between 1861 and 1874 and recently restored, this seat of the state government is known for its fine proportions and lofty dome, 237 feet (72 meters) above the street. The main building contains murals, historical exhibits and statuary; the surrounding park boasts shrubs, trees, and plants from all parts of the world. Free guided tours daily, 9 a.m.–4 p.m.; East Annex is open daily 7 a.m.–9 p.m. Bounded by 10th, 12th, L and N streets, Sacramento, tel: (916) 324-0333.

Vineyards and wineries of Santa Barbara County. One hour's driving time northwest of Santa Barbara lies the Scandinavian-style town of Solvang with its windmills and gas street lamps and from there a score of wineries are within easy reach. Most offer free tasting, tours and grounds in which to picnic, if not restaurants on the premises. Information from Santa Barbara Country Vintners Association, P.O.B Wine, Los Olivos, CA 93441, or call (805) 688-0881.
In the San Francisco Bay region there are a number of wineries open to visitors in both the Livermore and Gilroy areas, also the Napa and Sonoma Valleys. Call for information from Gilroy (408) 842-6436; Livermore (415) 447-1606; Los Gatos (408) 354-9300; Napa (707) 226-7455; and Sonoma (707) 996-1090.

Whale-watching is a popular pastime and the **American Cetacean Society** (P.O. Box 4416, San Pedro, CA 90731, tel: 548-6279) is among the many groups that organizes trips to see some of the thousands of 40-ton California gray whales that start their 10,000-mile migration south from Alaska to South America in the fall, returning in March and April. Traveling 80 to 100 miles (130–160 km) per day, some of these 40-foot mammals can be seen from high spots along the coast – particularly the Palos Verdes peninsula – and around the Channel Islands. Seals and sealions (the latter are more mobile because their rear flippers pivot from side to side) are also plentiful in the islands to which **Island Packers** (tel: 805/642-1393) run trips and about which the **Channel Island National Park** (tel: 805/644-8262) can provide a wealth of information. In addition, snowy plovers and cormorants are found on San Miguel; kestrels, larks and owls on Santa Barbara and brown pelicans – they nest between May and August – on Anacapa, the nearest island to the mainland. For information about Santa Cruz, the largest island, call the **Nature Conservancy**, tel: (805) 962-9111. Santa Catalina island is also a good place to find seals and sealions, especially on the 3-hour boat cruises operated out of San Pedro and Long Beach. Details from the **Catalina Island Chamber of Commerce**, P.O. Box 217, Avalon, CA 90704.

VISITING THE MISSIONS

From the beginning of California's history, the 21 missions set up along El Camino Real by Father Junipero Serra and his successors have played an important role. Today they are major tourist attractions. Seven of the missions are in Southern California, the quintet between Santa Barbara and San Diego being San Buenaventura, San Fernando, San Gabriel, San Juan Capistrano and San Luis Rey. Most are open every day of the year with a small admission fee.

Originally developed by Spanish clerics with virtually slave labor from local Indians, most of the missions were abandoned and fell into decay after the passing of the Secularization Act in 1834 and were forgotten for almost half a century. Helen Hunt Jackson's 1880 book, *A Century of Dishonor*, about mistreatment of the Indians revived

302

interest in the buildings whose architecture thereafter became a much-emulated style.

San Gabriel Arcangel is the nearest mission to Los Angeles, about 9 miles east off Highway 10. It has unusual architecture, wonderful statues and paintings and a September festival which celebrates its 1771 founding. Open: 9.30 a.m.–4.30 p.m. daily. Closed: Christmas, Thanksgiving and Easter. Tel: 282-5191.

San Fernando Rey de España prototype of the "mission style" with classical arches, thick adobe walls, contains statues of Serra and his successor, Fr Lasuen. Open: daily 9 a.m.–5 p.m., Sunday 10 a.m.–5 p.m. Tel: 361-0186.

San Juan Capistrano near Laguna Beach. This mission has Fr Serra's original chapel and ruins of an enormous church. Open: daily 7 a.m.–5 p.m. Tel: (714) 493-1424.

San Diego de Alcala first to be founded, originally 6 miles away. Open: daily 9 a.m.–5 p.m. Tel: (619) 281-8449.

San Buenaventura has ancient paintings, wooden bells, original tiles and rafters. Tel: (805) 643-4318.

San Luis Rey has a large collection of vestments, fiesta in July. Open: daily 9 a.m.–5 p.m., Sunday 11.30 a.m.–4 p.m. Tel: (619) 757-3651.

Santa Barbara "Queen of the Missions"; 60 Franciscan friars in residence. Open: daily 9 a.m.–5 p.m., Sunday 1–5 p.m. Tel: (805) 966-3153.

In the northern part of the state, the missions include the oldest structure in San Francisco:

Mission Delores, founded in 1776 by the Franciscans, boasts decorations from Spain and Mexico and a lovely garden. Open daily 9 a.m.–4 p.m. Tel: (415) 621-8203.

San Jose is a restoration of the once wealthy mission founded in 1797. Open daily 10 a.m.–5 p.m. except New Year's Day, Easter, Thanksgiving and Christmas. Tel: (415) 657-1797.

Santa Clara de Asis the 8th of the original 21 California missions. Open daily 7 a.m.–7 p.m. Museum open Tuesday–Sunday, 11 a.m.–4 p.m. Tel: (408) 554-4023.

Santa Cruz nearby the Casa Adobe. Santa Cruz's oldest building, this mission has a chapel open to visitors daily 9 a.m.–5 p.m. Tel: (408) 426-5686.

MOVIE STUDIO TOURS

Universal Studios Tour will put you in the midst of more mayhem than you've ever thought you'd be willing to pay for. For an hour and 45 minutes the hapless tour tram will dodge an avalanche, part the Red Sea, escape a tourist hungry King Kong, and survive a major earthquake. Disembark to explore the largest film studio in the world, see stunt and animal shows, beam aboard the starship *Enterprise* of *Star Trek* fame, and there's more. Summer and holiday hours: 8 a.m.–6 p.m. daily; off-season weekdays 10 a.m.–3 p.m., off-season weekends 9.30 a.m.–3 p.m. Admission: adults, $22; children age 3–11, $16; senior citizens 60+, $15.10. 100 Universal City Plaza, Universal City, tel: (818) 508-9600.

Burbank Studio Tour, home of Warner Bros, and Lorimar Productions; may be the antidote to the Universal tour. For the more serious student of movie and television production this 12-person "VIP tour" is unstaged and educational. Tour includes whatever may be on the day's production schedule, plus a look at the prop and special effects shops as well as an historical back lot. Two-hour tours weekdays 10 a.m. and 2 p.m. (by reservation only). Admission: $22 per person (no children under age 10). 4000 Warner Blvd, Burbank, tel: (818) 954 1744.

PARKS

California State Parks & Recreation Dept. 128 Paseo de la Plaza, Los Angeles, CA, tel: (213) 620-3342.

US Park Service. Dept of Interior, Washington, DC 20240, tel: (202) 343-4747.

US Park Service. Southwest Region (S. California), P.O. Box 728, Santa Fe, NM

87501, tel: (505) 988-6375.

US Park Service. Western Region (N. California), 450 Golden Gate Ave, P.O. Box 36063, San Francisco, CA 94102, tel: (415) 556-4196.

US Forest Service. Southwest Region (S. California), 517 Gold Ave SW, Albuquerque, NM 87102, tel: (505) 842-3292.

US Forest Service. Pacific Northwest Region (N. California), 630 Sansome St, San Francisco, CA 94111, tel: (415) 556-0122.

US Forest Service. Dept of Agriculture, Washington, DC 20250, tel: (202) 447-3760.

SHOPPING

NORTHERN CALIFORNIA

From elegant malls to farmers' markets, Northern California offers a wide array of shopping opportunities. In San Francisco alone, there are 20 distinct shopping areas. The most famous is probably **Union Square**, where most of the large, prestigious department stores are located, including I. Magnin, Neiman-Marcus and Saks. A block away from Union Square Park is **Maiden Lane**, a cute pedestrian street with boutiques, stationery stores, and an outdoor cafe. **The Galleria**, a collection of 60 specialty shops, restaurants and services housed under a vaulting glass dome modeled after Milan's Galleria Vittorio Emmanuelle, is also located nearby.

Visitors will also find an abundance of shopping in the **Fisherman's Wharf** area. The shopping area extends from Pier 39 to Ghirardelli Square and includes the Cannery, the Anchorage and a host of street vendors. Once a cargo wharf, Pier 39 now offers two levels of shops, restaurants, amusements, and free outdoor entertainment by some of the city's best street performers. Both the Cannery and Ghirardelli Square are converted factories. The Cannery was once a Del Monte peach canning plant, and Ghirardelli Square once housed a chocolate factory. The Anchorage, a colorful, modern shopping complex, is also located along the Northern Waterfront. Along with specialty shops and galleries, each complex offers unique landscaping, live entertainment, open-air walkways and breathtaking views of Alcatraz, the Golden Gate Bridge and the Bay.

The **Embarcadero Center** is also located on the waterfront, east of Pier 39, near the Financial District. This is San Francisco's largest mall, with about 175 shops, restaurants and nightclubs in four complexes between Sacramento and Clay streets.

Other shopping areas in San Francisco tend to reflect the character of the neighborhood. They include Columbus Avenue and Grant Street in North Beach (Little Italy), Grant Street in Chinatown, Castro Street between 20th and Market and from Market to Church, Haight Street along the Golden Gate Park Panhandle, Union Street at Cow Hollow, and Japan Center.

In the **East Bay**, visitors will find a distinctly collegiate shopping atmosphere along Telegraph Avenue in Berkeley, and Berkeley's famous "Gourmet Ghetto" along Shattuck Avenue. Other locations in the Bay Area boasting boutiques, restaurants and specialty stores include Solano Avenue in Albany, Piedmont Avenue and Jack London Square in Oakland, University Avenue in Palo Alto and the entire business district of Sausalito.

SOUTHERN CALIFORNIA

For intrepid shoppers, Southern California is right up there with the big guns like Paris, New York and Hong Kong. No matter what your taste or budget, you are bound to find whatever it is you're looking for.

Of course, the glitziest shopping street is Los Angeles' renowned **Rodeo Drive**. And while Rodeo has become quite a tourist trap, with more folks window shopping than buying, there are some terrific, world class shops along the drive like **Chanel**, **Armani**, **Ungaro**, **Alaia** and **Bottega Veneta**. Also in Beverly Hills are two first-rate department stores, **I. Magnin** and **Neiman-Marcus**.

Rodeo Drive's luxurious amenities were suddenly increased by 40 percent late in 1990 with the ingenious addition of a new street, **Two Rodeo** – a curving, cobble-stoned walkway lined with such top-name stores as **Tiffany**, **Christian Dior** and **Cartier** whose classy emporiums feature granite colonnades and copper-toned roofs. Developer Douglas Stitzel and his Japanese partners compare Via Rodeo with its Rome counterpart, Via Condoti, and believe that its European ambiance will lure most visitors to Beverly Hills for at least a look around. An underground parking lot offering free valet parking feeds shoppers right into the middle of the street.

A trip down **Melrose Avenue** is a must, where the shops range from the preppiness of the **Gap** to the forward-fashion at stores like **Ecru** and **Roppongi**. Some of Southern California's best people-watching goes on here, and there are plenty of little cafés to serve as rest stops. Those into avant-garde high fashion can go to **Maxfield**, near Doheny and Melrose, an austere temple of haute style, where stars like Jack Nicholson, Robin Williams and a host of rock 'n' rollers find labels like **Gaultier**, **Lagerfeld**, and **Katherine Hamnett**. For a change of pace you might want to browse among one of the country's largest collections of antique books at the **Heritage Book Store** in the 8500 block of Melrose, where an extensive autograph collection includes those of Mark Twain and Charles Dickens.

Although such trendy shopping streets as La Brea Avenue off Melrose and Santa Monica's Montana Avenue have not lost their lustre there always seems to be some up-and-coming newcomer, the latest of which is Venice's Abbot Kinney Boulevard (named after the visionary developer who created Venice at the turn of the century). Palm trees have been installed and art galleries, vintage clothing and jewelry stores are opening to supplement the existing handful of shops.

One of the Southland's most famous landmarks, the outstanding former Uniroyal tyre plant beside the highway in the City of Commerce (about 10 miles southeast of town on the Santa Ana Freeway) has re-emerged as an excitingly enticing shopping plaza. Fronted by the distinctive 7th century BC Assyrian-style wall that has dominated the site for years and which featured in William Wyler's *Ben Hur*, the new **Citadel Outlet Collection** (5675 E. Telegraph Road) now spreads around a tree-flanked courtyard whose 42 stores include such well-known names as Perry Ellis, The Gap and Benetton. Open: Monday–Saturday 9 a.m.–9 p.m., Sunday 11 a.m.–6 p.m.

It mustn't be forgotten that for mall lovers, Southern California is a shoppers' Valhalla. The mind reels at the number of mega-malls dotted throughout the region: **Century City**, **Beverly Center**, **Topanga Plaza**, **Del Amo Fashion Square** and **Fashion Island**. But our advice is to concentrate your energies on the **South Coast Plaza** in Costa Mesa (just a stone's throw from Newport in Orange County), which is the textbook example of what a mall should be. It's huge, to be sure, but all the shops are absolutely first rate: J. Crew (of mail-order fame) has the best, least expensive, quality sportswear around; the first Southern California branch of New York's Tony Barney's features modish designer clothing at all price ranges, as well as fabulous accessories, Kiehl's toiletries, and Molton-Brown, a wonderful British line of cosmetics that uses only pure ingredients and does not test on laboratory animals. There's a Rizzoli bookshop at the South Coast Plaza as well as Joan & David, Yves St Laurent, Chanel, the West Coast's first Calvin Klein boutique and a wide range of eateries to choose from (we like Ruby's in the Crystal Court section of the mall). There's also a full-size merry-go-round on the premises – perfect for keeping the little ones happy.

Because of its upscale nature the Palm Springs region is understandably one big shopping area, with the Desert Fashion Plaza on the city's main street – Palm Canyon Drive – maybe even outclassed by the Town Center of nearby Palm Desert where 130 shops and an outdoor ice skating rink are flanked by five major department stores. Equally attractive is the charm and ambiance of Santa Barbara's **La Arcada** shopping paseo, a cheerful Spanish-style courtyard adorned with tile, ornamental ironwork and bright flags. Yet another era is evoked by San Diego's Gaslamp Quarter shopping district. In addition to that city's Seaport Village and the multi-level Horton Plaza, it is also a short excursion to the Mexican border town of Tijuana where there are different souvenirs and lower prices.

This table gives a comparison of American, Continental and British clothing sizes. It is always best to try on any article before buying it, however, as sizes can vary.

Women's Dresses/Suits

American	Continental	British
6	38/34N	8/30
8	40/36N	10/32
10	42/38N	12/34
12	44/40N	14/36
14	46/42N	16/38
16	48/44N	18/40

Women's Shoes

American	Continental	British
4½	36	3
5½	37	4
6½	38	5
7½	39	6
8½	40	7
9½	41	8
10½	42	9

Men's Suits

American	Continental	British
34	44	34
—	46	36
38	48	38
—	50	40
42	52	42
—	54	44
46	56	46

Men's Shirts

American	Continental	British
14	36	14
14½	37	14½
15	38	15
15½	39	15½
16	40	16
16½	41	16½
17	42	17

Men's Shoes

American	Continental	British
6½	—	6
7½	40	7
8½	41	8
9½	42	9
10½	43	10
11½	44	11

NIGHTLIFE

Evening diversions in California are as varied and all-encompassing as the state itself. Visitors can entertain themselves with events that range from world-class operas, theater and symphonies to first-rate comedy and funky live blues, jazz and rock-n-roll.

The traveler in California looking for nightlife would do best by referring to the local newspaper as a guide to what's on in town. In San Francisco the Examiner's section of the *Sunday Los Angeles Times* will fill you in on the action in the Southland. The concierge at many hotels can help you in your quest for fun when the sun goes down in the Golden State.

SPORTS

SPECTATOR

BASEBALL

California possesses some of the finest teams in professional sports. Baseball season runs from April to October. In Southern California, the Los Angeles Dodgers play at Dodger Stadium; the California Angels play at Anaheim Stadium, and the San Diego Padres play at San Diego Jack Murphy Stadium. In Northern California, the San Francisco Giants play at Candlestick Park, and the Oakland A's play at Oakland Stadium.

BASKETBALL

The regular National Basketball Association season runs from October through April, with championship playoffs continuing in June. The Los Angeles Lakers, who are almost always a league powerhouse, play home games at the Forum in Inglewood. The LA Clippers play their games at the LA Sports Arena, and the Golden State Warriors play at Oakland Coliseum Arena.

FOOTBALL

The National Football League season begins in September and runs through December. There are pre-season games in August and post-season playoffs in January. In Southern California, the Los Angeles Rams play their games at Anaheim Stadium. The Los Angeles Raiders play at Los Angeles Memorial Coliseum, and the San Diego Chargers play at San Diego Jack Murphy Stadium. The Rose Bowl is held every year on New Year's Day between the best team in the Pac-10 conference and the best team in the Big Ten. It's such a popular event that Rose Bowl Stadium holds 104,699 people, and it's still difficult to get seats. There is only one professional football team in Northern California, the San Francisco '49ers. They play at Candlestick Park.

HOCKEY

California has only one professional hockey team, the Los Angeles Kings. Hockey season runs from October to April, and the Kings play at the Forum in Inglewood.

HORSE RACING

For those who prefer the sport of kings, Southern California has three tracks to choose from. Hollywood Park, in Inglewood, hosts thoroughbred racing from April to July and harness racing from August to December. Santa Anita Park, in Arcadia, hosts thoroughbred racing from December to April and from October to November. The season at the Del Mar Track, about 30 minutes north of San Diego, runs from mid-July to early September. There are two tracks in the San Francisco Bay Area. Bay Meadows is located on the Peninsula south of San Francisco. It is one of the oldest, busiest and most beautiful tracks in the state. Golden Gate Fields is located in the East Bay.

FURTHER READING

GENERAL

Back Roads of California, by Earl Thomas. (Clarkson N. Potter, 1983.)

California: A Guide to the Golden State, Federal Writers Project. (Hastings House, 1939.)

California Coast, by the editors of *Sunset* magazine. (Lane Publishing, 1978.)

California Coastal Access Guide, California Coastal Commission.

California: The Golden Coast, by Philip L. Fradkin. (Viking Press, 1973.)

California Political Almanac, edited by Dan Walters. (Pacific Data Resource, 1990.)

California: Ranch Days, by Helen Bauer. (Doubleday, 1953.)

California Southern Country, by Carey McWilliams. (Duell, Sloan Pearce, 1946.)

California's Missions, edited by Ralph B. Wright. (Hubert A. Lowan, 1978.)

City Guide: San Francisco and Northern California, by Bella Levin and Dan Whelan. (Cityguide, 1983.)

The Dolphin Guide to San Francisco and the Bay Area, by Curt Gentry and Tom Horton. (Doubleday, 1982.)

Exploring California's Byways, by Russ Leadabrand. (Westernlorne Press, 1972.)

Exploring Death Valley, by Ruth Kirk. (Stanford University Press.)

Field Guide to Southern California, by Robert P. Sharp. (Kendall/Hunt.)

Free and Easy, by the editors of *Bay Guardian*. (Downwind Publications, 1980.)

A Guide to Architecture in Los Angeles & Southern California by Gebhard and Winter.

Guidebook to Rural California, by Russ Leadabrand. (Ward Ritchie, 1972.)

Hidden Country Villages of California, by Francis Cleberd. (Chronicle Books, 1977.)

LA Access, by Richard Saul Wurman. (Access Press, 1987.)

Los Angeles: Biography of a City, by John & LaRee Coughey. (University of California Press, 1976.)

Los Angeles: A City Apart, by David L. Clark. (Windsor Publications, 1981.)

North of San Francisco, by Robert W. Matson. (Celestial Arts, 1975.)

San Francisco Access, by Richard Saul Wurman. (Presidio Press, 1982.)

San Francisco Insider's Guide, by John Bailey. (Non-Stop Books, 1980.)

Seeing California: A Guide to the State, by Blair Tavenner. (Little, Brown & Co, 1948.)

Southern California: An island on the Land, by Carey McWilliams. (Peregrine Smith, 1946.)

The Tree at the Center of the World, by Bruce W. Barton. (Ross-Erikson, 1980.)

Take a Walk Through Mission History: Walking Tours Through San Francisco's Inner Mission, Stanford Research Institute. (Stanford University, 1974.)

Timeless Walks in San Francisco: A Historical Walking Guide, by Michelle Brant. (1979.)

A Walker's Yearbook: 52 Seasonal Walks in the San Francisco Bay Area. (Presidio Press, 1983.)

Walks and Tours in the Golden Gate City, by Randolph Delehanty. (Dial Press, 1980.)

PEOPLE

The Great Movie Stars: The Golden Years, by David Shipman. (Crown, 1970.)

Life and Good Times of William Randolph Hearst, by John Tebbel. (E.P. Dutton & Co, 1952.)

The Life of Raymond Chandler, by Frank McShane. (E.P. Dutton & Co, 1976.)

This is Hollywood, by Ken Schessler. (Universal Books, 1989.)

GEOGRAPHY & NATURAL HISTORY

California Patterns: A Geographical and Historical Atlas, by David Hornbeck. (Mayfield, 1983.)

California Wildlife Map Book, by Vinson Brown and David Hoover. (Naturegraph Publishers, 1967.)

California: The Geography of Diversity, by Crane Miller and Richard Hyslop. (Mayfield, 1983.)

The City and the Country, by Harry Ellington Brook. (Kingsley, Barnes & Newner, 1987.)

Coast Walks, by John McKinney. (Olympus Press.)

The Environmentalist's Guide to the East Bay Shoreline, by Stephen Fisher and Anita Rubin. (1973.)

Grape Expeditions in California, by Lena Emmery & Sally Taylor. (1442 Willard St San Francisco, CA 94117, 1987.)

The Last Days of the Late, Great State of California, by Curt Gentry. (Comstock Editions.)

Natural Los Angeles, by Bill Thomas. (Harper & Row, 1989.)

The Natural World of San Francisco, by Harold Gilliam and Michael Bry. (Doubleday, 1967.)

Roadside Geology of Northern California, by David Alt and Donald Hyndman. (Mountain Press, 1975.)

San Francisco's Wilderness Next Door, by John Hart. (Presidio Press, 1979.)

Southern California: Off the Beaten Path, by Kathy Strong. (Globe Pequot Press.)

Spring Wildflowers of the San Francisco Bay Area, by Helen Sharsmith. (University of California Press, 1965.)

Walks of California, by Gary Ferguson. (Prentice Hall Press, 1987.)

Where to see Wildlife in California, by Tom Taber. (Oak Valley Press, 1983.)

PLACES

The Beach Towns: A Walker's Guide to LA's Beach Communities, by Robert John Pierson. (Chronicle Books, 1985.)

The Encyclopedia of Hollywood, by Scott and Barbara Siegel. (Facts on File, 1990.)

Fantasy by the Sea, by Tom Sewell Moran. (Beyond Baroque Foundation, 1979.)

Guide to Hollywood & Beverly Hills, by Charles Lockwood. (Crown, 1984.)

Hollywood, Land & Legend, by C. C. & B. Crane. (Arlington House, 1980.)

Out with the Stars, by Jim Heimann. (Abbeville, 1985.)

Venice of America, by Jeffrey Stanton. (Donahue Publications, 1987)

HISTORY

Berkeley: The Town and Gown of It, by George Pettitt. (Howel North Books, 1973.)

California: A Bicentennial History, by David Lavender. (W.W. Norton, 1976.)

The California Missions: A Pictorial History, by the editors of *Sunset* magazine. (Lane, 1979.)

A Century of Dishonor, by Helen Hunt Jacson. (Scholarly Press, 1880.)

A Companion to California, by James Hart. (Oxford University, 1978.)

Good Life in Hard Times, by Jerry Flamm. (Chronicle, 1976.)

Guide to the Missions of California, by Marjorie Camphouse. (Pasadena: Ward Ritchie, 1974.)

History of the San Fernando Valley, by Frank M. Keffner. (Stillman, 1934.)

Indians of Early Southern California, by Edna B. Ziebold. (Sapsis, 1969.)

Los Angeles, Biography of a City, by John and LaRee Coughey. (University of California Press, 1977.)

Los Angeles: A Profile, by W. W. Robinson. (University of Oklahoma, 1968.)

Los Angeles: From Pueblo to City of the Future, by Andrew Rolls. (Boyd & Fraster, 1981.)

Los Angeles Two Hundred, by David Lavender. (Harry N. Abrams, 1980.)

The Missions of California, by Melba Levick and Stanley Young. (Chronicle Books, 1988.)

Oakland: The Story of a City, by Beth Bagwell. (Presidio Press, 1982.)

Pictorial History of California, by Paul C. Johnson. (Bonanza, 1970.)

The San Fernando Valley, Past & Present, by Lawrence C. Jorgensen. (Pacific Rim Research, 1982.)

San Francisco Almanac, by Gladys Hansen. (Presidio Press, 1980.)

San Francisco as It Was, and It Is, by Paul Johnson and Richard Reinhardt. (Doubleday, 1979.)

A Short History of San Francisco, by Tom Cole. (Monte Rosa, 1981.)

Suddenly San Francisco, by Charles Lockwood. (California Living, 1978.)

Yesterday's Los Angeles, by Norman Dash. (E.A. Seamann Publishing, 1976.)

USEFUL ADDRESSES

TOURIST INFORMATION

Visitors' Bureaus: When in doubt, use the telephone. Local Visitors' Bureaus are happy to give information over the phone and will mail maps, lists of upcoming events or other literature in advance of your trip.

Anaheim Area Visitors' and Convention Bureau. 800 W. Katella Ave, Anaheim, CA 92802, tel: (714) 999-8999.

Beverly Hills Visitors' and Convention Bureau. 239 S. Beverly Drive, Beverly Hills, CA 90212, tel: (213) 271-8174.

Buena Park Visitors' and Convention Bureau. 6280 Manchester Blvd, Buena Park, CA 90621, tel: (714) 994-1511.

Escondido Visitors' and Information Bureau. 720 N. Broadway, Escondido, CA 92025, tel: (619) 745-4741.

Long Beach Convention and Tourism Bureau. 1 World Trade Center, Long Beach, CA 90802, tel: (213) 436-3645.

Greater Los Angeles Visitors' and Convention Bureau. 515 S. Figueroa, Los Angeles, CA 90071, tel: (213) 624-7300.

Palm Springs Convention and Visitors' Bureau. Municipal Airport Terminal, Palm Springs, CA 92270, tel: (619) 770-9000.

San Diego Convention and Visitors' Bureau. 1200 Third Ave, Suite 824, San Diego, CA 92101, tel: (619) 232-3101.

San Francisco Visitors' and Convention Bureau. Powell and Market streets, San Francisco, CA 94103, tel: (415) 974-6900.

Ventura Visitors' and Convention Bureau. 785 S. Seward Ave, Ventura, CA 93001, tel: (805) 648-2075.

CHAMBERS OF COMMERCE

Berkeley Chamber of Commerce. 1834 University Ave, Berkeley, CA 94703, tel: (415) 845-1212.

Big Bear Lake Valley Chamber of Commerce. 40588 Big Bear Blvd, Big Bear Lake, CA 92315, tel: (714) 866-4601.

Goleta Valley Chamber of Commerce. 5730 Hollister Ave, Goleta, CA 93117, tel: (805) 967-4618.

Hollywood Chamber of Commerce. 6255 Sunset Blvd, Hollywood, CA 90028, tel: (213) 469-8311.

Monterey Chamber of Commerce. 380 Alvarado St, Monterey, CA 92940, tel: (408) 649-1770.

Oakland Chamber of Commerce. 1330 Broadway, Oakland, CA 94612, tel: (415) 839-9000.

Sacramento Chamber of Commerce. 1311 "I" St, Sacramento, CA 95814, tel: (916) 442-5542.

Santa Barbara Chamber of Commerce. 1301 Santa Barbara, P.O. Box 299, Santa Barbara, CA 93102, tel: (805) 965-3023.

San Jose Chamber of Commerce. 1 Pasco de San Antonio, San Jose, CA 95113, tel: (408) 998-7000.

Santa Cruz Chamber of Commerce. Civic Auditorium, P.O. Box 1476, Santa Cruz, CA 95061, tel: (408) 423-6927.

CONSULATES

Foreign visitors looking for home country representatives can find consulates in San Francisco and Los Angeles. Check in the Yellow Pages of local telephone books available in libraries and post offices, or call "Information" (1-area code of city-555-121 if calling from out of town).

ART/PHOTO CREDITS

INDEX

C

D

R

Y

Z

A
B
D
E
F
G
H
I
J
a
b
d
e
f
g
h
i
j
k
l